ʾAŠERAH:

Extrabiblical Evidence

HARVARD SEMITIC MUSEUM

HARVARD SEMITIC MONOGRAPHS

edited by
Frank Moore Cross

Number 37

ʾAŠERAH:

Extrabiblical Evidence

by
Walter A. Maier, III

Walter A. Maier, III

ʾAŠERAH:
Extrabiblical Evidence

Scholars Press
Atlanta, Georgia

ʾAŠERAH:
Extrabiblical Evidence

Walter A. Maier, III

Library of Congress Cataloging in Publication Data

Maier, Walter A., 1952–
Aserah, extrabiblical evidence.

(Harvard Semitic monographs ; no. 37)
1. Asherah (Semitic deity) I. Title. II. Series.
BL1605.A7M35 1986 299'.26 86-15596
ISBN 1-55540-046-9

Printed in the United States of America
on acid free paper

To my parents,

Dr. Walter A. and Leah Maier

PREFACE

This monograph is a minor revision of my 1984 doctoral dissertation presented to Harvard University. My main advisor for the dissertation, and sole advisor for the monograph, the one to whom I owe the most, was Professor Frank Moore Cross, Jr., and to him I express my deepest thanks. His penetrating analysis, insights and guidance were invaluable. In working with Dr. Cross I came to an even greater appreciation of him not only as a scholar with a remarkable grasp of the various aspects of ancient Near Eastern studies, but also as a teacher displaying the highest professionalism, in addition to warmth and a sense of humor.

Professor Michael D. Coogan gave me much help as I was writing my dissertation, for which I am very grateful. Our discussions of the evidence relating directly and indirectly to ʾAšerah were an important part of the background out of which the dissertation and this monograph were derived.

Also, I am indebted to Professor Thomas O. Lambdin for his assistance with the Egyptian texts, his advice, and his encouragement; to Professor William L. Moran, for his aid with the Akkadian and Sumerian material; and to Professor Paul D. Hanson, for helpful comments made at the time of the final review of my dissertation. Finally, I wish to extend a word of thanks to the typist of the present monograph, Mrs. Joan Stahl.

Walter A. Maier III

Concordia College
River Forest, Illinois
Spring, 1986

TABLE OF CONTENTS

PREFACE vii

ABBREVIATIONS xi

INTRODUCTION 1

Chapter I. ʾAŠERAH IN THE TEXTS FROM UGARIT 3

ʾAṯirat in the Ugaritic Mythological Texts 3
ʾAṯirat in the Ugaritic Cultic Texts 38
ʾAṯirat in an Omen Text? 41
qdš, an Epithet of ʾAṯirat? 42

NOTES TO CHAPTER I 45

Chapter II. TWO GREEK WORKS 57

The *Phoenician History* 57
The Syrian Goddess 64

NOTES TO CHAPTER II 69

Chapter III. REPRESENTATIONS AND ADDITIONAL EPITHETS 81

qdš 81
tnt 96
Derketo/Phanebalos 118

NOTES TO CHAPTER III 123

Chapter IV. MISCELLANEOUS WRITTEN AND REPRESENTATIONAL MATERIALS 165

Amarna 165
Lachish 166
ʾEl-Khaḍr 166
Taanach 168
Kuntillet ʿAjrud 168
Khirbet el-Kom 172
Arslan Tash 173
Tyre 175

NOTES TO CHAPTER IV 177

CONCLUSIONS 193

NOTES TO CONCLUSIONS 197

Appendix A. MESOPOTAMIAN AND ARABIC EVIDENCE 199

NOTES TO APPENDIX A 203

Appendix B. ADDITIONAL UGARITIC TEXTUAL MATERIAL 209

NOTES TO APPENDIX B 215

Appendix C. HATHOR 217

NOTES TO APPENDIX C 223

Appendix D. CORRESPONDING TEXT NUMBERS 229

DRAWINGS 231

BIBLIOGRAPHY 241

ABBREVIATIONS

AfO	*Archiv für Orientforschung*
AJA	*American Journal of Archaeology*
AJSL	*American Journal of Semitic Languages and Literature*
ANEP	J. B. Pritchard, ed., *The Ancient Near East in Pictures Relating to the Old Testament*
ANET	J. B. Pritchard, ed., *Ancient Near Eastern Texts Relating to the Old Testament*
AnOr	Analecta orientalia
AOAT	Alter Orient und Altes Testament
AOS	American Oriental Series
ARI	W. F. Albright, *Archaeology and the Religion of Israel*
ASOR	American Schools of Oriental Research
BA	*Biblical Archaeologist*
BAR	*Biblical Archaeologist Reader*
BASOR	*Bulletin of the American Schools of Oriental Research*
Bib	*Biblica*
BJRL	*Bulletin of the John Rylands University Library of Manchester*
CBQMS	Catholic Biblical Quarterly -- Monograph Series
CIS	*Corpus Inscriptionum Semiticarum*
Clifford	R. J. Clifford, *The Cosmic Mountain in Canaan and the Old Testament*

CMHE	F. M. Cross, Jr., *Canaanite Myth and Hebrew Epic*
Coogan	M. D. Coogan, ed. and trans., *Stories from Ancient Canaan*
CTA	A. Herdner, *Corpus des tablettes en cunéiformes alphabétiques découvertes à Ras Shamra-Ugarit de 1929 à 1939*
Driver	G. R. Driver, *Canaanite Myths and Legends*
EA	J. A. Knudtzon, O. Weber, E. Ebeling, *Die El-Amarna-Tafeln*
Gaster	T. H. Gaster, *Thespis: Ritual, Myth, and Drama in the Ancient Near East*
GCS	Griechische christliche Schriftsteller
Gibson	J. C. L. Gibson, *Canaanite Myths and Legends*
Ginsberg	H. L. Ginsberg, trans., "Ugaritic Myths, Epics, and Legends," in *ANET*
GKC	E. Kautzsch, ed., and A. E. Cowley, trans., *Gesenius' Hebrew Grammar*
Gray	J. Gray, *The KRT Text in the Literature of Ras Shamra*
Gröndahl	F. Gröndahl, *Die Personennamen der Texte aus Ugarit*
HSM	Harvard Semitic Monographs
HTR	*Harvard Theological Review*
HTS	Harvard Theological Studies
HUCA	*Hebrew Union College Annual*
IDB	G. A. Buttrick, ed., *Interpreter's Dictionary of the Bible*
IEJ	*Israel Exploration Journal*
JAOS	*Journal of the American Oriental Society*
JBL	*Journal of Biblical Literature*
JCS	*Journal of Cuneiform Studies*
Jirku	A. Jirku, *Kanaanäische Mythen und Epen aus Ras Schamra - Ugarit*
JNES	*Journal of Near Eastern Studies*

JPOS — *Journal of the Palestine Oriental Society*

KAI — H. Donner and W. Röllig, *Kanaanäische und aramaische Inschriften*

Lachish II — O. Tufnell, C. H. Inge, and L. Harding, *Lachish II: The Fosse Temple*

LCL — Loeb Classical Library

NTA — A. Herdner, "Nouveaux textes alphabétiques de Ras Shamra - XXIVe campagne, 1961," in *Ugaritica VII*

Obermann — J. Obermann, *Ugaritic Mythology*

OIP — Oriental Institute Publications

OLP — Orientalia lovaniensia periodica

Or — *Orientalia*

OrAnt — *Oriens antiquus*

PBPH — H. W. Attridge and R. A. Oden, Jr., *Philo of Byblos: The Phoenician History*

PEQ — *Palestine Exploration Quarterly*

PF — J. B. Pritchard, *Palestinian Figurines in Relation to Certain Goddesses Known Through Literature*

PRU 2 — C. Virolleaud, *Le Palais Royal d'Ugarit II*

PRU 5 — C. Virolleaud, *Le Palais Royal d'Ugarit V*

PSI — W. F. Albright, *The Proto-Sinaitic Inscriptions and Their Decipherment*

PW — Pauly-Wissowa, *Real-Encyclopädie der classischen Altertumswissenschaft*

RAC — *Reallexikon für Antike und Christentum*

RB — *Revue biblique*

RES — *Répertoire d'épigraphie sémitique*

SBL — Society of Biblical Literature

SBLDS — SBL Dissertation Series

SBLMS — SBL Monograph Series

SBLTT — SBL Texts and Translations

SGAL	H. W. Attridge and R. A. Oden, Jr., *The Syrian Goddess (De Dea Syria). Attributed to Lucian*
StudOr	Studia orientalia
TOML	A. Caquot, M. Sznycer, and A. Herdner, *Textes ougaritiques. I. Myths et légendes*
UF	*Ugaritische Forschungen*
Ug 5	J. Nougayrol, E. Laroche, C. Virolleaud, and C. F. A. Schaeffer, *Ugaritica V*
UL	C. H. Gordon, *Ugaritic Literature*
UT	C. H. Gordon, *Ugaritic Textbook: Grammar, Texts in Transliteration, Cuneiform Selections, Glossary, Indices*
VA	W. F. Albright, "A Vow to Asherah in the Keret Epic," in *BASOR*
YGC	W. F. Albright, *Yahweh and the Gods of Canaan*
ZA	*Zeitschrift für Assyriologie*
ZAW	*Zeitschrift für die alttestamentliche Wissenschaft*
ZDPV	*Zeitschrift des deutschen Palästina-Vereins*

INTRODUCTION

Today almost every student of ancient Near Eastern religion has some familiarity with ʾAšerah, encountered in sources both biblical and extrabiblical. The present study of the goddess deals with extrabiblical sources, mainly religious texts and/or representations from Syria-Palestine, the city of Hierapolis, Egypt, the Sinai peninsula, and Punic settlements in the western Mediterranean (a brief review of relevant Mesopotamian and Arabian textual data is given in Appendix A). Also examined are descriptions of worship in Syria-Palestine and Hierapolis. Various time periods are involved, extending from the second millennium B.C. to the third century of the Christian Era.

A primary task is to demonstrate (except for most of the cited Ugaritic texts and the Hittite text) that the material pertains to ʾAšerah. To do this, information about the goddess provided by a corpus of evidence from one specific location and time -- the main example being the Ugaritic texts -- is frequently used to identify and/or clarify her worship in another region and period. Recurring characteristics of ʾAšerah are unifying factors in the study and can serve as the basis for drawing a composite picture of the goddess.

Chapter I

ᵓAŠERAH IN THE TEXTS FROM UGARIT

A study of ᵓAšerah has the literature of Ugarit as its chief source of information. In Chapter 1 those texts of most importance for this study will be examined. The material will be presented as follows: mythological passages in which ᵓAṯirat (=ᵓAšerah) plays a direct or indirect role; cultic texts (god lists, sacrifice lists); what seems to be an omen text; and mythological passages with the word *qdš*, which according to the context could be regarded as an epithet of ᵓAṯirat/ᵓAšerah.

ᵓAṯirat in the Ugaritic Mythological Texts

This section subdivides into two main parts: I) the relevant Ugaritic passages (vocalized for the sake of clarity,[1] and arranged poetically), their translations, explanations concerning context, and notes (where most required) dealing with elements in the vocalization and/or translation of a passage; and II) a discussion of the mythological texts drawing together and analyzing the evidence concerning ᵓAṯirat.

I.

1. *CTA*[2] 3.6.9-25

About ten lines are missing from the beginning of column 6. At the end of *CTA* 3.5 ᶜAnat had come to ᵓEl seeking to obtain his permission for a house to be built for Baᶜl. *CTA* 3.5 then breaks off (a lacuna of about 22 lines). When the action resumes in column 6, a messenger is being sent to Koṯar-wa-Ḫasis, probably by Baᶜl (cf. 3.6.24-5), possibly by ʿAnat (acting in the name of Baʿl). The command is given to pass over Byblos (*gabla*, line 7) and other localities (lines 7-9) and proceed to Egypt, the home of Koṯar.

(9) šamšir[a] (10) la-daggayyu[b] ʾaṯirati
(11) miǵī la-qadušu ʾamraru[c]
(12) ʾiddaka ʾal tattina (13) panīma
tôk ḥi{q}kupti[d] (14) ʾili kullihu
kaptāru (15) kissiʾu ṯibtihu
ḥikuptu[d] (16) ʾarṣu naḥlatihu
(17) bi-ʾalpi šadi rabbati (18) kumāni
la-paʿnê kôṯa⟨r⟩i (19) hubur wa-qīl
tištaḥ(20)wiya wa-kabbid huwati
(21) wa-rugum la-kôṯari (22) wa-ḫasisi
ṯanāyu la-ha(23)yyini dī ḥaraši yadêmi
(24) taḥmu ʾal[ʾiyāni[e] baʿli]
(25) ha[watu ʾalʾiyi qarrādīma][e]

(9) pass on,[a] (10) O Fisherman[b] of ʾAṯirat,
(11) proceed, O Qaduš ʾAmrar.[c]
(12) Then indeed set (13) (your) face
toward Egypt,[d] (14) (toward) the god of it all.
Kaphtor (15) is the throne of his sitting,
Egypt[d] (16) is the land that he possessed.
(17) (Go) at the thousand-field, the ten thousand(18)-
hectare pace.
At the feet of Koṯar (19) bow down and fall.
Pros(20)trate yourself and honor him.
(21) And say to Koṯar (22) wa-Ḫasis,
repeat to Ha(23)yyin the Handcraftsman:
(24) "Message of ʾAlʾiyan[e] Baʿl,
(25) word of the Conqueror of Warriors:[e]

Notes

a) Cf. Akkadian *wašārum* (also *mašārum*), which in the D is rendered "to abandon, leave (to), let go, release, send off."

b) See Cross for the formation of a name from a natural element plus the adjectival suffix -*ay* -*ayyu* (*CMHE*, 56 and 56 n. 45).[3]

c) At the suggestion of Cross, taking ʾ*amrr* as a formation (from √*mrr*) comparable to the Arabic elative. See GKC (no. 85 b and p. 429 n. 1).[4] A form of the verb *mrr* apparently occurs parallel to a form of *brk* in *CTA* 15.2.14-15, 19-20; 17.1.24-25, 35-36; and 19.4.194-195. Accordingly, ʾ*amrr* could have a meaning such as "most blessed," and the full name be rendered "Holy (and) Most Blessed One." This is also the interpretation of Coogan (96).[5]

d) See, e.g., Albright (*YGC*, 137 and 137 n. 69)[6] and *TOML* (99 and 99 n. 2).[7] Cf. Gibson (55 and 55 n. 1).[8]

e) For these epithets see Albright (*ARI*, 73 and 195 n. 11)[9] and Cross (*CMHE*, 66-7).

2. *CTA* 4.1.20-25

About twenty lines are missing at the end of *CTA* 3.6, and approximately the same number at the beginning of *CTA* 4.1. The position of the writer is that the messenger addressed in *CTA* 3.6 is speaking in *CTA* 4.1.4-23, proclaiming the words of Baʿl to Koṯar. The missing lines perhaps contained the message dictated by Baʿl, then a description of the messenger's trip to Egypt and his arrival at Koṯar's abode, followed by the beginning of his speech to that deity. In *CTA* 4.1.4-19 the basic reason is presented for the sending of the messenger and for the petition directed to the divine craftsman in lines 20-23. The writer's understanding of 4.1.4-19 (and his reconstruction of these lines) will be given in the treatment of *CTA* 4.4.47-57.

(20) ʾap maṯnī rigamīma (21) ʾargumaka[a]
šaskin[b] maʿ (22) maggana[c] rabbati ʾaṯirati yammi
(23) maǵẓī[d] qāniyati ʾilīma
(24) hayyinu ʿalaya la-mappūḫêmi
(25) badê ḫasisi maṣbaṭêmi

(20) Also something else (21) I[a] would say to you:
Provide,[b] I beseech you, (22) a present[c] for
Lady ʾAṯirat of the Sea,
(23) a gift[d] for the Creatress of the Gods."
(24) Hayyin went up to the bellows;
(25) in the hands of Ḫasis were the tongs.

Notes

a) Understanding the "I" to be in reality Baʿl; the messenger is simply repeating the words of the god.

b) Taking √*skn* as "to provide (for), prepare" in the Š. *TOML* (194 n. 6) and Gibson (153) refer to the use of Hebrew *hiskîn* in Ps 139:3, and to the use of *sakānu ana*, "to provide (for), care for, take care of," in the Akkadian of Tell Amarna. See *EA* (2.1499).[10]

c) Here regarding *mgn*, following *šskn*, as a noun; the verb *mgn* (D: "to give [presents]") occurs in *CTA* 4.3.25-36. Cf. Hebrew *mgn* (only in the *piel*), "to deliver up, deliver, give" (note Prov 4:9); Phoenician *mgn*, "to give," and "benefactor"; and Arabic *majjān*, "free, free of charge."

d) Also treating *mǵẓ* as a noun, from √*ǵẓy*. The verb, primarily on the basis of context, perhaps can be translated in the G "to present (a petition, offering, gift)" (below, *CTA* 4.3.26-35), in the D "to entreat, implore" (below, *CTA* 4.2.11). Cf. Hebrew *ʿāṣāh*, "to shut (eyes)."

3. *CTA* 4.2.3-11

Beginning with *CTA* 4.2, and continuing to 4.5.81, ʾAṯirat plays a direct role in the epic. For the sake of convenience this section will be divided into smaller units. About sixteen lines are missing from the beginning of column 2; the first two of the extant lines are too fragmentary to translate.

(3) ʾaḫadat pilkaha [bi-yadiha]
(4) pilka [qa]llati[a] bi-yamīniha
(5) napyanêha[b] maksê bašariha
(6) tamtuʿu[c] maddaha bi-yammi

ṯanê (7) napyanêha bi-nahari-mi
(8) šatat ḫuppatara[d] la-ʾišati
(9) ḫubruṯa[e] la-ẓāri paḥamīma
(10) taʿāpipu[f] ṯôra ʾila dī paʾida
(11) taǵaẓẓiyu[f] bāniya banawāti

(3) She took her spindle in her hand,
(4) the swift[a] spindle in her right hand.
(5) Her two garments,[b] the coverings of her flesh --
(6) her robe she carried[c] into the sea,
her two (7) garments into the river.
(8) She placed a pot[d] on the fire,
(9) a kettle[e] on top of the coals.
(10) She entreated[f] Bull ʾEl the Compassionate,
(11) she implored[f] the Creator of Creatures.

Notes

a) At the suggestion of Cross, taking *qlt* -- Herdner reads (*tʿ/q*)*lt* -- as a noun, "swiftness," from a verbal root *qll*, "to be swift" (cf. Hebrew).

b) Translation based on context; vocalization attempted for the sake of metrics.

c) Cf. Arabic *mataʿa*, "to carry off, carry away, take away."

d) Cf. Akkadian *ḫuppataru*, *ḫuppatru* (a Hurrian loan word), a kind of ewer.

e) Cf. Akkadian *ḫuprušḫu*, *ḫurpušḫu* (a Hurrian loan word), a container.

f) These two verbs are dealt with mainly on the basis of the writer's understanding of the context. For the latter verb, see text no. 2 n. d above. The former is vocalized as the L impf. of a root *ʿpp*.

4. *CTA* 4.2.12-26

(12) bi-nušuʾi ʿênêha wa-tipāhu-na
(13) huluka baʿli ʾaṯ{t}iratu (14) kī taʿīn
huluka batulti (15) ʿanati
tadraqa yabāmti (16) [laʾmi-mi]

bi-ha paʿnāmi (17) [taṭṭutā[a]
baʿ]d-anna kislu (18) [tiṯṯabir[b]
ʿal-anna pa]nūha! tadi[ʿū]
(19) tiǵǵaṣū [pinnātu kis]lêha
(20) ʾanš dt[c] zāri[ha]
(21) tiššaʾu gīha wa-taṣīḥu
[ʾê]kā̆ (22) maǵaya ʾalʾiyānu [ba]ʿlu
(23) ʾêkā̆ maǵayat ba[tu]ltu (24) ʿanatu
māḫiṣāya humā [mā]ḫiṣā (25) banīya
humā [mukalliyā ṣu]brati (26) ʾar(a)yīya[d]

(12) When she lifted her eyes she perceived
(13) the coming of Baʿl, ʾAṯirat (14) indeed saw
the coming of Virgin (15) ʿAnat,
the approach of the Sister-in-Law (16) of People.
At that (her) feet (17) shook,[a]
behind (her) loins (18) were broken,[b]
above her face sweated,
(19) her loin joints trembled,
(20) [c] of her back.
(21) She lifted her voice and shouted,
"Why (22) has ʾAlʾiyan Baʿl arrived,
(23-4) why has Virgin ʿAnat arrived?
Are my enemies going to smite (25-6) my sons?
Are they going to destroy my pride of lions?"[d]

Notes

a) Understanding the root of *ṭṭ* to be *nṭṭ*, perhaps meaning "to shake." This verb also occurs with *pʿnm* in *CTA* 3.3.30 and 19.2.94, and without in 4.7.35, where the text may possibly be translated "the high places [of the earth] shook." Cf. Hebrew *nûṭ*, "to dangle, shake, quake" (Ps 99:1). However, *TOML* (198 n. k, 166 n. b) and Gibson (56, 152), render *ṭṭ* "(her feet) stamp(ed)," citing Arabic *naṭṭa*, "to leap, jump, skip," besides mentioning Hebrew *nûṭ*.

b) Since the subjects of the other verbs in lines 16-20 are regarded by the writer as the various body parts of ʾAṯirat, *kislu* (a body part, thus conceivably feminine in Ugaritic) is viewed as the subject of *tṯbr*, the latter being treated as a 3rd f. s. impf. N (√*ṯbr*, "to break"). Cf. Coogan: "her back was as though shattered" (98); also *CTA* 16.1.54.

c) The vocalization and translation of ʾ*anš* -- and thus also of *dt* -- remain uncertain. Judging from the previous lines, *dt* possibly is nom. pl. f., and "those of her back" could = "vertebrae." Concerning ʾ*anš*, if one does not view the word as a broken plural (Gibson proposes such a solution [57, 141]; cf. Driver [93][11] and Jirku [40][12]), it should probably not be taken as a noun. A plural would be expected here, because the governing verb (in the previous line) most likely is plural (Herdner completes lines 16-20 according to *CTA* 3.3.29-32; cf. also 16.1.54 and 19.93-96). Moreover, taking ʾ*anš* as a verb is problematic: an imperfect would be more in keeping with the context.[13] Perhaps ʾ*anš* is an adverb, with a meaning, generally speaking, of "together with" or "likewise"; cf. Arabic *anisa*, "to be companionable, sociable, nice," and *anīs*, "close, intimate."

d) For *ṣbrt*, cf. Hebrew *ṣibbûr*, "heap," Aramaic *ṣibbūrā*, "total(ity), whole," and Arabic *ṣubrat*, "grain heap." ʾ*ary*, appearing in the Ugaritic mythological texts either in the phrase *ṣbrt* ʾ*ary* (// *bn* ʾ*aṯrt*, "sons of ʾAṯirat") or as a parallel of ʾ*aḫ*, "brother," clearly signifies a relative of some sort. The strongest etymological reference for ʾ*ary* is Hebrew ʾ*ărî*, "lion." As *ḫnzr*, "boar," could be used as a term for a page/lad (in *CTA* 5.5.9 // *ǵlm*), *ṯr*, "bull," and *ẓby*, "gazelle," for elements in the population of Kirta's realm (*CTA* 15.4.6-8; see, e.g., Gibson [92 n. 6] and Gray [62][14]), so "lion" could have been used for a kinsman (cf. the use of *ḫzr*, "swine, boar" in *PRU 2* 24.3.4, 7, 9 and 91.6).[15] For "pride of lions," see Coogan (98).

5. *CTA* 4.2.26-35

(26) [puʿla] kaspi [ʾa]t̠iratu (27) kī taʿīnu
puʿla[a] kaspi wa-n[ughata] (28) ḫurāṣi
šamāḫu rabbatu ʾa[t̠iratu] (29) yammi
gā-ma la-ǵalmiha kī [taṣīḥu]
(30) ʿīn makat̠t̠iru ʾap t[ipāhu][b]
(31) daggayyu rabbati ʾat̠ira[ti yammi]
(32) qaḥ rit̠ta badika[c]
t[---?][d] (33) rabbata ʿalê yadêmi
[-----] (34) bi-môdadi ʾili ya[mmi----]
(35) bi-yammi ʾili d[-----n]

(26-7) When ʾAt̠irat saw the work of silver,
the work[a] of silver and the gleam (28-9) of the gold,
Lady ʾAt̠irat of the Sea rejoiced.
Aloud to her lad indeed she cried,
(30) "See, Deft One, also behold,[b]
(31) Fisherman of Lady ʾAt̠irat of the Sea!
(32-3) Take a net in your hand,[c]
a large holder [?][d] in both of (your) hands.
(34) into [?] the beloved of ʾEl, Yam ,
(35) into [?] Yam, god of

Notes

a) With Cross and *TOML* (199 and 199 n. m), reading *pʿl* (cf. Hebrew *pāʿal*, "to do, make," and *pōʿal*, "doing, deed, work") instead of the *ẓl* of Herdner. Cf. also Gaster (178)[16] and Ginsberg (132).[17]

b) Restoring [*ph*] at the suggestion of Cross.

c) After *bdk* the interpretation of the text (from the end of line 32 through line 35) becomes very uncertain. For the rest of column 2 (following line 35) only the beginning portion of a number of the lines is recognizable.

d) Herdner suggests that, if the sign preceding the lacuna is indeed a *t*, perhaps *t*[*ʿrt*] should be restored, a noun which designates a holder/container in *CTA* 18.4.18, 29 and 19.207. Cf. Hebrew *taʿar*, "razor, sheath."

6. *CTA* 4.3.23-36

In lines 5-9 of column 3 someone (perhaps ᶜAnat) is speaking, but the text is too fragmentary to determine what is being said. Baᶜl responds in lines 10-22, describing (possibly) various insults he experienced.

(23) ᵓaḫra maǵaya ᵓalᵓiyānu baᶜlu
(24) maǵayat batultu ᶜanatu
(25) tamaggināni[a] rabbata [ᵓa]ṯirata yammi
(26) taǵẓiyāni[b] qāniyata ᵓilīma
(27) wa-taᶜnī rabbatu ᵓaṯiratu yammi
(28) ᵓêka tamaggināni rabbata (29) ᵓaṯirata yammi
taǵẓiyāni (30) qāniyata ᵓilīma
maggantumā (31) ṯôra ᵓila dī paᵓida
himma ǵaẓêtumā (32) bāniya banawāti
wa-taᶜnī (33) batultu ᶜanatu[c]
namaggin (34) [-]m[d] rabbata ᵓaṯirata yammi
(35) [naǵ]ẓī qāniyata ᵓilīma
(36) [---][e] namagginu huwati[f]

(23) After ᵓAlᵓiyan Baᶜl arrived,
(24) Virgin ᶜAnat arrived.
(25) They gave (presents)[a] to Lady ᵓAṯirat of the Sea,
(26) they presented (gifts)[b] to the Creatress of the Gods.
(27) And Lady ᵓAṯirat of the Sea answered,
(28-9) "Why do you give (presents) to Lady ᵓAṯirat
of the Sea,
(why) do you present (gifts) (30) to the Creatress
of the Gods?
Have you given (presents) (31) to Bull ᵓEl the
Compassionate,
or have you presented (gifts) (32-3) to the
Creator of Creatures?"
And Virgin ᶜAnat answered,[c]
"Let us give (presents) (34) to ,[d] Lady ᵓAṯirat
of the Sea,
(35) let us present (gifts) to the Creatress of the Gods;
(36) afterwards [?][e] we shall give him presents[f]

Notes

a) See text no. 2 n. c above.

b) See text no. 2 n. d above.

c) Due in part to the condition of the text any rendering of lines 33-36 is uncertain.

d) Driver (94-5), Gaster (180), and Gibson (58) suggest the restoration "(our) mother" -- [ʾ*u*]*m*.

e) Driver (94-5), Gaster (180), and Gibson (58) here propose "afterwards" or "thereafter" -- [ʾ*aḫr*].

f) Perhaps line 37 should be read [ʾ*ila* ʾ*abī*] ʾ*al*ʾ*iyāni baʿli*, "ʾEl, the father of ʾAlʾiyan Baʿl" (suggestion of Cross).

7. *CTA* 4.4.1-7

The end of *CTA* 4.3 (lines 38-53) may have in part described a banquet scene involving ʾAṯirat, Baʿl, and ʿAnat. About twelve lines are missing from the beginning of *CTA* 4.4, and the first five of the extant lines of the column (4.4.1-5) are themselves quite fragmentary. Herdner explains that the restoration of line 1 is conjectural, that of line 2 is based on line 8 (the execution of the orders given by ʾAṯirat), and that of line 3 on *CTA* 3.6.10-11; for lines 4-15, Herdner compares *CTA* 19.52-54, 57-60.

(1) [wa-taʿnī rabbatu] (2) ʾaṯira[tu yammi
šamaʿ la-qadušu] (3) wa-ʾam[raru
la-daggayyu rabbati] (4) ʾaṯirati yammi
[maddil[a] ʿêra] (5) ṣammid paḥla[b]
[šīt gapanīma[c] dūtu] (6) kaspi
dūtu yar[qi naqibānīma][d]
(7) ʿudub gapanī ʾatānati[ya]

(1-2) And Lady ʾAṯirat of the Sea answered,
"Hear, O Qaduš (3) wa-ʾAmrar,
O Fisherman of Lady (4) ʾAṯirat of the Sea,
equip[a] an ass, (5) bridle a donkey.[b]
Put on the reins[c] of (6) silver,

the trappings[d] of gold,
(7) prepare the reins of my (she-)ass."

Notes

a) The majority of scholars translate the verb *mdl* as "to saddle," but, as Cross has pointed out to the writer, there were no saddles in this period.[18]
b) Cf. Arabic *faḥl*, "stallion"; also Akkadian *puḫālu*, "breeding-ram/bull/stallion."
c) Cf. Hebrew *gepen*, "vine."
d) Cf. Hebrew *nāqab*, "to pierce," and its nominal derivatives.

8. *CTA* 4.4.8-22

(8) yišmaᶜ qadu[šu] wa-ᵓamra[ru]
(9) maddala ᶜêra ṣammada paḥla
(10) šata gapanīma dūtu kaspi
(11) dūtu yarqi naqibānīma
(12) ᶜadaba gapanī ᵓatānatiha
(13) yaḥbuqu qadušu wa-ᵓamraru
(14) yašītu-na ᵓaṯirata la-bamti ᶜêri
(15) la-yasamsimati[a] bamti paḥli
(16) qadušu yuᵓḫidu-mi šabᶜira[b]
(17) ᵓamraru kī kabkabi la-panīma
(18) ᵓaṯarā batultu ᶜanatu (19) wa-baᶜlu
tabaᶜā murayyimī ṣapāni
(20) ᵓiddaka la-tattinu panīma
(21) ᶜim(ma) ᵓili mabbūkê naharêmi
(22) qirba ᵓapīqê tihāmatêmi[c]

(8) Qaduš wa-ᵓAmrar obeyed.
(9) He equipped an ass, he bridled a donkey.
(10) He put on the reins of silver,
(11) the trappings of gold;
(12) he prepared the reins of her (she-)ass.
(13) Qaduš wa-ᵓAmrar clasped (his hands),
(14) he placed ᵓAṯirat on the back of the ass,
(15) on the sleek[a] back of the donkey.
(16) Qaduš took a torch,[b]

(17) ʾAmrar was like a star in front.
(18-9) Virgin ʿAnat and Baʿl went on,
they two departed for the heights of Ṣapan.
(20) Then (her) face indeed she set
(21) toward ʾEl at the sources of the two rivers,
(22) in the midst of the springs of the double-deep.[c]

Notes

a) Cf. Akkadian *(w)asāmu*, "to be(come) proper, fit, right, suitable," *(w)asmu*, "suitable, appropriate, fit," Arabic *wasāma*, "grace, gracefulness, charm, beauty." "Sleek (back)" is the suggestion of Cross.

b) Taking *šbʿr* as a substantive from √*bʿr*, "to burn, be kindled" (cf. Hebrew *bāʿar*) with *š* preformative (cf. *TOML* [203 n. d]; also GKC [nos. 85 o and 55 i]).

c) Choosing here the translation of Cross (*CMHE*, 36). *thmtm* is frequently rendered "two oceans."

9. *CTA* 4.4.23-39

(23) tagliyu[a] ḏadī[b] ʾili wa-tabāʾu
(24) qarašī[c] malki ʾabī šanīma
(25) la-paʿnê ʾili tahburu wa-taqīlu
(26) tištaḥwiyu wa-takabbiduhu
(27) halumma ʾilu kī yipāhunaha
(28) yapruqu liṣba[d] wa-yiṣḥaqu
(29) paʿnêhu la-hudumi yaṯpudu[e]
wa-yakarkiru[f] (30) ʾuṣbaʿātihu
yiššaʾu gīhu wa-ya[ṣīḥu]
(31) ʾêka maǵayat rabbatu ʾaṯira[tu ya]mmi
(32) ʾêka ʾatawat qāniyatu ʾi[līma]
(33) raǵābu raǵibti wa-tǵt[??][g]
(34) himma ǵamāʾu ǵamiʾti wa-ʿasê[ti][h]
(35) laḥmī himma šatyī-mi
laḥ[mī] (36) bi-ṯulḥanāti laḥma
šatī (37) bi-karpānīma yêna
bi-kā<sī>[i] ḫurāṣi (38) dama ʿiṣīma
himma yadu[j] ʾili malki (39) yaḫāsisuki[k]
ʾahbatu ṯôri taʿāriruki

(23) She opened[a] the tent[b] of ᵓEl and she entered
(24) the tent-shrine[c] of the King, the Father of Years.
(25) At the feet of ᵓEl she bowed down and fell,
(26) she prostrated herself and honored him.
(27) As soon as ᵓEl saw her
(28) he opened his mouth[d] and laughed.
(29) He put[e] his feet on the footstool
and twiddled[f] (30) his fingers.
He lifted his voice and shouted:
(31) "Why has Lady ᵓAṯirat of the Sea arrived?
(32) Why has the Creatress of the Gods come?
(33) Are you indeed hungry and [g]
(34) or are you indeed thirsty and parched?[h]
(35) Eat or drink!
Eat (36) from tables bread,
drink (37) from goblets wine,
from cups[i] of gold (38) the blood of vines.
Or does the love/member[j] of ᵓEl the King (39) move you,[k]
the love of Bull arouse you?"

Notes

a) See Clifford, who follows the suggestion of Conrad L'Heureux (49, 52).[19]

b) See Clifford (48-9, 51-4).

c) Cf. Hebrew *qereš*, "board, frame" (used frequently in Exod 26-40 in connection with the tabernacle. See Clifford (48-9, 54) and Cross (*CMHE*, 36 and 36 n. 144, 321-2).

d) Cf. Arabic *liṣb*, "defile, (narrow) pass."[20] Ugaritic *lṣb* may have denoted not only the mouth (the narrow passage between the rows of teeth and/or the jaws) but also the throat. Cf. Coogan (100), Driver (97, 159), Gibson (59, 150), Ginsberg (133), Gordon (*UT*, 429 no. 1393),[21] and Jirku (45).[22]

e) Cf. Hebrew *šāpat*, "to set, put."

f) Cf. Hebrew *kārar*, occurring only as a *pilpēl* ptc., "dancing ([lit.] whirling)"; *kikkār*, "a round, round district, round loaf, round weight"; and Arabic *karkara*, "turn a mill" (II -- "spin in the air, turn about"). An alternate translation of *wykrkr* ᵓ*uṣb*ᶜ*th* is "[he] wiggled his toes" (Cross [*CMHE*, 37]; cf. 2 Sam 21:20).

g) Perhaps compare *tǵt* to Hebrew *tā*ᶜ*āh*, "to wander about, err"?

h) At the advice of Cross, restoring a *t* and referring to Arabic ᶜ*asā*, "to grow hard, dry." Cf. Ginsberg (133). An alternate solution would be to restore the *t* but compare the verb to Arabic ᶜ*assa*, "to keep night watch, patrol; spy; arrive late." Cf. Driver (96) and Gibson (59).

i) Cf. the comment in *TOML* (205 n. h) and *CTA* 3.1.12.

j) As Cross has explained to the writer, *yd* here is undoubtedly a pun, involving both "member/hand (=penis)" and "love" (cf. Arabic *wadd*, "love, affection").

k) Or "excite you." Cf. Akkadian *ḫasāsu*, "to think (of), consider, recall."

10. *CTA* 4.4.40-57

CTA 3.5.38-52 for the most part parallels 4.4.41-57. This is also the case for *CTA* 3.4.2*-6 and 4.4.50-57, *CTA* 4.1.4-19 and 4.4.47-57, and RS 24.263, lines 1-6 (NTA, 65)[23] and *CTA* 4.4.45-55 (cf. *CTA* 3.5.11-12 and 4.4.50-51). Variations between *CTA* 4.4.41-57 and its parallels will be mentioned below.

(40) wataᶜnī rabbatu ᵓaṯiratu yammi
(41) taḥmuka ᵓilu ḥakama
ḥukmuka (42) ᶜim(m)(a) ᶜālami
ḥayyatu ḥiẓẓati (43) taḥmuka
malkunu ᵓalᵓiyā[nu] baᶜlu
(44) ṯāpiṭunu wa-ᵓênᵃ dū ᶜal-anahu
(45) kullāniyyunuᵇ qī[ša]huᶜ na[bilu-na]ᵈ
(46) kullāniyyunu [na]bilu kāsahu

(47) [ʾanā]yu[e] la-yaṣīḥu[f] ṯôra ʾila ʾabīhu
(48) [ʾi]la malka dū yakāninuhu
yaṣīḥu (49) ʾaṯirata wa-banīha
ʾilata[g] wa-ṣubrata (50) ʾarayīha
wa-na ʾên bêtu la-baʿli (51) kī-mā[h] ʾilīma
wa-ḥaẓiru[i] kī banī ʾaṯirati[j]
(52) môṯabu ʾili maẓallu[k] binihu
(53) môṯabu rabbati ʾaṯirati yammi
(54) môṯabu[l] kallāti kanyāti[m]
(55) môṯabu pidrayyi[n] bitti ʾāri[o]
(56) maẓallu ṭallayyi bitti rabbi
(57) môṯabu ʾarṣa<yyi> bitti yaʿabdiri[p]

(40) And Lady ʾAṯirat of the Sea answered:
(41) "Your decree, ʾEl, is wise;
your wisdom (42) (is) forever.
A life of good fortune (43) is your decree.
Our king is ʾAlʾiyan Baʿl,
(44) our judge without[a] rival.
(45) All of us[b] his gift[c] must bring,[d]
(46) all of us must bring his cup.
(47) He laments,[e] indeed he cries out[f] to Bull ʾEl his father,
(48) ʾEl, the King who created him;
he cries out to (49-50) ʾAṯirat and her sons,
ʾElat[g] and her pride of lions:
'But Baʿl has no house (51) as do[h] the (other) gods,
and no court[i] as do ʾAṯirat's sons.[j]
(52) The dwelling of ʾEl is the shelter[k] of his son.
(53) The dwelling of Lady ʾAṯirat of the Sea
(54) is the dwelling of[l] the honored[m] brides:
(55) the dwelling of Pidray,[n] daughter of light,[o]
(56) the shelter of Ṭallay, daughter of rain,
(57) the dwelling of ʾArṣay, daughter of [p].'"

Notes

a) *CTA* 3.5.41 has simply ʾ*in*.

b) *CTA* 3.5.41-2: *klnyy*. The writer follows the explanation of Cross that *klnyn* is the adjective *kl*, plus the adjectival ending -*n*, plus the *nisbe* element *y* (thus *kl* has a double adjectival ending), plus the 1st c. pl. suffix.[24]

c) Cf. Akkadian *qiāšu*, *qâšu*, "to give," *qištum*, "gift."

d) Herdner restores *n[bln]* according to *CTA* 3.5.42; RS 24.263, line 1 has *nbl*.

e) Or, ᵓ*any* may be an interjection: "alas!" (perhaps ᵓ*anīya*). Cf. Ginsberg (133).

f) *ly* in RS 24.263, line 4 definitely shows Baᶜl is the subject of *yṣḥ* (twice) in that passage. Therefore, due to the importance of repetition and parallelism in Ugaritic poetry, Baᶜl should be regarded as the subject of the same verb in the parallel passages. Moreover, in the writer's opinion ᵓ*any lyṣḥ* . . . *yṣḥ* ᵓ*aṯrt* . . . in *CTA* 3.5.43-52 is still part of the speech of ᶜAnat (line 37), in 4.4.47-57 part of ᵓAṯirat's speech (line 40), and in RS 24.263, lines 1-6 part of the speech of ᶜAnat, ᵓAṯirat, or another deity. That is, the speakers are describing the condition and action of Baᶜl, and repeating his complaint. Concerning *CTA* 4.1.4-19, in all probability the Fisherman is repeating the first-person message of Baᶜl to Koṯar (cf. 3.6.9-25); thus the verbs and suffixes of lines 4-7 would have been first-person. In line 10 the reading could have been either *lbᶜl* or *ly*.

g) ᵓEl is the ᵓ*ilu*, "god," and ᵓAṯirat (as the "Creatress of the Gods") the ᵓ*ilatu*, "goddess," *par excellence*. Thus "ᵓElat" is an appropriate alternate name for ᵓAṯirat; she is the feminine counterpart of ᵓEl.

h) RS 24.263, line 4 has *k*ᵓ*ilm*.

i) *CTA* 3.5.47 reads *ḥẓr*, while in RS 24.263, line 5 Herdner restores *[wḥṭ(?)r]*.[25]

j) Or, line 51 could be interpreted as saying "like that/those of the (other) gods . . . like that/those of the sons of ᵓAṯirat" -- cf. Coogan (100), Cross (*CMHE*, 184), and Jirku (45).

k) RS 24.263, line 5 has *mṭll*.[26]

l) *CTA* 3.4.2-6 and 3.5.48-52 (according to the restoration of Herdner) have *mṯb klt knyt* after *mṯb ʾarṣy bt yʿbdr*. It is uncertain whether RS 24.263 has *mṯb klt knyt*.

m) Cf. Akkadian *kanūtu* (verbal adjective from *kanû*), "the honored, estimable, cherished," a title of goddesses. Ginsberg (133), Jirku (46), and Obermann (30, 92)[27] render this adjective "perfect."

n) Vocalizing the names of the three goddesses according to the discussions of Cross (*CMHE*, 56 and 56 nn. 45-7; 116 n. 17).

o) Driver (97, 135) and Gibson (60, 142) relate *ʾar* to Arabic *ʾary*, "dew, rain," rendering *ʾar* "mist."[28]

p) At the advice of Cross, understanding *yʿbdr* to be a quadriliteral -- *ʿbdr* -- with preformative *y*.[29]

11. *CTA* 4.4.58 - 5.63

(58) wa-yaʿnī luṭpānu[a] ʾilu dū paʾidu
(59) pa-ʿabdu ʾanǎ ʿananu[b] ʾaṯirati
(60) pa-ʿabdu ʾanāku ʾāḫ̮idu ʾulṯi[c]
(61) himma ʾamatu ʾaṯiratu talbunu (62) labināti[d]
yabnī bêta la-baʿli (63) kī-mā ʾilīma
wa-ḥaẓiru kī banī ʾaṯirati[e]

(58) And Luṭpan[a] ʾEl the Compassionate answered,
(59) "Then am I a servant, an attendant[b] of ʾAṯirat,
(60) then am I a servant who grasps the trowel,[c]
(61) or ʾAṯirat a slave girl who makes (62) bricks?[d]
Let a house be built for Baʿl (63) as was for the (other) gods,
and a court as was for ʾAṯirat's sons."[e]

Notes

a) Cf. Arabic *luṭf*, "kindness, benevolence, friendliness."

b) *ʿnn* is generally translated by a "servant" word, which fits its usage in this and a number of other Ugaritic passages. As Cross has explained to the writer, the root is best seen as *ʿnn*, which points to Hebrew *ʿānān*, "cloud mass, cloud" as an etymological reference. Conceivably, the ancient poets viewed the clouds gliding across the sky as the messengers/servants of the gods. The fact that Baʿl was the Rider on the Clouds (*rkb ʿrpt*) may be pertinent to an understanding of *ʿnn* (cf. *CTA* 2.1.18, 35). Cf. Arabic *ʿanan*, "appearing object, apparition."

c) Vocalizing *ʾulṯ* for the sake of metrics and translating according to context.

d) An alternate translation is: "Or (am I [ʾEl]) a slave girl of ʾAṯirat who makes bricks?" Cf. Coogan (101) and *TOML* (206).

e) See text no. 10 n. j above.

12. *CTA* 4.5.64-81

(64) wa-taʿnī rabbatu ʾaṯiratu yammi
(65) rabêta ʾilu-mi la-ḥakamta
(66) šêbatu daqanika la-tasiruka
(67) rḫntt d[-] la-ʾirtika[a]
(68) wê-na-ʾap[b] ʿaddānu[c] maṭarihu (69) baʿlu
yaʿaddinu ʿaddānu ṯikkāti[d] bi-gulṯi[e]
(70) wa-‹ya›ttinu qôlahu bi-ʿurpāti
(71) šururhu[f] la-ʾarṣi baraqīma
(72) bêta ʾarazīma yakālilanahu
(73) himma bêta labināti yaʿmusanahu[g]
(74) la-yarguma la-ʾalʾiyāni baʿli
(75) ṣīḥ ḫarrāna bi-bahatī!ka
(76) ʿiḏḏabāti[h] bi-qirbi hêkalika
(77) tabilūka ǵūrūma maʾda kaspa
(78) gibaʿūma maḥmada ḫurāṣi
(79) yabiluka ʾudru[i] ʾilquṣīma[j]
(80) wa-banī bahatī kaspi wa-ḫurāṣi
(81) bahatī ṭahurīma ʾiqniʾīma

(64) And Lady ʾAṯirat of the Sea answered,
(65) "You are great, ʾEl, indeed you are wise;
(66) the grey hair of your beard indeed instructs you.

(67) your breast.[a]

(68-9) Yea also[b] Baʿl will make fertile[c] with his rain, with water[e] he will indeed make fertile harrowed land;[d]

(70) and he will put his voice in the clouds,

(71) he will flash[f] lightning to the earth.

(72) A house of cedars let him complete,

(73) or a house of bricks let him construct.[g]

(74) Indeed let it be said to ʾAlʾiyan Baʿl,

(75) 'Call a caravan into your house,

(76) wares[h] into the midst of your palace.

(77) The mountains will yield you much silver,

(78) the hills the choicest of gold;

(79) camels [?][i] will bring you gems.[j]

(80) And build a house of silver and gold,

(81) a house of pure lapis lazuli.'"

Notes

a) The writer did not find a convincing treatment of this line, neither does he have any proposal of his own.

b) At the advice of Cross, comparing *w-* to Arabic *wai*, "woe!, oh!" (also *waika*, "woe to you!, well done!, bravo!"), and understanding *-n-* as an additional, emphatic particle. Cross has suggested to the writer that ʾEl could actually be speaking lines 68-81, rather than ʾAṯirat.

c) In the Aramaic text from Tell el-Fakhariyeh (line 4) √*ʿdn*, as a participle (*mʿdn*), is used as an epithet of Hadad, with the possible meaning of "to make prosper" or "to make fertile."[30]

d) Cf. Akkadian *šikkatum* II, pl., "harrowed land."

e) In *CTA* 8.13 *glṯ* occurs before *ʾisr*; perhaps the text is saying "I [Baʿl] shall bind the *glṯ*." In RS 24.245, line 7 (*Ug 5*, 557)[31] the reading is *bglṯ bšm*[*m*] ("heavens"?). In *PRU 5* 1.1.5[32] *tglṯ* may be a verb, with *ʿṯtrt* as subject and *thmt* as object. Hebrew *gālaš* -- only Cant 4:1 and 6:5 -- possibly means "to flow down, stream (down), descend." Mishnaic Hebrew *gālaš* should also be mentioned: "to bubble, froth up, boil." Based on this rather meager evidence, the tentative conclusion reached here is that *gl<u>t</u>* as a substantive could be a "water" word; as a verb, it could signify water/liquid action or motion.

f) Postulating a root *šrr*, "to flash, shine, blaze." Cf. Akkadian *šarūrum*, "rays, beams, flashes"; Arabic *šarār*, "spark(s)."

g) Cf. Hebrew *ᶜāmas*, "to load, carry a load." *TOML* (208 n. w) and Gibson (154) refer to the use of *ᶜāmaś* in Neh 4:11.

h) Or, perhaps *ᶜḏbt* should be vocalized as a singular and translated "merchant train" (cf. Coogan [101] and Driver [97]). Cf. Hebrew *ᶜizzābôn*, only pl., "wares, goods"; Akkadian *uzubbûm*, "parting money"; and Old South Arabic *ᶜḏb*, "to repair, restore."

i) Translating as a collective. However, as Coogan has pointed out to the writer, camels may not have been domesticated in this period. Cf. Gibson ("the noblest"; 61).

j) Vocalizing *ᵓilqṣm* for the sake of metrics and translating according to context.

13. *CTA* 4.6.44-46

Having just completed his palace, Baᶜl prepares a great feast in celebration.

(44) ṣaḥa ᵓaḫḫīhu bi-bahatīhu
ᵓarayīhu[a] (45) bi-qirbi hêkalihu
ṣaḥa (46) šabᶜīma banī ᵓa<u>t</u>irati

(44) He invited his brothers into his house,
his lions[a] (45) into the midst of his palace;
he invited (46) the seventy sons of ᵓA<u>t</u>irat.

Note

a) See above text no. 4 n. d.

14. *CTA* 6.1.38-61

After Baʿl dies, ʿAnat buries him and slaughters many animals as a *gmn ʾalʾiyn bʿl*. She then starts out for and reaches the abode of ʾEl, entering his tent.

(38) tištaḥwiyu wa-takabbiduhu
(39) tiššaʾu gīha wa-taṣīḥu
tišmaḫū hitta (40) ʾaṯiratu wa-banūha
ʾilatu wa-ṣub(41)rati ʾarayīha
kī mita ʾalʾiyānu (42) baʿlu
kī ḫalaqa zubūlu baʿlu (43) ʾarṣi
gā-ma yaṣīḥu ʾilu
(44) la-rabbati ʾaṯirati yammi
šamaʿ (45) la-rabbatu ʾaṯira[tu] yammi
tinī (46) ʾaḥada bi banīki
[wa-]ʾamallikunnu
(47) wa-taʿnī rabbatu ʾaṯiratu yammi
(48) bal(a) namallika yadiʿa yilḥana[a]
(49) wa-yaʿnī luṭpānu ʾilu dū paʾi(50)du
daqqu ʾānīma[b] la-yarūẓu
(51) ʿimma baʿli la-yaʿdubu[c] murḥa[d]
(52) ʿimma bini dagani kī timmasā-mi[e]
(53) wa-ʿanê rabbatu ʾaṯiratu yammi
(54) biltī namallika ʿaṯtara ʿarīẓa
(55) yamluka ʿaṯtaru ʿarīẓu[f]
(56) ʾappinaka[g] ʿaṯtaru ʿarīẓu
(57) yaʿlī bi-ṣirārāti ṣapāni
(58) yaṯibu la-kaḥṯi[h] ʾalʾiyāni (59) baʿli
paʿnāhu la-tamgiyāni (60) huduma
riʾšuhu la-yamgiyu (61) ʾapsahu

(38) she prostrated herself and honored him.
(39) She lifted her voice and shouted,
"Let now rejoice (40-3) ʾAṯirat and her sons,
ʾElat and her pride of lions,
because ʾAlʾiyan Baʿl has died,
because the Prince, Lord of the Earth, has perished."

ʾEl shouted aloud
(44) to Lady ʾAṯirat of the Sea,
"Hear, (45) O Lady ʾAṯirat of the Sea,
give (46) one of your sons,
and I will make him king."
(47) And Lady ʾAṯirat of the Sea answered,
(48) "Shall we not make Yadiʿ Yilḥan[a] king?"
(49-50) And Luṭpan ʾEl the Compassionate answered,
"He, small of strength,[b] cannot race,
(51) he cannot throw[c] a lance[d] with Baʿl,
(52) with the son of Dagan in contest."[e]
(53) And Lady ʾAṯirat of the Sea answered,
(54) "Shall we not make ʿAṯtar the Terrible king?
(55) Let ʿAṯtar the Terrible be king."[f]
(56) Thereupon[g] ʿAṯtar the Terrible
(57) went up to the heights of Ṣapan.
(58) He sat on the seat[h] of ʾAlʾiyan (59) Baʿl.
His feet did not reach (60) the footstool,
his head did not reach (61) its top.

Notes

a) With Coogan (111), Cross (*CMHE*, 66-7, 67 n. 84), and Ginsberg (140), understanding *ydʿ ylḥn* as the sentence name of a god. It consists of two G imperfect verbal elements: "He knows, he understands." Concerning the latter verb, cf. Arabic *laḥana*, "to understand, comprehend," *laḥina*, "to be intelligent."

b) Taking *ʾanm* as a pl. intensive. Cf. Isa 40:26, 29; Prov 11:7.

c) Translating √*ʿdb* here basically according to context.

d) Cf. Hebrew *rōmaḥ*, "lance, spear."

e) As Cross has explained to the writer, a verb *msy/h* could have existed as a biform of Hebrew *nāsāh* (*piel*), "to test, try," or more likely, as a denominative of *massāh*, "test, trial, proving." *tms* is the short form of the verb (note the preceding *kī*), which in the N dual would have the meaning "they two enter into contest" (reciprocal sense;

cf. Hebrew *lāḥam* [*niphal*], "to engage in battle"). The translation "in contest" is that of Coogan (111).

f) Cross has suggested to the writer that ʾEl is the speaker of line 55, rather than ʾAṯirat.

g) Vocalizing for the sake of metrics.

h) Or "throne."

15. *CTA* 6.5.1-11

This passage is a recapitulation of Baʿl's conflicts with Yam and Mot. The fighting seems to have gone on for seven years.

(1) yaʾḫudu baʿlu banī ʾaṯirati
(2) rabbīma[a] yimḫaṣu bi-katipi
(3) dukayīma[a] yimḫaṣu bi-ṣimdi[b]
(4) ṣaḥura[c] môta yamṣuḫu[d] la-ʾarṣi
(5) [yaṯibu][e] ba[ʿ]lu la-kissiʾi mulkihu
(6) [la-nūḫati] la-kaḥṯi darkatihu
(7) la-[yômī]ma la-yaraḫīma
la-yaraḫīma (8) la-šanāti
[ma]ka bi-šabiʿi (9) šanati[f]
w[--] binu ʾili-mi môtu
(10) ʿimma ʾalʾiyāni baʿli
yiššaʾu (11) gīhu wa-yaṣīḥu

(1) Baʿl seized the sons of ʾAṯirat,
(2) he smote *Rabbīma*[a] on the shoulder,
(3) *Dukayīma*[a] he smote with a club.[b]
(4) Sallow[c] Mot he struck[d] to the earth.
(5) Baʿl sat[e] on the throne of his kingship,
(6) on the place of serenity, on the seat of his dominion.
(7) The days became months,
the months (8) years.
Lo, in the seventh (9) year[f]
the son of ʾEl, Mot, spoke [?]
(10) with ʾAlʾiyan Baʿl.
He lifted (11) his voice and shouted,

Notes

a) At the suggestion of Cross, regarding *rbm* and *dkym* as epithets of Yam. The former is likely an ellipsis for an expression identical to the Hebrew *mayīm rabbîm*, "mighty/great waters" (so also *TOML* [167 n. h, 265 and 265 n. b]). Cf. Pss 29:3, 93:4; also *CTA* 3.3.36. For *dkym*, "pounders, breakers" of the sea, cf. Hebrew *dŏkî*, "(crushing), pounding" of waves (Ps 93:3).

b) Cf. Arabic *ṣamada*, "to beat"; Hebrew *ṣemed*, "yoke."

c) Cf. Hebrew *ṣāḥōr*, "tawny."

d) *TOML* (173 n. e) raises the question whether *mṣḫ* might be a variant of the more common *mḫṣ*.

e) Coogan renders *yṯb* "returned" (114), Gordon "returns" (*UL*, 47).[33] An alternate restoration could be [*yʿl*]; cf. Ginsberg ("mounts"; 141).

f) Or, possibly, *bšbʿ šnt* is "after seven years" (Ginsberg [141]).

16. *CTA* 12.1.12-18

In lines 9-11 of *CTA* 12.1 the maidservants *tlš* and *dmgy* (lines 14, 16) apparently are complaining before ʾEl about sufferings they are experiencing.[34] ʾEl reacts by laughing (because the pains of the women come from approaching childbirth? -- see *TOML* [328, 336-7 n. q]) and ordering the women to go out into the wilderness (line 21), where they are to give birth to the ʾ*aklm* (line 26) and the ʿ*qqm* (line 27).[35]

(12) ʾilu yiẓḥaqu bi-mā (13) libbi
wa-yagmuḏu[a] bi-mā kabidi
(14) ẓiʾī ʾatti la-tulišu[b] (15) ʾamatu yariḫi
(16) la-dāmigayyu[c] ʾamatu (17) ʾaṯirati
qaḥī (18) kusʾanaki[d] ḥidāgaki

(12) ʾEl laughed in (13) (his) heart
and he inwardly convulsed (with laughter).[a]
(14) "(You) Go out, O Tuliš,[b] (15) maidservant of Yariḫ,
(16) O Damigay,[c] maidservant (17) of ʾAṯirat.
Take (18) your (sedan) chair,[d] your litter,

Notes

a) Choosing with some hesitation the suggestion of *TOML* (336 n. p). Referring to the Judaeo-Aramaean verb *gmd*, "to contract, shrink, twist, writhe," which might be written here with a *ḏ* (cf. ʾ*ḫd*, "to seize," written ʾ*ḫḏ* in *CTA* 12.2.32-36), *TOML* translates *wygmḏ* "he is convulsed with laughter."

b) With *TOML* (337 and 337 n. 5), Driver (71 and 71 n. 5), and Gordon (*UL*, 53), taking *tlš* as a proper name, attested elsewhere at Ugarit -- see Gordon (*UT*, 498 no. 2561) and Gröndahl (314, 420).[36] Vocalizing after Akkadian *tu-li-ša* (RS 8.333, line 8).[37]

c) Gröndahl lists, under the *qātil* form, the entry "+*dāmigay*- (dmgy, f.), vgl. asa., arab. dāmiǧ 'der zu Hilfe kommt'" (70).

d) Cf. Hebrew *kissē*ʾ, Akkadian *kussû*, "seat, chair, throne." Perhaps the *ks*ʾ*an* is a seat for childbirth (*TOML* [338 and 338 n. w]).

17. *CTA* 14.4.197-206

In the following passage from the Kirta Epic, the eponymous hero is on his way to ʾ*udm* with the goal of obtaining *ḥry*, that she might be his wife.

(197) yam[ǵiyǔ] la-qudši[a] (198) ʾa[ṯirati] ṣurri-mi[b]
wa-la-ʾilati (199) ṣid[yāni-]mi[b]
ṯam(m)(a) (200) yaddu[ru ki]rta ṯāʿu[c]
(201) ʾê-ʾiṯat[d] ʾaṯiratu ṣurri-mi
(202) wa-ʾilatu ṣidyāni-mi
(203) himma ḥurriya bêtiya (204) ʾiqqaḥa
ʾašaʿriba ǵalmata (205) ḥaẓiriya
ṯanêha[e] ka!spa-mi (206) ʾattina
wa-ṯalāṯaha[e] ḫurāṣa-mi

(197) they/he came to Qudšu,[a] (198) (to) ʾAṯirat of Tyre,[b]
and to ʾElat (199) of Sidon.[b]
There (200) Kirta the Noble[c] vowed,

(201) "As ᵓAṯirat of Tyre lives,[d]
(202) and ᵓElat of Sidon,
(203) if Ḥurriya (into) my house (204) I take,
(if) I bring the lass (205) (into) my court,
two times her weight[e] in silver (206) I will give
and three times her weight[e] in gold."

Notes

a) Understanding *qdš* as "Holiness." A "sanctuary" translation would be awkward here, especially in view of the following *wlᵓilt*.

b) Following the proposal of Albright and regarding the *-m* in both words as enclitic (VA, 30 n. 5).[38] *ṣdyn* is a peculiar spelling for "Sidon"; Gray suggests that perhaps it is a variant spelling of expected *ṣdn* (56).

c) An alternate translation of *ṯᶜ* could be "the Generous": see *TOML* (529-30 n. u), Gibson (87 n. 3), and Gray (56).

d) Or "is present, exists." With Albright (VA, 30-1 and 30-1 nn. 11, 12), taking the initial *ᵓi* as an asseverative particle (cf. Arabic *ay*, "that is [to say], i.e.," and *ī*, "yes [!]") and *ᵓiṯt* as a feminine form of *ᵓiṯ*, the particle of existence (cf. Hebrew *yēš*, "existence; is, are, was, etc."). Admittedly, *yēš* is invariable (no feminine form; cf. *ᵓiṯ* with *šmt* [f.] in *CTA* 19.3.110, 125, 139).[39]

e) Or "price/value." *ṯn* and *ṯlṯ* (lines 205-206) have been interpreted as "two-thirds" and "one-third" (e.g., by *TOML* [530 and 530-1 n. x]; Gray [16, 57]; Jirku [91]), with reference being made to the description of Gilgamesh (I.2.1): *šittašu ilu-ma šullultašu amēlutu*, "two parts of him are divine, his third human."

18. *CTA* 15.2.21-28

ᵓEl, at the urging of Baᶜl, blesses Kirta.

(21) ᵓaṯṯata (22) tiqqaḥu bêtika
ǵalmata tašaᶜribu (23) ḥaẓ!irika

talidu šabʿa banīma la-ka
(24) wa-ṯamānê tiṯtamminu-mi[a] (25) la-ka
talidu yaṣṣiba[b] ǵalma
(26) yênaqu ḥalaba ʾa[ṯi]rati
(27) maṣāṣu ṯadê batulti [ʿanati]
(28) mušêniqa[tê ʾilīma][c]

(21) the woman (22) you take (into) your house,
the lass you bring (23) (into) your court,
will bear seven sons for you,
(24) and eight will she produce[a] (25) for you.
She will bear Yaṣṣib[b] the Lad.
(26) He will suck the milk of ʾAṯirat,
(27) he will drain the breasts of Virgin ʿAnat,
(28) the two wet nurses of the gods.[c]

Notes

a) Regarding the verb *ṯmn* as a denominative of *ṯmn*, "eight," and vocalizing as a Dt. For the translation, cf. Ginsberg (146).

b) Cf. Hebrew *nāṣab*, *hiphil* impf. 3rd m. s., "he sets (up)."

c) With Driver (36-7), Ginsberg (146), Gordon (*UL*, 75) and others, restoring [*t ʾilm*]. However, simply *mšnq* (Š m. s. passive participle of √*ynq*) may be the correct reading; see, e.g., *TOML* (539 and 539 n. k).

19. *CTA* 15.3.22-30

After the gods bless Kirta, his wife soon bears him children.

(22) maka bi-šabʿi šanāti
(23) banū kirta kī-mā-hum(u)[a] tuddarū[b]
(24) ʾap banātu ḥurriya (25) kī-mā-hum(u)
wa-taḫsusu ʾaṯiratu (26) nidrahu
wa-ʾilatu p[ilʾahu][c]
(27) wa-tiššaʾu gīha wa-[taṣīḥu]
(28) pāh maʿ ʾap ki[rta pārara][d]
(29) ʾū-ṯanī nidra[hu malku][e]

(30) ʾapāriru h/ʾi [-------]

(22) Lo! in seven years
(23) the sons of Kirta were as many as[a] were vowed,[b]
(24) also the daughters of Ḥurriya (25) were so many.
And ʾAṯirat thought (26) of his vow,
and ʾElat his pledge.[c]
(27) And she lifted her voice and shouted,
(28) "See, I beseech you, has Kirta then broken,[d]
(29) or the king changed his[e] vow?
(30) I will break

Notes

a) *TOML* (541 n. r) and Gray (60) suggest *k* plus *mhm*, relating the latter word to Arabic *mahmā*, "whatever, whatsoever; however much."

b) At the suggestion of Cross, understanding *kmhm tdr* basically to have the sense of "as many as Kirta had asked for in his vow." Clearly Kirta requested eight sons, no doubt to replace the eight who had died (*CTA* 14.1.6-11; see also the previous text). Perhaps this petition was assumed to be part of Kirta's vow to ʾAṯirat (*CTA* 14.4.197-206; text no. 17) and not included in the text, or perhaps it was part of a later vow to the goddess which has not been preserved. *tdr* is vocalized as a G passive. A "to promise" translation for $\sqrt{ndr}$ is too weak.

c) Restoring [*lʾah*] with Driver (38). Alternatively, if *ndrh* is regarded as plural, one could restore [*lʾih*] with Ginsberg (cf. 146; cf. also *TOML* [542 n. t]). Cf. Hebrew *peleʾ*, "wonder," *pālāʾ*, in the *piel* with *neder*, "to make a special votive offering."

d) Restoring . *pr*] after *k*[*rt* with Driver (38) and Gibson (92). Or, one might choose to restore *ypr* (cf. Ginsberg [146]).

e) Restoring [*h mlk*] with Driver (38) and Gibson (92). An alternative reading (plural): *nd*[*rm mlk*] (cf. Ginsberg [146]).

20. *CTA* 23

The present study's scope precludes a discussion of the relationship of the first portion of *CTA* 23 (lines 1-29; "ʾAṯirat" in lines 13, 24, 28), which (according to the writer's viewpoint) is liturgical in nature, with the second part (lines 30-76), a myth telling of ʾEl with two women and the birth of his sons Šaḥar and Šalim.[40] However, due to the different genres of these two sections, and to the fact that the name of ʾAṯirat or one of her epithets is not mentioned (in the writer's opinion) in the second portion,[41] it is not at all certain that ʾAṯirat is one of the women/ goddesses in the mythological text. Therefore, only those lines in the liturgical section which contain the name ʾ*aṯrt* will be treated.[42]

(13 [28]) wa-šadu šadu ʾili-mi šadu ʾaṯirati wa-raḥma yyi [a]
(13 [28]) And the field is the field of ʾEl, the field of ʾAṯirat wa-Raḥmay[a]

Note

a) With Cross and *TOML* (371 n. m), understanding *rḥmy*, "the one of the womb," as an epithet of ʾAṯirat. Another interpretation, less likely to be correct, is to identify *rḥmy* with ʿAnat on the basis of *CTA* 6.2.27 (*rḥm*).

(23) ʾiqraʾu-na ʾilêmi naʿimêmi [ʾagzariyyêmi banê] yômi[a]
(24) yāniqêmi bi-ʾappê zīdê ʾaṯirati [-------][b]
(23) I call the gracious gods, the circumcised ones, sons of a day,[a]
(24) those sucking on the nipples of the breasts of ʾAṯirat [b]

Notes

a) Choosing here the suggested translation of Cross ("circumcised ones, sons of a day"), who analyzes ʾ*agzrym* as an elative (see text no. 1 n. c above) from √*gzr* (cf. Hebrew *gāzar*, "to cut, divide") plus the adjectival ending.

b) Driver (122-3) and Gibson (124) restore [*wrḥmy*].

II.

In the Baᶜl cycle, ᵓAṯirat may conveniently be viewed as playing two roles, which in reality are complementary: she is the principal/senior wife/consort of ᵓEl, the supreme deity, and she is the mother of the gods. Before commenting on texts nos. 1-15 in the previous section, however, a review and interpretation of background events leading to ᵓAṯirat's being mentioned and becoming involved in the cycle is in order.[43]

The council of the gods, made up of the sons of ᵓEl (and ᵓAṯirat), is presided over by ᵓEl. Although ᵓEl is sometimes called "king," in the myths (and epics) he appears more as the grand patriarchal judge, the father of gods and men, head of the pantheon. There is, however, another position of prominence which carries the title "king." The god filling this position would share in ᵓEl's rule (primarily over the cosmos) and would have pre-eminence among the gods, being subordinate only to ᵓEl (who ultimately decides which god will fill this position).[44] Judging from the preserved texts, Yam and Baᶜl are the two most capable gods for this position.

ᵓEl apparently decides that Yam should be king, installs him as ruler (cf. *CTA* 1.4.12-20), and commissions a house to be built for him (cf. 2.3.4-10) so that Yam can exercise his power and reign. Soon after taking the throne Yam sends a message to the divine council, telling them to give up Baᶜl, whom "they are hiding," so that Baᶜl might become his slave and Baᶜl's inheritance fall into his possession. The sons of ᵓEl, seeing the approach of Yam's messengers, cower in fear, realizing that none of them can go against Yam or disobey his command. Baᶜl, though, who has been standing by ᵓEl, encourages them and promises to answer the messengers. However, when the message is delivered, ᵓEl consents to the order of Yam, despite Yam's arrogantly commanding his father and telling his messengers not to bow before the supreme god.[45]

Baᶜl becomes the prisoner of Yam; but with the help of Koṯar wa-Ḫasis he defeats his enemy (*CTA* 2.4). Now Baᶜl is free to succeed to the kingship formerly held by Yam. However, in order for Baᶜl to rule he needs to build and possess a house, and in order to build a house he needs the permission of ᵓEl. Baᶜl himself will not approach ᵓEl, though, probably because it is customary to use an intermediary in such cases, but perhaps also because Baᶜl realizes that such an action on his part would be politically unwise: Baᶜl had, after all, conquered ᵓEl's own son[46] and appointee. Therefore, Baᶜl sends for his ally ᶜAnat. When he finishes telling her about his problem, she immediately heads for the abode of ᵓEl with fire in her eye. Once there, the angry goddess addresses ᵓEl in a most disrespectful manner, and then presents the (indirect) petition of Baᶜl (cf. *CTA* 3.3 - 3.5). ᵓEl replies negatively to the plea of Baᶜl presented through ᶜAnat, as indicated by *CTA* 3.6 and *CTA* 4.[47]

In *CTA* 3.6.9-25 (text no. 1) the Fisherman (also known as "Qaduš wa-ᵓAmrar" and the "Deft One") is being sent to Egypt, the home of Koṯar wa-Ḫasis, in order to deliver a message of Baᶜl to the divine craftsman. In *CTA* 4.1.4-23 the Fisherman delivers this message, which consists of an explanation of Baᶜl's situation (lines 4-19) and a request that Koṯar make gifts for ᵓAṯirat (*CTA* 4.1.20-23; text no. 2). Koṯar responds by going up to the bellows, grasping the tongs, and producing beautiful presents (*CTA* 4.1.24-44). Evidently, after ᶜAnat failed to elicit ᵓEl's all-important permission, both she and Baᶜl decide that they will need the help of ᵓAṯirat. Only this goddess, they feel, the chief wife of ᵓEl and Creatress of the Gods, could succeed in gaining the desired answer from her husband. However, Baᶜl (and ᶜAnat) wants to improve the chance of ᵓAṯirat being won over to his cause; hence, the sending of the Fisherman, a servant of ᵓAṯirat, to Koṯar with Baᶜl's message.

In *CTA* 4.2.3-11 (text no. 3) ᵓAṯirat, engaged in a ritual, prays to ᵓEl (who is not there with her, as becomes clear in the following passages).[48] Suddenly, she sees Baᶜl and ᶜAnat approaching, with the result that she trembles and sweats, due to her intense fear and extreme anxiety. ᵓAṯirat wonders aloud if her enemies (Baᶜl and ᶜAnat) are going to smite her sons (*CTA* 4.2.12-26; text no. 4). The question arises as to why there is such a reaction on ᵓAṯirat's part.

Light is shed on the cause of ᵓAṯirat's terror by remnants of a myth -- written in Hittite but commonly regarded as Canaanite in origin -- contained on fragments considered to have belonged to the same tablet.[49] The extant portions of the myth for the most part deal with El-kuniršа (*qōnê ᵓarṣ*, "Creator of the Earth"), Ašertu, and the Storm God, the equivalents of West Semitic ᵓEl, ᵓAṯirat/ᵓAšerah, and Baᶜl. In the text, Ašertu, wife of El-kunirša, asks the Storm God to sleep with her, threatening him with verbal and physical harassment if he refuses. The Storm God, in turn, reveals Ašertu's desire to El-kunirša, who then tells the Storm God to yield to her advances and also humble her. Listening to El-kunirša, the Storm God sleeps with Ašertu and humiliates her by telling the goddess that he slew seventy-seven, even eighty-eight of her sons.[50]

Given this tradition preserved in the Hittite text, ᵓAṯirat's reaction readily becomes understandable. There is, additionally, Ugaritic evidence which helps explain her terror. Baᶜl has crushed ᵓAṯirat's son Yam; ᶜAnat, moreover, claims to have done likewise (*CTA* 3.3.35-36). Generally speaking, ᶜAnat is a warlike, bloodthirsty goddess (*CTA* 3.2.1-30; 3.3.35-43), and the insolence she demonstrated even towards ᵓEl has already been mentioned.

Therefore, when ᵓAṯirat notices the beautiful gifts (made by Koṯar) which Baᶜl and ᶜAnat are bringing, her mood quickly reverses into one of relief and joy, for she realizes that the two deities are coming on a peaceful, rather than a hostile, mission (*CTA* 4.2.26-35; text no. 5). After arriving, Baᶜl and ᶜAnat give the presents to ᵓAṯirat. She of course questions why they are doing so, asking if they have presented gifts also to ᵓEl. The reply of ᶜAnat evidently satisfies ᵓAṯirat (*CTA* 4.3.23-53; text no. 6).

Baᶜl and ᶜAnat succeed in their purpose: ᵓAṯirat does agree to be Baᶜl's intermediary, because she commands the Fisherman to prepare her donkey for a journey (*CTA* 4.4.1-7; text no. 7). Qaduš wa-ᵓAmrar obeys, and after helping ᵓAṯirat onto the animal's back, leads the way as ᵓAṯirat travels to the abode of ᵓEl at the sources of the two rivers.[51] Meanwhile, Baᶜl and ᶜAnat depart for Mt. Ṣapan (*CTA* 4.4.8-22; text no. 8).[52]

Arriving at the sources of the two rivers, ᵓAṯirat enters ᵓEl's tent, bowing before the supreme god. Such obeisance on her part surely is proper and not unusual, but ᵓAṯirat may feel that so honoring her husband would help put him in the right frame of mind. Whatever, ᵓEl is delighted to see his wife, and wonders if she wants food, drink, or if she has more private needs. The impression gained is that ᵓEl and ᵓAṯirat are on good terms with each other, and that the physical side of their marriage has been vigorous and mutually enjoyable (*CTA* 4.4.23-39; text no. 9).

Seemingly brushing aside the questions of her jovial husband, ᵓAṯirat immediately begins her plea on behalf of Baᶜl. Her speech, a repetition of ᶜAnat's before ᵓEl (*CTA* 3.5.37-52), strongly proposes Baᶜl for the kingship formerly held by Yam, and then quotes the complaint/lament of Baᶜl that he has no house (*CTA* 4.4.40-57; text no. 10). ᵓAṯirat succeeds in her purpose: after she speaks ᵓEl yields, granting his permission for a house to be built for Baᶜl (and thus also for Baᶜl to occupy the position of king). The success of ᵓAṯirat points to her power and prestige as the senior wife of ᵓEl and Creatress of the Gods.[53]

In the writer's opinion, ᵓEl appears to willingly give this answer. His reply seems to be laced with irony. Basically he is saying, "So Baᶜl has no house like the gods? All right, ᵓAṯirat, I see the problem and will remedy the situation in a way satisfactory to you. But you and I don't have to build the house; I command that it be built for Baᶜl [by someone else]" (*CTA* 4.4.58 - 5.63; text no. 11).

ᵓAṯirat next speaks, praising ᵓEl for his decision. Moreover, she encourages Baᶜl to get on with the project of having his house built, so that he can rule the cosmos. In his palace, Baᶜl will display his power as storm god -- sending forth thunder, lightning, and fertilizing rain (*CTA* 4.5.64-81; text no. 12).

CTA 4.6.44-46 (text no. 13) provides the information that ʾAṯirat has "seventy" sons -- "seventy" being a round number for a large quantity.[54] ʾAṯirat's sons, here also called the brothers of Baᶜl, are not actually his physical brothers (brothers via adoption?). They make up the council of ʾEl, of which group Baᶜl is still a member. However, he has just attained the rank of foremost among the gods after ʾEl, visually signified by the completion of his palace.

In text no. 14 (*CTA* 6.1.38-61) ᶜAnat, grieving and angry after the death of Baᶜl, shouts before ʾEl, ʾAṯirat, and the divine council, "Let ʾAṯirat and her sons now rejoice," because "Baᶜl has died."[55] ʾEl tells ʾAṯirat to nominate one of her sons, whom ʾEl will make king (if he finds her choice satisfactory). The proclamation of ʾEl evidences, as did *CTA* 4.4.20 - 5.63, ʾAṯirat's power and prestige, and the regard ʾEl has for her opinion and position as his chief wife and Creatress of the Gods (cf. *CTA* 1.4.13-17). Perhaps it is the right of ʾAṯirat as *qnyt ʾilm* to name (subject to the approval of ʾEl) the god who will rule with ʾEl, which would be an important consideration in the interpretation of *CTA* 3.6, 4.1.20 - 4.5.81.

ʾAṯirat no doubt exults in the opportunity to propose the son she wants to possess the kingship. However, her two choices, Yadiᶜ Yilḥan (= Koṯar wa-Ḫasis?) and ᶜAṯtar the Terrible, are for differing reasons incompetent; *CTA* 6.1. 48-61 indicates that Baᶜl is irreplaceable.[56] In sum, ʾAṯirat's behavior throughout the Baᶜl cycle may be viewed from the perspective of her role as senior/chief wife of ʾEl and Creatress of the Gods.

CTA 6.5.1-10 (text no. 15) specifically identifies Yam and Mot as sons of ʾAṯirat. *CTA* 12.1.12-17 (text no. 16) provides the information that ʾAṯirat has a maidservant named Damigay.

The passages from the Kirta Epic (texts nos. 17-19) depict ʾAṯirat operating in the earthly realm. More precisely, they recount her being worshipped by, and dealing with, a human king. Her importance is dramatically portrayed. On the third day of his march to the homeland of Ḥurriya, Kirta comes to "Qudšu, (to) ʾAṯirat of Tyre, and to ʾElat of Sidon," and makes a vow with generous promises to the goddess (*CTA* 14.4.197-206). A possible interpretation of these lines is that Kirta is standing before an image of ʾAṯirat, who is also known as "Qudšu"; the image, evidently well known, was associated with Tyre and Sidon.[57] According to the epic, then, ʾAṯirat enjoyed a special veneration by the inhabitants of both cities.

Significantly, ʾEl has in essence already promised the king that he would obtain Ḥurriya, and she would bear him offspring (cf. *CTA* 14.1.1 - 3.155, esp. 2.59-62 and 3.149-153). Kirta, nevertheless, feels the need to make the vow to ʾAṯirat, hoping that she will act on his behalf and grant success to his mission. He wants the added assurance of having ʾAṯirat on his side, thereby revealing his great respect for the goddess and her power.

Eventually Kirta does bring Ḥurriya into his house. Credit is due ʾAṯirat, at least partially, for later on, when sons and daughters are born to Kirta, she recalls his vow and, noting that he has not fulfilled it, angrily threatens, "I will break [ ]."[58] In the following section of the epic Kirta is grievously ill. Presumably, this sickness is ʾAṯirat's punishment of the king for not keeping his pledge, and shows that the goddess is able not only to bring great blessing, but also calamity, to an individual. ʾEl alone can drive out the disease brought upon Kirta by ʾAṯirat (*CTA* 16.5.9 - 6.14).

Finally, before the children of Kirta are born ʾEl announces that Kirta's future son Yaṣṣib would have the privilege of nursing at the breasts of ʾAṯirat and ʿAnat. In *CTA* 23 (text no. 20) the "gracious gods" are said to be sucking the breasts of ʾAṯirat (lines 23-24). The role of wet nurse well suits ʾAṯirat (the Creatress of the Gods, mother of "seventy" divine sons), as does her name "Raḥmay" (*CTA* 23.13, 28), "the one of the womb" (which may also be a play on "compassion").[59]

ʾAṯirat in the Ugaritic Cultic Texts

Before making reference to the specific texts mentioning ʾAṯirat, a few general comments concerning the cultic texts (in Ugaritic) are appropriate.[60] There are more gods and goddesses listed in this material, and occasionally more epithets for an individual deity, than appear in the extant Ugaritic myths and epics. Also, unlike the myths and epics, the rituals rarely provide information about the function(s) of the divinities named.[61] If, by chance, one would have at his/her disposal only the cultic texts, he/she would have a different conception of the pantheon of Ugarit than that gained by a reading of the mythological and epic texts.[62] The total corpus of preserved texts is, of course, relatively small, and such knowledge should always temper any opinion concerning the Ugaritic literature. Nevertheless, the divergence between the known mythological-epic material and the known cultic texts may perhaps be partially understood by regarding the material as connected to some extent with different periods. The texts of the cultic practice seem to be relatively late, dating from the last decades of the political and religious history of Ugarit. A large portion of the literary texts may derive from older accounts (reflecting an older tradition) carefully preserved by the scribes.[63]

RS 24.264 + 280, a Ugaritic god list, pertains to this study of ʾAṯirat.[64] The text has an Akkadian equivalent (a translation of a Ugaritic original): RS 20.24.[65] Both texts (given in Appendix B, no. 5) are commonly known as the "Pantheon of Ugarit," although not all the deities worshipped at the city are included in the list.[66] *CTA* 29, a duplicate of RS 24.264 + 280, but missing ten lines (lines 12-21 of RS 24.264 + 280), has an additional line at the beginning: *ʾil ṣpn*.[67]

The "Pantheon of Ugarit" can be divided into three parts: the first group of deities, lines 1-18; a small group of goddesses, lines 19-24; and finally other divinities, lines 25-33.[68] Probably the deities are given according to rank or importance, since at the head of the list are the leading gods of the pantheon, while the last four divinities are more minor in nature.[69] "ᵓAṯirat" occurs, then, in a position (line 19) somewhat lower than would be expected on the basis of the mythological and epic texts. Alternately, it is surprising to see certain divinities, namely *kṯrt* (line 12; the divine female sages?),[70] *yrḫ* (line 13), *kṯr* (line 15), *pdry* (line 16), and *ᶜṯtr* (line 17) listed before *ᵓaṯrt*. As has been mentioned, however, not all the information provided by the cultic texts exactly matches that coming from the other texts. Even ᵓEl in the "Pantheon of Ugarit" is preceded by *ᵓil ᵓib* (and by *ᵓil ṣpn*, according to *CTA* 29).[71] It is equally significant that "ᵓAṯirat" appears before "ᶜAnat" (line 20) and "ᶜAṯtart" (line 24).

The first five lines of *CTA* 30 are a god list. ᵓAṯirat is paired with ᵓEl in line 5.

(1) ᵓil b[n] ᵓil	(2) dr bn ᵓil
(3) mpḫrt bn ᵓil	(4) ṯk!mn wšnm
(5) ᵓil wᵓaṯrt	

(1) ᵓEl, the sons of ᵓEl, (2) the generation of the sons of ᵓEl,
(3) the assembly of the sons of ᵓEl, (4) *ṯkmn wšnm*[72]
(5) ᵓEl and ᵓAṯirat

The offering lists are for the most part rather loosely structured. None has the gods in an order identical to that of RS 24.264 + 280; moreover, the offering lists differ with each other in their sequences of divine names. Further, the offerings assigned to a deity vary not only from text to text, but not uncommonly also within the same text (the deity being designated several times in the list).

In *CTA* 34 "ᵓAṯirat" appears in line 6:[73]

[b]ᶜl š . ᵓaṯrt . š . ṯkmn wšnm . š

Baᶜl, a sheep [or, "head of small cattle"]; ᵓAṯirat, a sheep; *ṯkmn wšnm*, a sheep . . .[74]

The goddess is also mentioned in *CTA* 35.40:[75]

[ ] . ᵓaṯrt . ᶜṣr[m . lᵓinš . ᵓilm -]

ᵓAṯirat; birds for the ᵓ*inš* of the gods . . .[76]

Lines 23 and 24 of *CTA* 35 are interesting:[77]

(23) kdm . yn . prs . qmḥ . [mᶜ----]
(24) mdbḥt . bt . ᵓilt . ᶜṣr[m . lṣpn . š]

According to the pattern of this text the preposition *l* or *l* plus a word (in construct with *mdbḥt*, line 24) was in the lacuna at the end of line 23, and thus the writer proposes a translation such as "for the [/"for the ___ of the"] altar(s) of the house of ᵓ*ilt*: birds; for *ṣpn*: a head of small cattle . . ." ᵓ*ilt* could be either "the goddess" or "ᵓElat."[78]

"ᵓAṯirat" occurs in lines 6 and 8 of *CTA* 36:

(6) [--------ᵓi]l š . bᶜl š . ᵓaṯrt . š . ym š . [bᶜ]l knp
(8) [--------ᵓa]lp . lbᶜl . wᵓaṯrt . ᶜṣr[m] lᵓinš
(9) [ᵓilm --------]

(6) ᵓEl, a sheep; Baᶜl, a sheep; ᵓAṯirat, a sheep; Yam, a sheep; Lord of the Wing . . .
(8) an ox for Baᶜl and ᵓAṯirat; birds for the ᵓ*inš* of the
(9) gods . . .

For whatever reason, Baᶜl and ᵓAṯirat seem to be linked together in line 8.

The goddess's name is partially restored in *CTA* 37.3 (a poorly preserved text) and appears intact in RS 24.643, line 7.[79] Finally, "ᵓAṯirat" occurs in line 24 of RS 24.256,[80] a description of a religious ceremony:

(21) wqdš . yšr . bḫmš ᶜ
(22) [š]rh . šnpt . ᵓil š bᶜl ṣ
(23) pn š . bᶜl ᵓugrt š ṯ[n šm]
(24) lᵓaṯr[t] ṯn šm . l bt bt[

(21) and the consecrated one sings. On the fif-
(22) teenth (day), two-thirds [?], ᵓEl, a sheep; Baᶜl Ṣa-
(23) pan, a sheep; Baᶜl Ugarit, a sheep; two sheep
(24) for ᵓAṯirat; two sheep for *btbt*[81] . . .

In summary, the information concerning ᵓAṯirat provided by the cultic texts is tantalizing but incomplete, due to the very nature of the material. That which may be known about the goddess from these texts does not in every instance blend smoothly with the picture emerging from the extant mythological and epic texts. On the other hand, all the data from the cultic texts may not be easily harmonized. While ᵓAṯirat appears in the "Pantheon of Ugarit" in a position somewhat removed from those of ᵓEl and Baᶜl, in other cultic texts she is paired with ᵓEl (*CTA* 30) and Baᶜl (*CTA* 36), and follows Baᶜl in *CTA* 34, ᵓEl and Baᶜl in *CTA* 36, and ᵓEl, Baᶜl Ṣapan, and Baᶜl Ugarit in RS 24.256 (cf. also *CTA* 37). Generally speaking, the impression given by the cultic texts is this: ᵓAṯirat was an important goddess, who continued to be worshipped until the destruction of Ugarit.

ᵓAṯirat in an Omen Text?

RS 24.247, according to Herdner, is an omen text dealing with abnormal births.[82] Referring to the Akkadian literature, she explains that it is of the type for which the first words of the protasis are "If a woman gives birth."[83] However, this phrase (*ktld ᵓaṯt*) has not been preserved. Herdner thinks that it was expressed one time for the whole text in the beginning of the tablet, which has been lost.[84] The preserved part of the text, in Herdner's view, contains the rest of the protasis (and the apodosis), which has been reduced to the essential point: "and such an organ is missing" or "and such an organ presents such an anomaly."[85] Of note for this study are lines 24 and 25.

(24) [----] . ʾaṯrt . ʿnh . wʿnh . blṣbh
(25) [ʾibn . y]rps ḥwt

Understanding *ʾaṯrt* as "ʾAṯirat," Herdner suggests restoring at the beginning of line 24 a 3rd f. s. verb of a root signifying "to shut (up), close, seal (up)"; "ʾAṯirat" would be the subject.[86] These lines, then, could be translated:

(24) [and] ʾAṯirat has closed his eye(s) and his
eye(s) is/are by his mouth,
(25) our enemy will trample the villages.[87]

In the writer's opinion, RS 24.247 must be treated with caution. The text is fragmentary and the interpretation difficult. It may be an omen text,[88] but this view requires assuming a key phrase in a lost portion of the tablet. Be that as it may, the restoration and translation of the first part of line 24 ([ ] *ʾaṯrt*) remain uncertain. A deity is not mentioned in the extant portion of any other protasis of RS 24.247.[89] *ʾaṯrt* possibly means "place" -- "the place/ location of his eye" (cf. *PRU 2* 2.39; text no. 4 in Appendix B) -- or perhaps is the verb *ʾṯr*, "proceed, advance," with "his eye" as subject (cf. *ʿnh blṣbh*). If "ʾAṯirat" is correct, what precedes *ʾaṯrt* is still open to question, and thus no new or reliable information about the goddess is provided by line 24.

qdš, an Epithet of ʾAṯirat?

The reader already knows the position of the writer, since *qdš* in *CTA* 14.4.197 was translated as "Qudšu"

(= "Holiness") and taken in apposition to "ᵓA<u>t</u>irat." The epithet is also used in the phrase *bn qdš*, "sons of Qudšu," which parallels *ᵓilm*, "gods."[90] Further, *CTA* 16.1.9-11 (= 16.2.110-111) and 20-23 should be noted. In these passages the son of Kirta is mourning the impending death of the fatally ill king (before Kirta was healed by *šᶜtqt*, who was commissioned by ᵓEl).

(9) ᵓap (10) kirta binu-mi ᵓili
šapaḥu (11) luṭpāni wa-qudši

(9) "Then (10) is Kirta a son of ᵓEl,
an offspring (11) of Luṭpan and Qudšu?"

(20) ᵓêka-mi yargumu binu ᵓili (21) kirta
šapaḥu luṭpāni (22) wa-qudši
ᵓū ᵓilūma tamūtūna
(23) šapaḥu luṭpāni la-yaḥī

(20-1) "How can it be said that Kirta is a son of ᵓEl,
an offspring of Luṭpan (22) and Qudšu?
Or do the gods die?
(23) Will not the offspring of Luṭpan live?"

Kirta is the son of ᵓEl and ᵓA<u>t</u>irat via adoption (Yaṣṣib's nursing at the breasts of ᵓA<u>t</u>irat is a mark of his likewise being adopted). In the passages translated above Kirta's divine sonship is being emphasized, and his connection with the deities is reinforced by calling him the offspring not only of the father of the gods, but also of their mother. An epithet of ᵓEl (*lṭpn*) is followed by an epithet of ᵓA<u>t</u>irat (*qdš*).[91]

There is much more to be said about Qudšu/ᵓAšerah on the basis of evidence coming from Ugarit and elsewhere, as will be seen in Chapter 3. General conclusions concerning ᵓAšerah/ᵓA<u>t</u>irat to be derived from the Ugaritic mythological texts are that she was the chief wife/consort of the supreme god ᵓEl, a goddess of fertility ("Creatress of the Gods," mother of "seventy" divine sons, "Raḥmay"), and associated with the sea (ʾ*ṯrt ym*, her servant Fisherman). Furthermore, there are hints in ʾAṯirat's relationship with ʾEl that she was (linked with her fertility role) a goddess of the erotic (cf. *CTA* 4.2.3-11, text no. 3; also 4.4.38-39, text no. 9); this aspect is vividly portrayed in the Hittite myth. Finally, the goddess had a violent, combative, and/or warlike side to her disposition, as seen in the Kirta Epic (and the Hittite myth): it is significant that Kirta, at the head of an army, petitions ʾAṯirat for success. Later, she reacts in a fearful manner when the king fails to fulfill his vow.[92]

NOTES TO CHAPTER I

1. Anyone who has worked with these texts is well acquainted with the difficulties of vocalizing Ugaritic poetry, but the attempt is made here for the sake of a clearer picture of the metrics, the syntax, and the translator's understanding. Unless otherwise noted, all translations are my own.

2. Andrée Herdner, *Corpus des tablettes en cunéiformes alphabétiques découvertes à Ras Shamra-Ugarit de 1929 à 1939* (Mission de Ras Shamra 10; Text, and Figures and Plates; Paris: Imprimerie Nationale, 1963). For the Ugaritic texts cited (in Chaps. 1-4) from *CTA* and other sources, the corresponding numbers in M. Dietrich, O. Loretz, and J. Sanmartín's *Die keilalphabetischen Texte aus Ugarit* (AOAT 24; Neukirchen-Vluyn: Butzon and Bercker Kevelaer, 1976) are given in App. D.

3. Frank Moore Cross, Jr., *Canaanite Myth and Hebrew Epic* (Cambridge: Harvard University, 1973).

4. E. Kautzsch, ed., and A. E. Cowley, trans., *Gesenius' Hebrew Grammar* (2nd English ed.; Oxford: Clarendon, 1946).

5. Michael David Coogan, ed. and trans., *Stories from Ancient Canaan* (Philadelphia: Westminster, 1978).

6. William Foxwell Albright, *Yahweh and the Gods of Canaan* (Garden City, N.Y.: Doubleday, 1968); see also Albright, *From the Stone Age to Christianity* (2nd ed.; Garden City, N.Y.: Doubleday, 1957) 216.

7. André Caquot, Maurice Sznycer, and Andrée Herdner, *Textes ougaritiques. I. Mythes et légendes* (Littératures anciennes du Proche-Orient 7; Paris: Editions du Cerf, 1974).

8. J. C. L. Gibson, *Canaanite Myths and Legends* (Edinburgh: T. and T. Clark, 1977).

9. *Archaeology and the Religion of Israel* (Baltimore: Johns Hopkins, 1942).

10. Jørgen Alexander Knudtzon, Otto Weber, and Erich Ebeling, *Die El-Amarna-Tafeln* (2 vols.; Leipzig: J. C. Hinrichs, 1915).

11. Godfrey Rolles Driver, *Canaanite Myths and Legends* (Edinburgh: T. and T. Clark, 1956).

12. A. Jirku, *Kanaanäische Mythen und Epen aus Ras Schamra - Ugarit* (Gütersloh: Gütersloher Verlagshaus Gerd Mohn, 1962).

13. If ʾ*anš* is regarded as a verbal form, what the translation would be is uncertain. Relating the root (ʾ*nš*) to Hebrew ʾ*ānaš*, "to be weak, sick," is questionable, since the latter is better associated with √ʾ*nṯ*.

14. John Gray, *The KRT Text in the Literature of Ras Shamra* (2nd ed.; Leiden: E. J. Brill, 1964).

15. Charles Virolleaud, *Le Palais Royal d'Ugarit II* (Mission de Ras Shamra 7; Paris: Imprimerie Nationale, 1957). See Patrick D. Miller, "Animal Names as Designations in Ugaritic and Hebrew," *UF* 2 (1970) 177-80.

16. Theodor H. Gaster, *Thespis: Ritual, Myth, and Drama in the Ancient Near East* (Garden City, N.Y.: Doubleday, 1961).

17. H. L. Ginsberg, trans., "Ugaritic Myths, Epics, and Legends," in *Ancient Near Eastern Texts Relating to the Old Testament* (3rd ed. with Supplement; ed. James B. Pritchard; Princeton: Princeton University, 1969; hereafter *ANET*) 129-55.

18. According to the article "Harness and Saddlery" in *The New Encyclopaedia Britannica*, for "at least 12 centuries after horses were first ridden [in the second millennium B.C.], there were no saddles but only saddle-cloths attached by surcingles or bellybands. These cloths were gradually supplemented by cushions or rolls that improved the rider's comfort but did not add greatly to his stability. Rigid saddles without stirrups appear in China during the Han dynasty (206 BC-AD 220)" (Macropaedia 8 [1980] 657).

19. Richard J. Clifford, *The Cosmic Mountain in Canaan and the Old Testament* (HSM 4; Cambridge: Harvard University, 1972).

20. See Edward Ullendorff, "Ugaritic Marginalia," *Or* n.s. 20 (1951) 271-2.

21. Cyrus H. Gordon, *Ugaritic Textbook: Grammar, Texts in Transliteration, Cuneiform Selections, Glossary, Indices* (AnOr 38; 3 pts.; Rome: Pontifical Biblical Institute, 1965).

22. Herdner, "Nouveaux textes alphabétiques de Ras Shamra -- XXIVe campagne, 1961," in *Ugaritica VII* (Mission de Ras Shamra 18; Paris: Mission Archéologique de Ras Shamra, 1978; hereafter NTA) 56-7, has a different understanding of *lṣb*. She holds that the use of the word in RS 24.247 (lines 24 and 32: NTA, 46-8, 50), which Herdner takes as an omen text (discussed later in this chapter), shows that *lṣb* should be translated "forehead, brow." Herdner cites what she considers to be Akkadian parallels in support of her interpretation. Concerning *yprq lṣb wyṣḥq* (*CTA* 4.4.28, 6.3.16, and 17.2.10), Herdner compares *prq* to Aramaic *peraq*, "to disengage, disentangle; to deliver, set free," and Ethiopic *faraqa*, "to liberate, free," rendering the phrase "he smooths/unwrinkles (his) brow/forehead and laughs."

However, RS 24.247 is a difficult text, and I hesitate to take an uncertain meaning derived from such a context and transfer it to define the use of *lṣb* in the clearer mythological passages. Further, Herdner's reference to the Akkadian texts is inconclusive, since the Akkadian term which she considers parallel to *lṣb* may not actually signify the same part of the anatomy as *lṣb*. Finally, Herdner's explanation of *prq* (*yprq lṣb wyṣḥq*) seems weak. The Hebrew, Akkadian, and Arabic evidence points to a meaning such as "to tear apart, split, divide, separate" -- one of the factors leading me to prefer a "mouth" translation for *lṣb*.

23. See the previous note. Consult especially Herdner's study of this text (NTA, 64-7).

24. See Carl Brockelmann, *Grundriss der vergleichenden Grammatik der semitischen Sprachen* (2 vols.; Hildesheim: Georg Olms, 1961; a reprint of the 1908, 1913 work) 1: no. 220 h.

25. Herdner makes this restoration due to *mṭll* in line 5 and the appearance elsewhere of *ḥṭr* for *ḥẓr* (NTA, 67).

26. Herdner records *mṯll* for *CTA* 3.5.48 in the Texts volume (p. 20), but *mẓll* in the Figures and Plates volume (fig. 12). The correct reading is *mẓll* (pls. 5, 6).

27. J. Obermann, *Ugaritic Mythology* (New Haven: Yale University, 1948).

28. The three lines following *ʾar* in RS 24.263 have major lacunae, which Herdner concludes cannot be restored (NTA, 65-7).

29. For a good review of scholarly treatment of *pdry*, *ʾar*, *ṭly*, *rb*, *ʾarṣ⟨y⟩*, and *yʿbdr* consult *TOML*, 77-80.

30. See Ali Abou-Assaf, Pierre Bordreuil, and Alan R. Millard, *La statue de Tell Fekherye et son inscription bilingue assyro-araméenne* (Etudes Assyriologiques, Cahier 7; Paris: Editions Recherche sur les civilisations, 1982) 23, 30, 50, 53, 62.

31. Jean Nougayrol, Emmanuel Laroche, Charles Virolleaud, and Claude F. A. Schaeffer, *Ugaritica V* (Mission de Ras Shamra 16; Paris: Imprimerie Nationale, 1968).

32. Charles Virolleaud, *Le Palais Royal d'Ugarit V* (Mission de Ras Shamra 11; Paris: Imprimerie Nationale, 1965).

33. *Ugaritic Literature* (Rome: Pontifical Biblical Institute, 1949).

34. According to *TOML*, 329, 337 n. r, *tlš* and *dmgy* are the same person. The verbs and suffixes in lines 14-27 are, to be sure, singular. Yet due to the 1st c. pl. nominal suffixes in lines 9 and 11 I prefer to regard *tlš* and *dmgy* as two separate women.

35. For examples of scholarly opinion concerning *CTA* 12, see Driver, 10, and especially the discussion of *TOML*, 318-30.

36. Frauke Gröndahl, *Die Personennamen der Texte aus Ugarit* (Studia Pohl Dissertationes Scientificae de Rebus Orientis Antiqui 1; Rome: Pontifical Biblical Institute, 1967).

37. Jean Nougayrol, *Le Palais Royal d'Ugarit III* (Mission de Ras Shamra 6; Text and Plates; Paris: Imprimerie Nationale, 1955) 7.

38. "A Vow to Asherah in the Keret Epic," *BASOR* 94 (1944).

39. For further discussion, see *TOML*, 530 n. w, which gives two instances of ᵓ*iṯt* associated with *ndr* in letters; Gibson, 87 n. 4; Gray, 56-7; and Alice Lenore Perlman, "Asherah and Astarte in the Old Testament and Ugaritic Literature" (Ph.D. diss., Graduate Theological Union, Berkeley, Ca.: Ann Arbor, Mich.: University Microfilms, 1978) 66-7.

40. For a review of scholarly opinion concerning *CTA* 23, see *TOML*, 356-65, and R. J. Clifford, "Recent Scholarly Discussion of *CTCA* 23 (*UT* 52)," in *SBL 1975 Seminar Papers* (ed. George MacRae; vol. 1; Missoula, Mont.: Scholars Press, 1975) 99-106.

41. *št* in line 61 may be the verb "to set, place, put" (*TOML*, 377), less likely the verb "to drink" (Gaster, 433), or, if it is translated "the Lady" (Gibson, 126; Gordon, *UL*, 61; Jirku, 84), I think that this is an epithet of ᶜAnat (cf. *CTA* 18.4.6, 11, 27; 19.4.215-21; 3.2.5).

42. *TOML* (371), Driver (120-1), and Gaster (424) restore [ʾ*aṯrt*] (Driver: [ʾ*aṯrt mdbr*]) after *wtṣd* in line 16, which to me is debatable.

43. The myths of Ugarit to a certain extent reflect natural patterns and phenomena -- life, fertility, growth, death, dry seasons, rainy seasons, unpredictable forces of nature, and so forth -- and these are embodied in the myths' deities. Thus, for example, the conflict of Yam and Baᶜl is connected to the struggle between chaotic, destructive forces of nature and those which promote fecundity, generation, harvest. The Baᶜl cycle seems to depict the triumph of life- and fertility-promoting powers over unruly, disaster-bringing powers and death. Yet in the writer's opinion the people of Ugarit did not view the actions and deities of the myths only as symbolic of cosmic principles and patterns but as actual events involving real beings with individual characteristics and personalities. In other words, these deities were believed to exist and were assigned traits from the human sphere. The following discussion is based mainly on this consideration (at the risk of being overly rationalistic). It should be stressed that any reconstruction of Ugaritic mythology is tentative, due to the state of preservation of the tablets, uncertainty of the proper order of the tablets, etc.

44. Cf. Cross, *CMHE*, 42-3.

45. For possible reasons behind ʾEl's decision to hand Baᶜl over to Yam (emphasizing the "human-sphere" aspect), see the author's dissertation, "A Study of ʾAšerah: The Extrabiblical Evidence" (Ph.D. diss., Harvard University, 1984) 39-40.

46. Although Baᶜl is a member of the divine council, and called a son of ʾEl, he is not actually the offspring of ʾEl (and ʾAṯirat), but is instead the son of Dagan (e.g., *CTA* 2.1.19, 37; Baᶜl is ʾEl's adoptive son?). Cf. the *Phoenician History (Praeparatio evangelica* 1.10.18-19); see Harold W. Attridge and Robert A. Oden, Jr., *Philo of Byblos: The Phoenician History* (CBQMS 9; Washington, D.C.: Catholic Biblical Association of America, 1981; hereafter *PBPH*) 48-51 and 88 n. 94.

47. See Maier, "A Study of ʾAšerah," 41 for possible explanations (from the "human sphere") for ʾEl's rejection of ᶜAnat's intercession.

48. Conceivably, the ritual had fertility and sexual overtones, that is, ʾAṯirat may have been imploring ʾEl, her husband, to hasten to where she was and have conjugal relations with her. ʾEl, on his part, is very pleased when ʾAṯirat enters his tent (*CTA* 4.4.23-39; text no. 9).

49. For the fragments, and the Hittite text, see Heinrich Otten, "Ein kanaanäischer Mythus aus Boğazköy," *Mitteilungen des Instituts für Orientforschung* (Deutsche Akademie der Wissenschaften zu Berlin) 1 (1953) 125-6, 141-2; cf. Emmanuel Laroche, "Textes mythologiques hittites en transcription, 2e partie: Mythologie d'origine étrangère," *Revue Hittite et Asianique* 26 (1968) 25-7. For translations of the Hittite, see Otten, 127, 142-3, and Albrecht Goetze, trans., "Hittite Myths, Epics, and Legends," in *ANET*, 519.

50. As a result, according to the text, Ašertu becomes incensed with the Storm God. Shortly after this a number of lines are missing, which probably told about Ašertu's plan to get revenge. When the myth picks up again (?), Ašertu has regained her husband's favor, for El-kuniršа announces that he will turn over the Storm God to his wife, and she can deal with him as she pleases. Husband and wife sleep with each other; they apparently plot together to punish the Storm God.
The myth is interesting not only for the way Ašertu is depicted as relating with the two gods, but also for the aspects of the goddess's character and person which are portrayed. She is obviously a deity of great fertility, something which goes hand in hand with her erotic nature. Moreover, she has an angry, violent, and vengeful side to her disposition. Finally, Ašertu is a cunning goddess, a schemer, one who can make an ally of the very husband she has betrayed, and who undoubtedly is spinning an intricate plot to bring grief to the god she has previously asked to be her lover. These aspects of her character will be seen in other sources providing information about ᵓAṯirat/ᵓAšerah examined in this study.

51. If there was any question in the reader's mind that "Fisherman" and "Qaduš wa-ᵓAmrar" might designate two separate beings, rather than simply being alternate names (the position of this chapter), *CTA* 4.4.1-17 (with Herdner's restorations in lines 1-3) effectively resolves the matter. Whereas ᵓAṯirat utters both appellations in commanding that her donkey be prepared for a journey (lines 2-7), only Qaduš wa-ᵓAmrar is mentioned as obeying her order, helping the goddess onto a donkey, and accompanying her as she travels to see ᵓEl (lines 8-17). It seems best, therefore, to regard "Qaduš wa-ᵓAmrar" and "Fisherman" (also "Deft One," *CTA* 4.2.30) as different names of the same servant.

52. Why does ᵓAṯirat consent to help Baᶜl in his quest for a house? Strictly from a religious point of view, some kind of alliance between a fertility/mother goddess and the god of the fertilizing, life-sustaining rains is to be expected. However, the "human-sphere" aspect should not be ignored in interpretation. The presents given by Baᶜl and ᶜAnat had an influence on ᵓAṯirat's

decision, but to think that the gifts alone brought this about is, in the writer's opinion, too facile an assumption. In part, ʾAṯirat's compliance perhaps should be seen against the background of ancient Near Eastern court intrigues. See Maier, "A Study of ʾAšerah," 43-4. The mythology of the divine court undoubtedly reflected to some degree the events and activities of the human court. For a good discussion of women rulers in the ancient Near East (and life in the harem) see Ilse Seibert, *Women in the Ancient Near East* (trans. Marianne Herzfeld, rev. George A. Shepperson; New York: Abner Schram, 1974) 41-51. One queen of Ugarit, Aḫat-milki, intervened energetically after the death of her husband Niqmepa to secure the succession for her younger son Ammištamru II, even banishing two elder sons to Cyprus, whose rights she disregarded (Seibert, 48). For more on Aḫat-milki as queen mother, see Edward Lipiński, "Aḫat-milki, reine d'Ugarit, et la guerre du Mukiš," OLP 12 (1981) 79-115.

53. For further expansion of this "human-sphere" explanation, see Maier, "A Study of ʾAšerah," 45. Strictly from a religious point of view, ʾAṯirat's success reflects one fertility deity aiding another; it reflects the triumph of fertilizing, life-sustaining forces in nature.

54. F. C. Fensham, "The Numeral Seventy in the Old Testament and the Family of Jerubbaal, Ahab, Panammuwa and Athirat," *PEQ* 109 (1977), as the title of his article indicates, discusses (in addition to *šbʿm* in *CTA* 4.6.46) the use of "seventy" for the sons and/or brothers of a king/leader in biblical and extrabiblical sources (113-5). These examples, combined with other uses of "seventy" in the Hebrew Bible (see also *CTA* 6.1.18-28), lead Fensham to conclude that the number is "quite probably used as a kind of symbolic figure, just like seven. With the usage of seven and seventy the ancient Semites tried to make a difference between a smaller symbolic figure and a larger one . . . ["seventy"] is not intended as an exact number or even an approximate figure (with the exception of Ezra 8. 7). It is only a larger group of people taken as a whole" (115).

55. Why will ʾAṯirat rejoice, after having acted as Baʿl's ally? Here the tension in the relationship of ʾAṯirat and Baʿl is indicated: at times working together, at other times hostile toward each other. It is interesting to note that in the preserved texts there is no mention of ʾAṯirat mourning over the death of Baʿl, as did ʾEl (*CTA* 5.6.11-25). For further discussion, see Maier, "A Study of ʾAšerah," 46.

56. Possibly there is more to the interpretation of the passage, again taking into consideration the "human-sphere" aspect coupled with the background of ancient Near Eastern court intrigues. See Maier, "A Study of ʾAšerah," 47.

57. The language of the epic is similar to that of a letter written by the King of Mitanni to Amenophis III of Egypt, informing the gravely ill Pharaoh that he is sending to him "Ištar of Nineveh," undoubtedly a statue or cult picture of the goddess. While in Egypt, "Ištar of Nineveh" was believed to have twice wonderfully healed Amenophis. See Jaroslav Černý, *Ancient Egyptian Religion* (Hutchinson's University Library, World Religions; London: Hutchinson House, 1952) 128, and Rainer Stadelmann, *Syrisch-Palästinensische Gottheiten in Ägypten* (Probleme der Ägyptologie 5; Leiden: E. J. Brill, 1967) 106-7; see also Chap. 3 n. 100.

58. Hebrew √*prr* (*hiphil*) is used in Num 30:9, 13, 14, 16 of a husband "breaking" (nullifying) a vow(s) taken by his wife. Used elsewhere in the Bible the verb ordinarily has the sense of "to violate," "make ineffectual" (e.g., counsel/advice, the commandment(s), God's judgment). *prr* frequently has as direct object *bĕrît*, "covenant." Usually man "breaks" the covenant. However, Yahweh promises not to "break" the *bĕrît* in Lev 26:44 and Judg 2:1; in Jer 14:21, Yahweh is asked not to "break" his covenant. Cf. Zech 11:10 (discussed by Paul D. Hanson as part of the passage 11:4-17 in *The Dawn of Apocalyptic* [Philadelphia: Fortress Press, 1975] 338-54). In Ps 89:34, Yahweh promises concerning the Davidic heir, "But my goodness I will not break off [ʾ*āpîr*] from him" (cf. Cross, *CMHE*, 257, 259). In *CTA* 15.3.30 √*prr* perhaps carries the meaning that ʾAṯirat will "break" a covenant or special relationship she had entered into with Kirta.

59. Excerpts from the Ugaritic mythological texts which probably or possibly mention ʾAṯirat/ʾElat, and are not included in Chap. 1, are given in App. B. They are *CTA* 1.4.13-15, 3.1.13-15, 8.1-6, and *UT* 1002 (*PRU 2* 2) 38-40, 42-44, 59-61.

60. For studies of these texts, consult Johannes C. de Moor, "The Semitic Pantheon of Ugarit," *UF* 2 (1970) 187-228; Jean-Michel de Tarragon, *Le Culte à Ugarit* (Cahiers de la Revue Biblique 19; Paris: J. Gabalda, 1980), esp. 149-84; and Paolo Xella, *I testi rituali di Ugarit-I* (Studi Semitici 54; Roma: Consiglio Nazionale delle Ricerche, 1981). See also André Caquot and Maurice Sznycer, *Ugaritic Religion* (Iconography of Religions 15/8; Leiden: E. J. Brill, 1980), 15-8.

61. de Tarragon, 169, 176.

62. de Tarragon, 176, 183.

63. de Tarragon, 183-4.

64. NTA, 1-3.

65. *Ug 5*, 44-5. Cf. RS 26.142 (*Ug 5*, 321-2).

66. After examining the occurrence of divine names in the various types of Ugaritic literature, de Moor concludes that all the major gods and goddesses of the Ugaritic pantheon are included in RS 24.264 + 280, except for *ṯkmn wšnm* (217-8); I might add the god Mot also as an exception. Further, only a small minority of the names listed belong to deities who appear to have been relatively unimportant (cf. de Moor, 218).

67. The reading [ʾ*a*]*rṣ* of *CTA* 29 (rev., 1) should, in light of RS 24.264 + 280, line 22, be changed to [ʾ*a*]*rṣy*.

68. de Tarragon, 151.

69. See de Tarragon, 151-60, and de Moor, 218.

70. de Tarragon, 158.

71. For a discussion of ʾ*il* ʾ*ib* and ʾ*il ṣpn*, with a review of scholarly opinion, see de Tarragon, 151-7.

72. Perhaps *ṯkmn wšnm* designates the deified mountains (de Tarragon, 170; see also 179 n. 23 for bibliographical references). Cf. RS 24.258, lines 18-19 (*Ug 5*, 546-7).

73. *CTA* 34.6 = 35.15 = App. II. 16.

74. ʾ*ilt mgdl* and ʾ*ilt* ʾ*asrm* in line 11 are more likely anonymous goddesses rather than references to ʾElat: "the Goddess of the Tower," "the Goddess of the ʾ*asrm* ["prisoners," or "vows, obligations"?]." Cf. de Tarragon, 170; de Moor, 224. For *b*ʿ*lt bhtm*, "Lady of the House(s)," in line 21 and elsewhere in the cultic texts, note the discussion of de Tarragon, 163. Her identification remains uncertain; it has been suggested that she is ʾ*ušḫry* (line 23 of the "Pantheon"), ʿAnat, or a hierodule.

75. Cf. *CTA* App. II. 43-44.

76. The phrase ʿ*ṣrm l*ʾ*inš* ʾ*ilm* occurs frequently in the cultic texts. For ʾ*inš* ʾ*ilm*, possibly a term for personnel of the cult, see de Tarragon, 131-4.

77. Cf. *CTA* App. II. 26-27.

78. Cf. ʾ*ilt* in *CTA* 38.2, 4 and *PRU 2* 4.5, 8, 12, 21.

79. *Ug 5*, 580. RS 24.643 lines 1-9 apparently is an offering-list counterpart of the god list in RS 24.264 + 280, lines 1-31 and *CTA* 29. Variations in RS 24.643 include

an absence of *ʾil* before *ṣpn* (line 1; cf. *CTA* 29.1), *ʿṯtr* not occurring in the preserved text (line 6; cf. RS 24.264 + 280, lines 16-18), *ʾušḫry* and *ʿṯtrt* having a reverse order (lines 7-8; cf. RS 24.264 + 280, lines 23-24), and *ʾuṯḫ[t]* evidently not being listed (line 9; cf. RS 24.264 + 280, lines 28-31).

80. NTA, 21-3.

81. Perhaps *bt bt* is "Daughter of the House." De Moor classifies her with other deities belonging to buildings (224).

82. NTA, 44. For the Ugaritic text, see NTA, 45-9.

83. NTA, 44-5.

84. NTA, 45.

85. NTA, 45.

86. NTA, 50, 56.

87. Cf. the translation of Herdner, NTA, 50, 56-7, and see n. 22 above.

88. Herdner (NTA, 44 n. 115) states that the 24th campaign has furnished a second alphabetic example of this genre, unfortunately reduced to some beginnings of lines -- the fragment RS 24.302 (see NTA, 60-2).

89. *r[š]p*, "Rešep," apparently occurs in the apodosis of line 15; *ʾilm*, "the gods," in that of lines 16 and 31; *bʿl*, "master" (?), in that of line 11; and *bʿln*, "our master" (?), in that of line 15 (NTA, 46-50).

90. See *CTA* 2.1.20-21, 37-38; 2.3(?).19-20, 22-23; 17.1.3-4 (and the parallels 17.1.8-9, 10-12, 13-14, 22-23). *CTA* 2.3(?).19-20 -- (*ʾin*) *bt* [*l*]*y* [*km*] *ʾilm* [*w*]*ḥẓr* [*kbn*] [*qd*]*š* -- is parallel to *CTA* 3.4.2*-1, 3.5.11-12, 46-47, 4.1.10-12, 4.4.50-51, 62-63, and RS 24.263, lines 4-5, except for the *ly* (*CTA* 3 - 4: *lbʿl*) and, of course, the *qdš* (*ʾaṯrt*). *bn qdš* has been rendered "holy ones," yet for the latter *qdšm* would have been expected.

91. It is unlikely that *qdš* here is a title of ʾEl. The word does not appear as such in another Ugaritic text(s). Moreover, outside of these passages from *CTA* 16, *lṭpn* occurs 1) in the phrase *lṭpn ʾil dpʾid*; 2) in the phrase *lṭpn ḥtk*; 3) in the phrase *ṯr lṭpn*; and 4) alone. *lṭpn* is a hypocoristicon, as is *ʾalʾiyn*. I am not aware of an *ʾalʾiyn w epithet* form.

"Holiness" is one of a number of abstract names in Ugaritic literature. Included in this group are, e.g., "Death" (Mot), "Pestilence" (Rešep), and "ʿAṯtart-name-of-Baʿl" (*CTA* 16.6.56). Note also "Righteousness" (*ṣdq*) and "Justice" (*mšr*) in RS 24.271 A, line 14 (*Ug 5*, 583, 585). Cf. "Misor" and "Sydyk," as well as other abstract names, in the *Phoenician History* (*PBPH*, 44-5, 85 n. 74).

92. Before proceeding to the next chapter it should be mentioned that, with regard to personal names in the texts from Ugarit, ʾAṯirat is attested in the Akkadian *abdi-a-šar-ti* (Gröndahl, 103, 316). Cf. *bn ʾilt* (Gröndahl, 98, 370) and *ʿbdʾilt* (Gröndahl, 97, 374).

Chapter II

TWO GREEK WORKS

Two Christian Era Greek works which should be included in a study of the goddess ʾAšerah are the *Phoenician History* of Philo of Byblos, probably written in the late first or early second centuries,[1] and *The Syrian Goddess*, attributed to Lucian, the second century satirist and rhetorician.

The *Phoenician History*

Today the majority of the extant fragments of the *Phoenician History* are preserved in the *Praeparatio evangelica*, composed by the fourth century Church Father Eusebius of Caesarea. The great reliability of Eusebius in preserving and transmitting his sources has been demonstrated; in fact, there is a general consensus that his care is perhaps unequalled among ancient compilers.[2] The remains of the *Phoenician History* in the *Praeparatio evangelica* consist of remarks from Philo's preface and selections from the first volume of the work. Among the excerpts made by Eusebius are those dealing with a) the history of Kronos and b) accounts of later rulers.[3]

The *Phoenician History* purports to be, after the preface, a translation of a native source, authored by one Sanchuniathon.[4] Eusebius and the third century pagan philosopher Porphyry stress the great antiquity of Sanchuniathon (who, they believe, lived prior to, or at the time of, the Trojan era),[5] and Eusebius, Porphyry and Philo hold that Sanchuniathon had access to and used records and works which were old by his lifetime.[6]

There has been, as is well known to scholars of ancient Near Eastern religion, not a little debate regarding whether or not Sanchuniathon really existed, and, if he did, when he actually lived and wrote.[7] Recent scholarship concerning these questions generally supports one of two positions -- the first being that Sanchuniathon was undoubtedly a historical person antedating the Hellenistic period, with access to reliable tradition.[8] The second position asserts that Sanchuniathon may simply be a fiction of Philo, but if he did exist, he was a patriotic local ethnographer of the Hellenistic or Roman periods, who wrote on the basis of ancient traditions preserved in local priestly circles.[9]

For the purposes of this study it is happily unnecessary to enter into the debate about Sanchuniathon. Both positions agree that Philo or his source had access to at least some authentic, ancient local traditions. As will be seen below, there is no compelling reason (cf. n. 9) to doubt (especially comparing the Ugaritic literature) that, in the final analysis, the portions pertaining to ᵓAšerah in the excerpts Eusebius quotes from the *Phoenician History* are based on ancient Phoenician and Canaanite tradition.

The first text which almost certainly contains information relevant to a study of ᵓAšerah[10] is *Praeparatio evangelica* 1.10.22-24, a portion of the excerpt dealing with the history of Kronos.[11]

> "Χρόνου δὲ προιόντος Οὐρανὸς ἐν φυγῇ τυγχάνων θυγατέρα αὐτοῦ παρθένον Ἀστάρτην μεθ᾽ ἑτέρων ἀδελφῶν αὐτῆς δύο, Ῥέας και Διώνης, δόλῳ τὸν Κρόνον ἀνελεῖν ὑποπέμπει· ἃς καὶ ἑλὼν ὁ Κρόνος κουριδίας γαμετὰς ἀδελφὰς οὔσας ἐποιήσατο. γνοὺς δὲ Οὐρανὸς ἐπιστρατεύει κατὰ τοῦ Κρόνου Εἱμαρμένην καὶ Ὥραν μεθ᾽ ἑτέρων συμμάχων· καl ταύτας ἐξοικειωσάμενος Κρόνος παρ᾽ ἑαυτῷ κατέσχεν. ἔτι δὲ (φησίν) ἐπενόησεν θεὸς Οὐρανὸς βαιτύλια, λίθους ἐμψύχους μηχανησάμενος.
>
> "Κρόνῳ δὲ ἐγένοντο ἀπὸ Ἀστάρτης θυγατέρες ἑπτὰ Τιτανίδες ἢ Ἀρτέμιδες. καὶ πάλιν τῷ αὐτῷ γίνονται ἀπὸ Ῥέας παῖδες ἑπτά, ὧν ὁ νεώτατος ἅμα τῇ γενέσει ἀφιερώθη· καὶ ἀπὸ Διώνης θήλειαι <δύο>, καὶ ἀπὸ Ἀστάρτης πάλιν ἄρρενες δύο, Πόθος καὶ Ἔρως.

> "Some time later, while Ouranos was in exile, he secretly sent his maiden daughter Astarte together with two other sisters of hers, Rhea and Dione, to kill Kronos by stealth. Kronos, however, caught the lasses and made the sisters his wives. When Ouranos found out, he sent Destiny, Hour, and other allies into battle against Kronos. These too Kronos won over and kept at his side. Also," he says, "the god Ouranos further invented baetyls, by devising stones endowed with life.
>
> "Kronos had seven daughters, Titanids or Artemids, by Astarte, and again by Rhea he had seven sons, the youngest of whom was made an object of worship at the time of his birth. By Dione he had ⟨two⟩[12] female children and again by Astarte two male children, called Desire and Love.

The Greek names found in these lines and elsewhere in the excerpts from the *Phoenician History* evidently were supplied by Philo (or a preceding Hellenistic or Roman author). Cross has suggested that here Rhea and Dione appear to be alternate identifications of ʾAšerah, that is, Rhea = ʾAšerah and Dione = ʾElat.[13] In Greek mythology, generally speaking, Rhea is a Titaness, daughter of Ouranos and Gaia, full-sister and wife of the Titan Kronos, and mother of Hestia, Demeter, Hera, Pluto, Poseidon, and Zeus. She is the "Mother of the Gods,"[14] often being identified with Cybele, who was usually called at Rome the "Great Mother."[15] Since "Kronos" is, in the *Phoenician History*, the Greek name used for "ʾEl,"[16] an equation of Rhea with ʾAšerah (in light of the Ugaritic literature) seems clear.

At first it appears somewhat strange that another sister and wife of Kronos here should be named "Dione," since this goddess is perhaps best known, from the earliest Greek mythology, as the female counterpart and consort of Zeus in the oracular cult at Dodona.[17] As this oracle declined in importance, however, her place as the partner of Zeus was taken by Hera.[18] After being admitted to the general religious system of the Greeks, Dione was variously described.[19] In Hesiod (*Theogonia* 353) she is a daughter of Okeanus and Tethys.[20] Others make her a Titaness, a daughter of Ouranos and Gaia (e.g., Apollodorus I.1).

With these variations in the mythological genealogies it is possible to see how Philo could in the present passage name a Dione as a daughter of Ouranos and sister (and then also wife) of Kronos. His choosing of "Dione," though, is probably due mainly to a desire to find a Greek equivalent for "ʾElat." As stated above, Dione was regarded according to certain traditions as the female counterpart of the chief god Zeus; her name is simply the feminine form of "Zeus."[21] Since there was no corresponding feminine name/form to be paired with "Kronos," the Greek name he chose for the supreme god El, Philo decided instead to use "Dione" for "ʾElat."[22]

The dividing of ʾAšerah/ʾElat into two separate beings, Rhea and Dione,[23] is perhaps due to a misunderstanding, whether by a Sanchuniathon or Philo, of the ancient Phoenician and Canaanite mythology, but more likely to a euhemeristic analysis of the material. Clapham explains that "euhemerism may also treat the several epithets of a single old god as several human beings . . . a reconstruction of the old gods often requires a synthesis of several euhemeristic parties."[24]

The information given about Rhea and Dione in these lines from the *Phoenician History* can thus be seen as corresponding in large measure to what is known about ʾAšerah/ʾElat from the Ugaritic literature. That Rhea, according to the Greek text, had seven sons (versus the "seventy" of Ugaritic mythology), and only "one of these was made an object of worship" (cf. *Praeparatio evangelica* 1.10.10.34) is probably due to a combination of two factors: a Greek tendency to rationalize and a Semitic background.[25] Rhea and Dione are here called the sisters of Kronos and ʿAštart; this may or may not be a borrowing from Greek mythology. It is also reported that Rhea and Dione were originally sent (together with ʿAštart) by Ouranos to kill Kronos by stealth, but Kronos caught them and made the sisters his wives; and further, that Dione had (two) female children by Kronos. For these elements in the narrative there are no specific extant Canaanite/Phoenician or Greek parallels. The question then arises as to how this material should be regarded. In other words, where does this information come from, and approximately how old is it?

A few observations are in order. First of all, many of the other portions from the *Phoenician History* relating the history and activities of Kronos definitely do not come from Greek myths (apart from names), but show a dependence on or relation to Phoenician or Canaanite lore.[26] Secondly, the overall story of Kronos related in the citations from the *Phoenician History* (particularly *Praeparatio evangelica* 1.10.15-35), while in some points resembling Greek mythology,[27] does not reflect the basic outline of the latter.[28]

Additionally, while the mythological pictures presented by the Ugaritic texts and Philo are to a certain degree homogeneous, they are far from being completely similar. In fact, the two mythologies, especially when describing the life of Kronos/ʾEl, often seem to complement each other, the *Phoenician History* presenting events in the life of the god and others involved with him which chronologically occurred prior to the events in the preserved Ugaritic texts (as does *Praeparatio evangelica* 1.10.22-24). More precisely, as Cross and his student Mullen have observed, the stories of Kronos/ʾEl in Philo and the Ugaritic literature are of two different types: the mythology in Philo is chiefly theogonic in nature, that from Ugarit belongs more to the cosmogonic genre. The two sources reveal different levels of tradition.[29]

After these observations, it is most reasonable to suppose that the features of the secret mission of Rhea/Dione and the female children of Dione in the present passage are theogonic in nature and Canaanite or Phoenician in origin. Precisely how far back in time this information should be traced remains uncertain (unless one assumes here a complete fabrication by a Sanchuniathon or Philo). On the one hand, however, other elements in the Rhea/Dione material in this passage and *Praeparatio evangelica* 1.10.33-35 agree with what is contained in second millennium B.C. sources. On the other hand, there is no compelling reason (cf. n. 9) to assume that the secret mission and female children are not old traditions (certainly pre-Hellenistic). Thus, it seems likely that these elements are, indeed, ancient, roughly from the last centuries of the second millennium or first half of the first millennium.

The second text[30] which calls for examination is *Praeparatio evangelica* 1.10.10.33-35.[31]

> λοιμοῦ δὲ γενομένου καὶ φθορᾶς τὸν ἑαυτοῦ μονογενῆ υἱὸν ὁ Κρόνος Οὐρανῷ τῷ πατρι ὁλοκαρποῖ καὶ τὰ αἰδοῖα περιτέμνεται, ταὐτὸν ποιῆσαι καὶ τοὺς ἅμ᾽ αὐτῷ συμμάχους ἐξαναγκάσας. καὶ μετ᾽ οὐ πολὺ ἕτερον αὐτοῦ παῖδα ἀπὸ Ῥέας ὀνομαζόμενον Μοὺθ ἀποθανόντα ἀφιεροῖ· Θάνατον δὲ τοῦτον καὶ Πλούτωνα Φοίνικες ὀνομάζουσιν. καὶ ἐπὶ τούτοις ὁ Κρόνος Βύβλον μὲν τὴν πόλιν θεᾷ Βααλτίδι, τῇ καὶ Διώνῃ, δίδωσι, Βηρυτὸν δὲ Ποσειδῶνι καὶ Καβείροις Ἀγρόταις τε καὶ Ἁλιεῦσιν, οἳ καὶ τὰ τοῦ Πόντου λείψανα εἰς τὴν Βηρυτὸν ἀφιέρωσαν.

> "At the occurrence of a fatal plague, Kronos immolated his only son to his father Ouranos, and circumcized [*sic*] himself, forcing the allies who were with him to do the same. And not long after this, when another of his children died, one born of Rhea and called Muth, he made him an object of worship. The Phoenicians call him Death and Pluto. In addition, Kronos gave the city Byblos to the goddess Baaltis, who is also Dione, and the city Beirut to Poseidon and to the Kabeiri, the Hunters and the Fishers, who made the relics of Pontos an object of worship in Beirut.

The name "Muth" is obviously derived from that of the Canaanite god of the underworld, Mot, an important figure in the texts from Ugarit.[32] The *Phoenician History* indicates that Mot (Muth) was the son of ʾAšerah (Rhea), something which is also known from *CTA* 6.5.1, 4 (Chapter 1, text no. 15). It is not clear whether the "youngest" son of Rhea, mentioned in the previous passage, who was "made an object of worship," is the same as Muth in the present passage, whom Kronos made "an object of worship." In *Praeparatio evangelica* 1.10.24 the unnamed son was consecrated "at the time of his birth," while this happened to Muth when he "died."

Kronos's giving the city Byblos to Baaltis is noteworthy because he founded it as the first city:

> "Furthermore, Kronos surrounded his own dwelling with a wall, and founded the first city, Byblos in Phoenicia (*Praeparatio evangelica* 1.10.20).[33]

Baaltis, most scholars agree, must be the *bᶜlt gbl*, the "Lady of Byblos," addressed on several inscriptions of the Byblian kings.[34] The high position of Baᶜlat at Byblos is also demonstrated by the reference to *^{d}bēltu ša ^{uru}Gubla* in the Amarna letters[35] and Lucian's mention of 'Αφροδίτη Βυβλίη (*The Syrian Goddess*, 6).[36] This account of the transfer of Byblos to Baaltis must be based on her rise to prominence in that city, which strongly argues that the tradition reflects conditions sometime before the beginning of the first millennium, when she is firmly established there.[37]

Moreover, Baaltis/Baᶜlat in the text is identified as Dione. If this information as well as the conclusions reached above are correct, *bᶜlt gbl* = ʾElat/ʾAšerah. Such an equation will be further discussed in the next chapter.

The final text to be examined is all but the last lines of *Praeparatio evangelica* 1.10.11, a portion of the excerpt from the *Phoenician History* dealing with the history of culture.[38]

> Χρόνοις δὲ ὕστερον πολλοῖς ἀπὸ τῆς Ὑψουρανίου γενεᾶς γενέσθαι Ἀγρέα καὶ Ἁλιέα, τοὺς ἁλιείας καὶ ἄγρας εὑρετάς, ἐξ ὧν κληθῆναι ἀγρευτὰς καὶ ἁλιεῖς· ἐξ ὧν γενέσθαι δύο ἀδελφοὺς σιδήρου εὑρετὰς καὶ τῆς τούτου ἐργασίας, ὧν θάτερον τὸν Χουσὼρ λόγους ἀσκῆσαι καὶ ἐπῳδὰς καὶ μαντείας· εἶναι δὲ τοῦτον τὸν Ἥφαιστον, εὑρεῖν δὲ ἄγκιστρον καὶ δέλεαρ καὶ ὁρμιὰν καὶ σχεδίαν πρῶτόν τε πάντων ἀνθρώπων πλεῦσαι· διὸ καὶ ὡς θεὸν αὐτὸν μετὰ θάνατον ἐσεβάσθησαν.

> In much later times there were born, in the line of Hypsouranios, Hunter and Fisher, the inventors of fishing and hunting, from whom hunters and fishermen are named. From them were born two brothers who discovered iron and how to work it. One of these, Chousor, practiced verbal arts including spells and prophecies. He is, in fact, Hephaestos and he invented the hook, lure, line, and raft, and was the first of all men to sail. Therefore they honored him, too, as a god after his death.

Fisher, one might argue, should be associated with *dgy*, "Fisherman," the attendant of ʾAšerah in the Ugaritic texts.[39] If so, it is interesting to note that, according to the *Phoenician History*, the Ugaritic god Koṯar wa-Ḫasis, with whom Chousor is generally identified, is a descendant of the Fisherman.[40] Yet it must be kept in mind that the old traditions which served as sources for the *Phoenician History* have been subjected to a thorough euhemeristic analysis, which, as Clapham warns, "distorts old mythic genealogies and kinship patterns among the gods."[41]

To sum up the preceding discussion: the writer concludes that in the *Phoenician History* ʾAšerah/ʾElat is to be identified with Rhea and Dione. It is most probable that all the portions of the text (except perhaps for the matter of the sisterhood) dealing with Rhea and Dione are based on ancient Phoenician and Canaanite mythology. Accordingly, information derived from the *Phoenician History* about the goddess, which supplements that provided by the Ugaritic texts, is that she was sent by her father to kill ʾEl by stealth, but ʾEl caught her and made her his wife; that she possibly was the sister of ʾEl; and that she is to be identified with the *bʿlt gbl*, the chief goddess of Byblos.

Finally, a noteworthy observation is that in the level of tradition essentially reflected by the excerpts from the *Phoenician History* dealing with the history of Kronos/ʾEl and accounts of later rulers (which is basically different from the level of tradition chiefly characteristic of the Ugaritic literature), ʾAšerah does not play a greater role than ʿAštart (cf. also *Praeparatio evangelica* 1.10.10.31-2).[42] Nevertheless, the importance of Rhea/ʾAšerah in this mythology is evident, since it was her son(s) whom Kronos/ʾEl made "an object of worship." Also, the *History* includes the account (reflecting pre-first-millennium conditions) of Kronos/ʾEl giving Byblos, which he founded as the first city, to Dione/ʾElat.

The Syrian Goddess[43]

The Syrian Goddess (Περὶ τῆς Συρίης Θεοῦ) is attributed to Lucian, who was born in the second decade of the second century in Samosata (the capital of the Syrian province of Commagene) and whose literary career carried him throughout the Mediterranean basin.[44] The manuscript tradition is unanimous in ascribing *The Syrian Goddess* to Lucian, and until the nineteenth century the genuineness of the work was unquestioned; but during the past two centuries there have been numerous denials of Lucianic authorship.[45] One, or both, of two criteria are commonly adduced to distinguish *The Syrian Goddess* from the compositions which are certainly Lucian's: 1) the work is composed in Ionic Greek (a dialect distinct from Lucian's usual Attic), the use of which Lucian repudiates in *De Historia Conscribenda* 16, 18 and 40; and 2) the author does not seem as cynical as Lucian; the supposed hidden satire of *The Syrian Goddess* is too hidden for the work to be considered Lucianic.[46] However, both of these objections can be effectively answered. In the first place, the use of the Ionic dialect could well be due to Lucian's satirizing the pseudo-Ionic revival of the second century, and probably also to his parodying Herodotus.[47] Secondly, there are several passages in *The Syrian Goddess* which many have read as typically Lucianic satire.[48] The great majority of Lucianic scholars agree that the work should be ascribed to Lucian,[49] a decision with which the present writer concurs. At the very least it may be said that the dialect of *The Syrian Goddess* suggests a date of composition in the second century, and "the author's familiarity with the several levels of tradition at Hierapolis may indicate a knowledge of Aramaic and thus perhaps his upbringing in the Near East."[50]

By far the largest portion of *The Syrian Goddess* is concerned with the myths, temple and cult of Hierapolis (ancient Mabbug, modern Mambij).[51] Lucian's accounts and descriptions of these, the author indicates, are based upon information he obtained himself in visiting the city and questioning its inhabitants.[52] The basic trustworthiness of the observations related in *The Syrian Goddess* is supported by much ancient evidence and by observations of visitors to Hierapolis/Mambij in this century.[53] Abundant corroborating parallel accounts demonstrate that the satirical work has a firm factual foundation (which it then exaggerates and fancifully elaborates).[54]

The Near Eastern nature of the religion of Hierapolis is clear, despite the Greek names given the deities by Lucian. For example, in one tale related in *The Syrian Goddess* a large role is played by a steward named Kombabos; his name undoubtedly corresponds to that of Ḫumbaba, the guardian of Ištar's cedar forest in the epic of Gilgamesh.[55] Also, Lucian writes about the Syrian Goddess's consort, Zeus, a bearded Apollo, and other statues in the Hierapolitan temple. Zeus, it is generally agreed, is to be identified with Canaanite Baᶜl Haddu (Syrian Hadad),[56] while Apollo, who gives divine oracles, is possibly ʾEl, the grand patriarchal deity of Canaanite religion.[57] Both of these figures are well-known, of course, from the Ugaritic myths.[58]

The Syrian Goddess herself, who was worshipped at Hierapolis, and whom Lucian names "Hera," is, as other sources clearly show, Atargatis.[59] Today there is a consensus that Atargatis (Greek Ἀταργάτις, Aramaic *ᶜtrᶜth* or some variation of this form with a different *mater lectionis* at the end of the name) is a composite deity. Yet scholars disagree over which god(s) and/or goddess(es) Atargatis's name and attributes encompass. One view sees behind the first part of the name (Ἀταρ-/*ᶜtr*-) the goddess ᶜAštart,[60] Greek Astarte, and behind the second part (-γάτις/-*ᶜth*, or possibly *ᶜtʾ* or *ᶜt*) ᶜAte or ᶜAttah, either to be regarded as an unknown (Anatolian?) deity, or perhaps to be identified with the god Attis.[61]

While accepting this view concerning the first part of "Atargatis," Albright has demonstrated that the second part of the name represents the goddess ᶜAnat. He explains that "the Aramaeans replaced the Canaanite-Hebrew name *ᶜAnat* with the Aramaeized form *ᶜAttâ* and later amalgamated the sister-deities ᶜAttar and ᶜAttâ into the *dea syria*, Atargatis."[62] Thus, *ᶜtrᶜth* is **ᶜAṯtart* > Aram. *ᶜAttar(t)* > *ᶜAtar* > Gk. Ἀταρ-, and **ᶜAnat* > Aram. *ᶜAttâ* > *ᶜAtâ* > Gk. -γάτις.[63] In both cases, according to Albright, "the reduction of the doubling [*ᶜAttar* > *ᶜAtar*, *ᶜAttâ* > *ᶜAtâ*] is a normal phenomenon in early Aramaic."[64] With reference to this view the by-forms Ἀτταγάθη and Ἀταράτη should be noted: the first may preserve the memory of the older Aramaic form with the doubling (ᶜ*Attar*), while the second reflects the general situation in which Semitic ᶜ*ayin* was sometimes represented by Greek γ and sometimes by zero.[65]

Albright's position presently is that of the large majority of commentators. Recently, though, a new understanding of ᶜ*tr*ᶜ*th*/ Ἀταργάτις has been proposed by Oden, one in which the ᶜAštart-ᶜAnat viewpoint is not contradicted but rather supplemented. Oden thinks that there is an additional goddess behind Atargatis: ᵓAšerah. Only his stronger arguments for this conclusion[66] are briefly summarized here, as follows: a) Atargatis is to be identified with Derketo, and Derketo is best identified with ᵓAšerah (an identification with which this writer concurs; see Chapter 3);[67] and b) a comparison of ᵓAšerah material in the Ugaritic texts with information about Atargatis from *The Syrian Goddess* and other sources shows definite similarities between the two goddesses.[68] Another argument to be added to the preceding is that the object called σημήιον by Lucian, located in the inner chamber of the Hierapolis temple between the images of Zeus and Hera,[69] and pictured on coins of the city, was essentially the same object as the Punic caduceus, a symbol of the goddess Tannit (= ᵓAšerah).[70]

Taking into consideration the cumulative effect of the preceding arguments, this writer agrees with Oden's conclusion that in Atargatis there is a conflation of all three major Canaanite goddesses: ᶜAštart, ᶜAnat, and ᵓAšerah. Therefore a discussion about Lucian's *The Syrian Goddess* (the fullest and most immediate account of Atargatis and her cult at the main center of her worship, Hierapolis), and about Atargatis in general, has a proper place in a study of ᵓAšerah. At the same time, however, it becomes clear that such a discussion is of limited value for this inquiry. ᵓAšerah, under the figure of Atargatis, can never really be perceived alone, but always combined with ᶜAštart and ᶜAnat; thus the picture of ᵓAšerah is somewhat clouded. Furthermore, the decision that ᵓAšerah is included in the composite deity Atargatis was reached primarily on the basis of information from the ᵓAšerah/Derketo/Tannit texts and representations. Material concerning Atargatis, then, adds very little new information about ᵓAšerah herself to what is known about the goddess from these other sources, elsewhere examined in this study.

That the Syrian Goddess's name (Atargatis) and attributes encompass all three major Canaanite goddesses does point to two well-known phenomena of the ancient Near East, necessary to keep in mind for a proper perspective of ᵓAšerah and her worship at various times and places. On the one hand, as Pritchard writes, "At a particular place and time one female deity seems to be predominant as the divine lady of that particular time and place."[71] Or, as Oden puts the matter:

> Although our view is doubtlessly distorted by the fragmentary nature of the evidence, that evidence we have suggests that ᵓAšerah, ᶜAštart, or ᶜAnat surpassed her sister goddesses in importance at different times and places, but also that each continued to be worshipped as a distinct goddess somewhere . . .[72]

until at least the last centuries before the present era. On the other hand, the three great goddesses began to share attributes and to be blended together, or confused, by their worshippers already in the second millennium B.C., a process which continued in the following millennium.[73]

In conclusion, it may be said that Lucian's *The Syrian Goddess* gives a reliable (albeit satirical) account of Atargatis and her cult at Hierapolis. This deity, in encompassing ᶜAštart, ᶜAnat, and ᵓAšerah, still retained many of the features of Canaanite religion.[74] Wherever[75] and whenever[76] the worship of the Syrian Goddess took place, ᵓAšerah, to the extent that she was perceived to be comprehended in Atargatis, was also worshipped.

NOTES TO CHAPTER II

1. The medieval dictionary, the Suda, which gives Philo's dates and a list of titles of his work, apparently indicates that Philo was born in the reign of Nero (54-68) and survived at least into the reign of Hadrian (117-138). See *PBPH*, 2 and 2 n. 6, and 16-7, no. 1, with nn. 1-4.

2. For bibliographical references, see *PBPH*, 2 n. 5.

3. Other excerpts deal with a) cosmogony and b) the history of culture. The portions in *Praeparatio evangelica* on a) human sacrifice and b) snakes may not be from Philo's *Phoenician History*. See *PBPH*, 93 n. 148 and 94 n. 151.

4. Porphyry, *de abstinentia* 2.56 (*PBPH*, 16-7); *Praeparatio evangelica* 1.9.20 (*PBPH*, 18-9), 1.9.23 (*PBPH*, 28-9), 1.9.30 (*PBPH*, 36-7), 1.10.42 (*PBPH*, 60-1).

5. *Praeparatio evangelica*, 1.9.20-21 (*PBPH*, 18-21). The fall of Troy traditionally was dated to 1184 B.C. and was the earliest historical event in Greek chronography. See *PBPH*, 23-4 n. 17.

6. *Praeparatio evangelica*, 1.9.20-21, 24-26 (*PBPH*, 18-21, 28-31). See also *PBPH*, 4-5.

7. For surveys of the history of scholarship on the *Phoenician History*, see Carl Clemen, *Die phönikische Religion nach Philo von Byblos* (Mitteilungen der vorderasiatisch-ägyptischen Gesellschaft 42/3; Leipzig: J.C. Hinrichs, 1939) 1-16 and James Barr, "Philo of Byblos and his 'Phoenician History,'" *BJRL* 57 (1974) 18-21.

8. Otto Eissfeldt ("Phönikische und griechische Kosmogonie," *Kleine Schriften* 3 [1966] 510-2; for other references, see *PBPH*, 6 n. 27), accepting the tradition placing Sanchuniathon somewhere about the time of the Trojan War, thinks that Sanchuniathon lived in the second millennium B.C., while Albright ("Neglected Factors in the Greek Intellectual Revolution," *Proceedings of the American Philosophical Society* 116 [1972] 240) advances a date around the mid-first millennium B.C. Albright explains that Sanchuniathon, probably originally a native of Tyre, presumably escaped from that city before, during, or after

the long siege (585-572 B.C.) and final capture of Tyre by Nebuchadnezzar. Sanchuniathon then lived, according to Albright, at the court of Abedbalos, king of Berytus, where he wrote between ca. 585 and ca. 550. Briefly, the main evidence cited for the position that there was a Sanchuniathon who lived and wrote a *Phoenician History* in pre-Hellenistic times is the fact that the name *sknytn* definitely could have belonged to a native Phoenician, and, especially, the similarities between Philo's source and the Ugaritic and Hittite mythological material discovered in the twentieth century. The name *sknytn* has been found in a Punic inscription from Hadrumetum, North Africa (see Mark Lidzbarski, *Handbuch der nordsemitischen Epigraphik* [2 vols.; Weimar: Emil Felber, 1898] 1: 432 b.2.2). Additional names compounded with the theophorus element *skn* are also evidenced: e.g., *ᶜbdskn*, found in a Phoenician inscription perhaps dating to ca. 600 B.C. (*Corpus Inscriptionum Semiticarum* [Ab Academia inscriptionum et litterarum humaniorum; Paris: e Republicae typographeo, 1881-; hereafter *CIS*] Pars Prima, no. 112a) and other inscriptions, and *grskn*, which occurs in numerous inscriptions from Carthage, some perhaps from the very early period of that city. See, conveniently, Frank L. Benz, *Personal Names in the Phoenician and Punic Inscriptions* (Studia Pohl 8; Rome: Biblical Institute Press, 1972).

9. *PBPH*, 9. Attridge and Oden argue that although *sknytn* could have been a native Phoenician name, this does not prove the antiquity or even the historicity of Sanchuniathon. Also, they point out that since the religion of which the Ugaritic texts are one manifestation lived on long after the fall of Ugarit, a correspondence between the Ugaritic material and the *Phoenician History* of Philo is not adequate proof that Philo used an ancient Phoenician source, and if he did, it need not have been one dating from remote antiquity (*PBPH*, 6). Attridge and Oden further argue against seeing the *Phoenician History* as a translation of an ancient work (authored by a Sanchuniathon) by explaining that the material in Philo lacks any apparent structure which might correspond to that of other ancient Semitic documents (*PBPH*, 6-7). They additionally state that the highly developed, thorough and consistent euhemeristic analysis of mythology in the *Phoenician History* indicates a date in the Hellenistic or Roman periods for this compilation of ancient myth, as does a) the fact that a large part of the surviving text deals with the history of culture and the progress in human civilization achieved through the contributions of various inventors (the Hellenistic world witnessed a great interest in this issue), and b) a dependence at some points on Greek myths and an ignorance of the meaning of some of the Semitic names given in the *Phoenician History* (*PBPH*, 7-9). Oden, in his article "Philo of Byblos and Hellenistic Historiography" (*PEQ* 110 [1978] 118-26) sees certain tendencies exhibited in the entire *Phoenician History*,

which, he states, demonstrate that the *History* is a typical specimen of Hellenistic historiography. These tendencies, also witnessed in the surviving fragmentary historical texts from subject lands in the Hellenistic and Roman eras, are a) to write in euhemeristic fashion, b) to write history on a universal scale, c) to compose patriotic cultural history, d) to have a belligerent and defensive stance with respect to Greek civilization and particularly Greek mythography, and e) to claim that the material used was better, in age and reliability, than that used by competitors or adversaries. Oden cautions that even when a piece of datum in the *Phoenician History* is remarkably similar to information provided by the Ugaritic texts, this correspondence does not mean that the remainder of Philo's text is of second millennium B.C. vintage, nor that it is even natively Phoenician of whatever date (the *Phoenician History* in certain instances clearly relies upon Egyptian material, some of which, Oden concludes, indicates that Philo drew directly upon Hermopolitan tradition).

10. Lynn R. Clapham, "Sanchuniaton: The First Two Cycles" (Ph.D. diss., Harvard University, 1969) 102-4 proposes that the anonymous mothers of Samemroumos and Oosoos (*Praeparatio evangelica* 1.10.9; *PBPH*, 42-3) are ᶜAnat and ᵓAšerah. While this may be correct, the reasons Clapham advances for including ᵓAšerah in this pair are not very strong or convincing, particularly when he says that it seems both ᵓAšerah and ᶜAnat are mates of ᵓEl and mothers of Dawn and Dusk in *CTA* 23 (cf. the treatment of this text in Chap. 1 above). Therefore, *Praeparatio evangelica* 1.10.9 will not be included in the examination of other material from the *Phoenician History*, which has more compelling reasons for being included in a discussion of ᵓAšerah.

Also, *Praeparatio evangelica* 1.10.15 mentions "a certain Elioun, called Most High, and a woman called Berouth, who settled the area around Byblos" (*PBPH*, 46-7). Various suggestions have been put forward regarding the identity of Berouth. Albright ("The North Canaanite Epic of ᵓAlᵓêyân Baᶜal and Môt," *JPOS* 12 [1932] 190) connects the name with *bᵓrwt*, "fountains." He argues for viewing *bᵓrwt* as an ᶜAnat epithet, but Attridge and Oden think it is more plausibly a title of ᵓAšerah, "whose association with the sea and its fecundity is well established" (*PBPH*, 86 n. 81). As they point out, however, since ᵓAšerah's consort is regularly ᵓEl, one would expect the "Elioun" of 1.10.15 to be an ᵓEl epithet, but in fact ᵓEl/Kronos does not appear until 1.10.16. Therefore, an identification of Berouth with ᵓAšerah is problematic.

11. The text and translation used in this chapter are from *PBPH*. *Praeparatio evangelica* 1.10.22-4 (with translation) may be found on pp. 50-3. Their text of the *Phoenician History*, Attridge and Oden explain (*PBPH*, 9-10), is basically that of Karl Mras, *Eusebius Werke*, achter Band,

Die Praeparatio Evangelica (GCS 43; Berlin: Akademie, 1954), and that Mras's text has been compared with that of Felix Jacoby, *Die Fragmente der griechischen Historiker* (Dritter Teil, C.; Leiden: E. J. Brill, 1958) 790. Attridge and Oden also list the manuscripts on which Mras's edition is based (*PBPH*, 10).

12. These words are conjecturally restored. Attridge and Oden explain that in parallel with this section's other pieces of genealogical information, one would expect the number (most likely two, as with ᶜAštart's children, Desire and Love) and the names of Dione's daughters. This information, they conclude, has probably fallen out of the text (*PBPH*, 89 n. 106).

13. *CMHE*, 28. Cross (*CMHE*, 29 n. 90) points out the transparent etymological relation between Dione and Zeus (gen. *Dios*), ᵓElat (ᵓ*ilatu*) and ᵓEl (ᵓ*ilu*).

14. See, e.g., Brookes More, trans., "Atalanta" (from Ovid, *Metamorphoses*, Book 10), in *Great Classical Myths* (ed. F. R. B. Godolphin; Modern Library; New York: Random House, 1964) 332, par. 2, line 12.

15. Cf., e.g., More, 332, par. 3, line 9. See also J. Heckenbach, "῾Ρέα," PW 1 (Zweite Reihe; 1914) cols. 340-341.

16. *Praeparatio evangelica* 1.10.16 (*PBPH*, 48-9).

17. At Dodona Dione was worshipped together with Zeus in his quality of a god of springs, being regarded as wife of the supreme god and herself a spring goddess and giver of oracles (C. Kerényi, *The Gods of the Greeks* [London: Thames and Hudson, 1951] 68).

18. "Dione," *Encyclopedia Britannica* 8 (11th ed., 1910-11) 283; Alexander Duthie, *The Greek Mythology* (Edinburgh: Oliver and Boyd, 1949) 17.

19. In the Iliad (v. 370) she is the mother (by Zeus) of Aphrodite, who is herself in later times called "Dione." See J. Escher-Bürkli, "Dione," PW 5 (1905) col. 879.

20. In the sacred books of Orpheus there is a tale according to which Kronos and Rhea were the eldest children of Okeanos and Tethys, who, in turn, were the offspring of Ouranos and Gaia (Kerényi, 42, where the reference is given).

21. Cf. the name "Juno," which some derive from the same root as that of "Jupiter." See Herbert Jennings Rose, "Juno," *The Oxford Classical Dictionary* (1949) 471-2.

22. As a spring goddess, and wife of Zeus νάιος at Dodona, Dione came to be reckoned as one of the ναιάδες , the feminine divinities of the (fresh) water (see Escher-

Bürkli, col. 880). One is reminded of ʾAšerah/ʾAṯirat's connections with the sea in the Ugaritic literature.

23. Robert Graves, *The Greek Myths* (2 vols.; Baltimore: Penguin Books, 1955) 1: 39, 41, 50, 181 mentions that the oak tree was thought by some to be sacred to Rhea (Scholiast on Apollonius Rhodius: i. 1124). Since the oak was also sacred to Dione, as evidenced by the cult at Dodona (which, he explains, was taken over by Zeus), Graves holds that the two goddesses may be equated. Such a conclusion is intriguing but far from certain. However, it is interesting to note that, along with other descriptions of her relation to Hera, Dione was regarded as the mother of Hera. See Escher-Bürkli, col. 879.

24. Clapham, 18.

25. The smaller numbers, particularly the seven, are a result of rationalization; but "seven" is also a "good" Semitic number, symbolizing a smaller (versus a larger) group of people taken as a whole. See Chap. 1 n. 54.

26. *Praeparatio evangelica* 1.10.15 (first sentence), 16 (first sentence), 19-20, 25, 27, 31, 32, 34, 35 (*PBPH*, 46-57; see also the accompanying notes for these passages).

27. E.g., portions of *Praeparatio evangelica* 1.10.17, 18, 29, and the last sentence of 32 (*PBPH*, 48-51, 54-7; see also the notes to the text). The story of Ouranos's castration by Kronos is also attested in the Hittite myth of Kumarbi; see, conveniently, Goetze, 120.

28. The main outline is provided primarily by Hesiod in his *Theogony* (116-820). According to Greek mythology the children of Ouranos and Gaia were the Titans/esses, Cyclopes, and hundred-armed monsters. However, Ouranos thrust the Cyclopes and monsters into Tartarus. Grieved by this, Gaia thought of a treacherous plan. Taking her Titan son Kronos, she hid him in an ambush, arming him with a sickle which she had made. When the time was right, Kronos, from his hiding place, castrated his father Ouranos with the sickle.

Kronos reigned in his father's stead, taking to wife his sister Rhea. They had six children, but Kronos swallowed them one by one as they were born, until Rhea saved her sixth child, Zeus, by giving to Kronos in his place a stone wrapped in swaddling clothes, which Kronos swallowed. Zeus was hidden until he grew to maturity. Then, aided by the counsels of Rhea and Gaia, he proceeded to take vengeance on his father. A potion was given to Kronos, causing him to disgorge the stone, followed by his five sons and daughters.

Zeus and his allies fought against Kronos and most of the Titans. The conflict raged for years until finally, at the advice of Gaia, Zeus set free from

Tartarus the Cyclopes and hundred-armed monsters, and by their aid defeated the party of the older gods. Kronos either fled to the west or was thrown into captivity by Zeus (see Duthie, 3-6 and Kerényi, 20-5).

29. See Cross, *CMHE*, 40-3 and E. Theodore Mullen, Jr., *The Divine Council in Canaanite and Early Hebrew Literature* (HSM 24; Chico, Ca.: Scholars Press, 1980) 43-5.

30. The first line of *Praeparatio evangelica* 1.10.26 and the beginning of the next read Ἐγεννήθησαν δὲ καὶ ἐν Περαίᾳ Κρόνῳ τρεῖς παῖδες. . . : "Three more children were born to Kronos in Peraea . . ." (*PBPH*, 52-3). Attridge and Oden give as an alternate translation for ἐν Περαίᾳ "by Peraea," explaining (*PBPH*, 89 n. 111) that the text may have originally mentioned not the place in which further children of Kronos were born, but the mate by whom he fathered them. Moreover, Attridge and Oden comment that Περαία possibly is corrupted from Ῥέα, Kronos's wife and the mother of Zeus (Hesiod, *Theogony*, 453-58). However, judging from the writing style of the *Phoenician History*, it is doubtful that "by Peraea ["Rhea"?]" is correct, since ἀπὸ Περαίας or ἐξ Περαίας would be expected for such a translation. See especially *Praeparatio evangelica* 1.10.16, 17, 24; cf. 1.10.44 (*PBPH*, 46-9, 52-3, 62-3).

31. *PBPH*, 56-7.

32. "Muth" reflects the normal Iron Age shifts á > ā > ō and ō > ū. The figure of Mot in the excerpt dealing with cosmology (*Praeparatio evangelica* 1.10.1-2; *PBPH*, 36-7) may possibly derive from the Canaanite god, Mot. See the discussion of Attridge and Oden, *PBPH*, 76-7 n. 29.

33. *PBPH*, 50-1.

34. See, for example, Herbert Donner and Wolfgang Röllig, *Kanaanäische und aramäische Inschriften* (3 vols.; Wiesbaden: Otto Harrassowitz, 1966-69; hereafter *KAI*) nos. 6 (ᵓElibaᶜl inscription, ca. 920 B.C.), 7 (Shipiṭbaᶜl inscription, ca. 900 B.C.), and 10 (Yeḥawmilk stele, ca. 5th-4th century B.C.); cf. no. 4 (Yeḥimilk inscription, ca. 960 B.C.).

35. See *EA*, 2: 1583.

36. This reference of Lucian will be discussed in Chap. 3.

37. Clapham, 120.

38. *PBPH*, 42-5.

39. So Attridge and Oden, *PBPH*, 84 n. 64.

40. Since Hephaestos was the smith of Olympus, the syncretistic identification of Chousor with this Greek deity is not surprising. The association of Hephaestos with the sea is less clear in Greek tradition (*PBPH*, 84 n. 67). However, Koṯar is possibly called "son of the sea" in *CTA* 4.7.15-16.

41. Clapham, 20.

42. *PBPH*, 54-5. Her role is not much larger than that played by ᶜAnat, if Athena is to be identified with ᶜAnat. See *Praeparatio evangelica* 1.10.18 and 1.10.10.32-3 (*PBPH*, 48-9, 56-7; consult also the notes to the text).

43. For the following section of Chap. 2 I rely heavily on a) the translation, introduction, and notes in Attridge and Oden's *The Syrian Goddess (De Dea Syria). Attributed to Lucian* (SBLTT 9; Missoula, Mont.: Scholars Press, 1976), hereafter *SGAL*, and b) Oden's *Studies in Lucian's De Syria Dea* (HSM 15; Missoula, Mont.: Scholars Press, 1977).

44. *SGAL*, 2.

45. *SGAL*, 2.

46. *SGAL*, 2; Oden, *Studies*, 11.

47. *SGAL*, 2; Oden, *Studies*, 11-2. See the references supporting this opinion cited by Oden in his *Studies*, 12 n. 42.

48. *SGAL*, 2. For examples of satire and other rhetorical tricks in *The Syrian Goddess* consult Oden, *Studies*, 16-24.

49. See Oden, *Studies*, 7-11.

50. *SGAL*, 2-3.

51. Four main sections are evident in the work, as Oden notes (*Studies*, 3-4). After an introduction (par. 1), the reader is led through several cities lying "in Syria," as does Hierapolis itself (par. 2-9). Then, Lucian gives a more detailed description of the founders of both the cult of Hierapolis and the temple there (par. 10-27). The third section (par. 28-41) is a description of the temple at Hierapolis (as it stood in Lucian's day), including descriptions of the sacred area around the temple as well as of the temple's interior, particularly the representations of the deities. All these deities are given Greek names. The final section (par. 42-60) consists of an account of the cultic rites practiced by the inhabitants of Hierapolis and by those making pilgrimages to the city.

52. *SGAL*, 1.

53. *SGAL*, 1, 3. See, conveniently, the references cited by Attridge and Oden, *SGAL*, 3 and 7 n. 1, and by Oden, *Studies*, 43-6.

54. *SGAL*, 3; Oden, *Studies*, 43, 46.

55. *SGAL*, 4; Oden, *Studies*, 36-40.

56. See Oden, *Studies*, 48, 53-5.

57. *SGAL*, 4 and 8 n. 14 (where reference is made to René Dussaud, who first suggested this identification).

58. Previously, John Garstang and Herbert A. Strong (*The Syrian Goddess* [London: Constable, 1913], esp. 11-2) and H. Stocks ("Studien zur Lukians 'De Syria Dea,'" *Berytus* 4 [1937] 1-40) argued (incorrectly) for the Anatolian, perhaps originally Hittite, character of the religion of Hierapolis (*SGAL*, 4).

59. For the evidence, see Oden, *Studies*, 48-53, 55-8.

60. The original form of ᶜAštart's name was ᶜ*ṯtrt* (occurring in the Ugaritic texts), but **ṯ* merged with *t* in Aramaic, while in Phoenician and Hebrew **ṯ* merged with *š* and is represented by the grapheme ש. On the matter of the reduction of the doubling, see the main text and n. 64 below.

61. See Oden, *Studies*, 61-3.

62. "The Evolution of the West-Semitic Divinity ᶜAn-ᶜAnat-ᶜAttâ" (*AJSL* 41 [1925]) 101. Cf. Albright, *YGC*, 133.

63. The syncope of ᶜ*Anat* > ᶜ*Antâ* (> ᶜ*Attâ*) is a characteristic Aramaic development. Note Albright's formula, "ᶜ*Anat* : ᶜ*Attâ* : : *šanat*, 'year' : *šattâ*" ("Evolution of the West-Semitic Divinity," 88). The ending -*â*, however, is problematic. Independently or as the second part of a compound name, ᶜAnat's name is usually written ᶜ*th* or ᶜ*t*ᵓ = ᶜ*Atâ* (Oden, *Studies*, 67 and 67 n. 95). Oden suggests that "if this -*â* is the article, the memory of the etymological origin of ᶜAnat's name may have been preserved in Syria, which would be unexpected though not without parallel." Nevertheless, Oden concludes that "the ending on ᶜAtâ remains a puzzle for which no satisfactory solution has been adduced" (*Studies*, 67 n. 95).

64. *YGC*, 133 n. 58. As Oden writes, this claim by Albright "is seductive in its resolution of the doubling problem, though one would like some evidence for it" (*Studies*, 64 n. 88).

65. Oden, *Studies*, 65 and 65 n. 92.

66. "Weaker" arguments, in this writer's opinion, are a) Oden's reasoning that since Ugaritic ᶜ*ṯtrt*, Hebrew-Phoenician ᶜ*štrt* is ᶜ*tr* in Aramaic, so too Ugaritic ᵓ*ṯrt*, Hebrew ᵓ*šrh*, is ᵓ*tr* in Aramaic. Thus, these Aramaic forms are so similar that in the Aramaic ᶜ*tr*- and Greek Ἀταρ- there might be "a congeneric assimilation of ᵓ*tr* and ᶜ*tr* and a conceptual assimilation of ᵓAšerah and ᶜAštart" (*Studies*, 66). Such "assimilations," however, are far from certain; moreover, an Aramaic goddess ᵓ*tr* is as yet unattested. Oden also argues that b) the Aramaic by-form ᵓ*tr*ᶜ*t*ᵓ might preserve the memory of ᵓAšerah's place in the compound name Atargatis. As Oden himself admits, though, ᵓ*tr*ᶜ*t*ᵓ could be the result of a dissimilation of the two ᶜ*ayin*'s in ᶜ*tr*ᶜ*t* or an ᶜ*ayin*-ᵓ*aleph* confusion (both of which are widely evidenced especially in later material). Still, Oden's counterargument is noteworthy: ". . . it is at least intriguing that one never finds a spelling ᶜ*tr*ᵓ*th*, with the second ᶜ*ayin* dissimilated to ᵓ*aleph*, though this phenomenon is witnessed elsewhere" (*Studies*, 68-9). Finally, Oden mentions that c) Punic Tannit (= ᵓAšerah; see Chap. 3) was identified with Hera in the western Mediterranean, and Hera is the Greek goddess Lucian chooses to identify with Atargatis at Hierapolis (*Studies*, 101-2). However, Tannit was also identified with Ops, the Latin counterpart of Greek Rhea (see Cross, *CMHE*, 32).

67. Oden's evidence for both identifications may be found on pp. 69-72 of his *Studies*.

68. *Studies*, 99-101. Specifically, both have clear marine associations, both have "mother" roles, and both are mentioned as holding a spindle.

69. *The Syrian Goddess*, par. 33 (*SGAL*, 44-5).

70. This connection is proposed by Oden, *Studies*, 149-55. See the next chapter.

71. James B. Pritchard, *Palestinian Figurines in Relation to Certain Goddesses Known Through Literature* (AOS 24; New Haven: American Oriental Society, 1943) 85.

72. *Studies*, 105-6. Oden summarizes the evidence nicely: "ᶜAštart dominates in the names of Phoenicians on the mainland in the first millennium B.C., as she shares a place of honor among the references to foreign worship in the Old Testament. ᵓAšerah is heard of more often than ᶜAštart in the Ugaritic texts, and under the epithet Tannit, again plays a role of major importance in Carthage and elsewhere in the western Mediterranean. Except for as the theophorous element on a few [Punic] names and several inscriptions from Cyprus, the name ᶜAnat is little heard in the first millennium B.C., yet hers is the preeminent role in the Ugaritic texts" (*Studies*, 106).

73. For example, ᶜAnat and ᶜAštart are mingled together in an incantation text from Ugarit (RS 24.244, line 20; *Ug 5*, 565, 567), in which Šapaš is directed to carry a "message" to ᵓEl, Baᶜl, Dagan, and then "to ᶜAnat-and-ᶜAštart" (*ᶜim ᶜanati-waᶜaṯtarti*, lines 19-20). R. B. Coote has observed that of the divine pairs to whom Šapaš is to go, "the group *ᶜntwᶜṯtrt* is the only one spelled without a word divider" ("The Serpent and Sacred Marriage in Northwest Semitic Tradition" [Ph.D. diss., Harvard University, 1972] 29). In Egypt, ᶜAnat and ᶜAštart are often indistinguishable (see Oden, *Studies*, 96 n. 243 for references). The two names are combined into one in Egypt: a treaty between Ramesses II and Hattusilis names a Syrian goddess *ᶜntrt* as a witness (Oden, *Studies*, 96 and 96 n. 246). An Egyptian relief (discussed in Chap. 3) dating approximately from the time of Ramesses III presented to Winchester College gives the names Qudšu, ᶜAštart, and ᶜAnat to a typical Qudšu (ᵓAšerah) representation (I. E. S. Edwards, "A Relief of Qudshu-Astarte-Anath in the Winchester College Collection," *JNES* 14 [1955] 49-51 and pl. 3). Each of these goddesses receives in Egypt a title translated by Stadelmann "'Herrin des Himmels'" (92-5 [ᶜAnat], 106 [ᶜAštart], 120 [Qudšu/ᵓAšerah]; see Chap. 3 n. 30). Finally, a seventh-sixth century B.C. Phoenician inscription (discussed in Chap. 3) records the dedication of a statue to the conflate goddess "Tannit-ᶜAštart" (J. B. Pritchard, *Recovering Sarepta, A Phoenician City* [Princeton: Princeton University, 1978] 104-6 and 104 fig. 103).

74. Since "Zeus"/Hadad was regularly linked with Atargatis, apparently Baᶜl Haddu during the first millennium B.C. came to be regarded as the chief consort of all three goddesses, a situation which many scholars see reflected in the Hebrew Bible with regard to ᵓAšerah and ᶜAštart. Atargatis/"Hera" and "Zeus" were the chief deities of Hierapolis: e.g., their statues occupied a special chamber within the Hierapolis temple (cf. *The Syrian Goddess*, 31 and 34; *SGAL*, 42-5), their statues are described first by Lucian (*The Syrian Goddess*, 31-32; *SGAL*, 42-5), and the twice-daily sacrifices of Hierapolis were in honor of "Hera" and "Zeus" (*The Syrian Goddess*, 44; *SGAL*, 50-1); note also the evidence from the island of Delos cited by Oden (*Studies*, 48-50). Of the two, Atargatis generally had the pre-eminence (at Hierapolis and elsewhere). This is seen, first of all, in Lucian's *The Syrian Goddess*: e.g., the temple of Hierapolis was built at the order of "Hera" (19; *SGAL*, 28-9); she is mentioned before "Zeus" (31; *SGAL*, 42-3); her statue is described in greater length and detail than that of "Zeus" (see above); the self-castrations in the temple may have been performed as an honor to "Hera" (26-27; *SGAL*, 36-7); and specific sentences in the work indicate as much, such as, "She [Semiramis] established a law for the inhabitants of Syria that they should worship her as a goddess

and that they should ignore the other deities, even Hera herself" (39; *SGAL*, 48-9). Secondly, note the relief of Hadad and Atargatis from Dura-Europos mentioned by Oden (*Studies*, 50 and 50 n. 13, 51-2).

The bearded "Apollo" (= ᵓEl?) was not considered to be of the same rank as "Hera" and "Zeus" at Hierapolis, judging, e.g., from his statue being described after those of "Hera" and "Zeus" in *The Syrian Goddess* (35; *SGAL*, 46-7), and its location in the temple (*The Syrian Goddess*, 34-35; *SGAL*, 44-7). Evidently, however, the god was believed to deliver oracles, which were not only collected, but also used to guide religious and personal business (*The Syrian Goddess*, 36; *SGAL*, 46-9).

75. The worship of Atargatis with her consort Hadad was not limited to Hierapolis, but spread throughout Syria and eventually the entire Mediterranean world (Oden, *Studies*, 50). Listings of her cult sites are given in F. R. Walton's "Atargatis," *RAC* 1 (1950) cols. 856-859. Specifically in the Near East, locations of Atargatis worship included Dura-Europos, Palmyra, ᶜAkko (Ptolemais), Carnaim (2 Macc 12: 26) and Nabataea.

76. It is likely that worship of Atargatis continued at least into the third century of the Christian Era. Among pieces of evidence which support such an assumption are two coins of Hierapolis from the early part of that century, one issued under Alexander Severus (see Stocks, pl. 1.1), the other under Caracalla (Stocks, pl. 1.5), which picture Atargatis with Hadad in a manner similar to Lucian's descriptions of the representations of the deities.

Chapter III

REPRESENTATIONS AND ADDITIONAL EPITHETS

This chapter will deal with *qdš*, *d̲t bt̲n*, *bᶜlt gbl*, *tnt*, Derketo, and Phanebalos. *d̲t bt̲n* and *bᶜlt gbl* are included in the *qdš* section, which immediately follows.

qdš

Representations of a nude female figure have been found at almost every excavated site in Syria-Palestine. Pritchard, in his monograph *Palestinian Figurines in Relation to Certain Goddesses Known Through Literature*,[1] deals with these objects, concentrating mainly on the small terra cotta figurines and plaques uncovered in Palestine.[2] After cataloguing the then-published examples of these Palestinian figurines and plaques and classifying them according to seven types, he discusses the connections of each of the types with similar objects in other cultural areas.

Of particular interest here is Pritchard's Type I: the arms of the standing (with legs together), frontally-viewed figure are extended sideward and upward so that the forearm and the upper arm form the letter V. Included in this group are those plaques on which the figure holds stalks (unidentified stalks, papyrus stalks, or lotus stalks with three-petal bloom),[3] on which nothing is represented in the hands,[4] and those on which a serpent(s) is pictured.[5] Pritchard concludes that "on the whole the evidence of the contextual dating" places the Type I plaque in the Late

Bronze Period,[6] but some fragments of plaques which seem to belong to this type come from strata E (eighteenth-seventeenth centuries) and D (seventeenth-sixteenth centuries) of Tell Beit Mirṣim.[7]

Most of the figures in Type I wear what appears to be a wig (two massive locks, usually curved outward at the ends in spiral or semi-spiral fashion, extending to the shoulders or breasts), which in Egypt is characteristic of the goddess Hathor, and dates from the Twelfth Dynasty[8] or earlier.[9] A number of the figures, however, have two slender locks, sometimes spiral, hanging to the shoulders or the breasts; the general appearance is that of natural hair. This latter treatment of the hair probably is to be regarded as earlier than the Hathor wig: the double slender locks have been traced to prototypes from third millennium Mesopotamia, the earliest coming from the period of Entemena (a ruler of the Early Dynastic III Period).[10]

Parallel to and (although exhibiting somewhat differing features) belonging to the same classification as the Palestinian terra cotta plaques of Pritchard's Type I are metal plaques from various locations in Syria-Palestine, as far north as Zincirli and as far south as Tell el-ᶜAjjul.[11] Certain of these plaques show only a face with Hathor hairdress, breasts, and genital triangle.[12] The remainder depict the full Type I figure -- shown from the front, nude, in standing position, wearing a Hathor wig, raising her arms to the sides in the V shape.[13] Each, though, is unique in the total picture it presents.[14] Almost all of these plaques (both the "representational" and the complete-figure groups) date from approximately the same time period (Late Bronze) as the Palestinian terra cotta plaques.[15]

Furthermore, there are several Egyptian portrayals occurring on reliefs which match Pritchard's Type I,[16] generally dating from the Nineteenth and Twentieth Dynasties.[17] While there are minor variations in the examples, the main pattern for depicting the female figure is strikingly apparent: viewed from the front, nude, wearing the Hathor wig, standing on a lion striding to the (viewer's) right, with arms held out at the sides and bent in the V shape, one hand holding a serpent(s), the other a (lotus) blossom(s).[18] Generally, the Egyptian stelai may be grouped into two categories, those (whether with or without representations of worshippers) on which the female figure is portrayed alone, and those on which she is portrayed as part of a triad. The other two members of this triad always stand on either side of the female figure and face her. They are, with two exceptions, the Egyptian god Min (to the viewer's left) and the Canaanite god Rešep (to the viewer's right).[19] At least four of these reliefs, which must all be grouped with the Type I terra cotta plaques and corresponding metal examples discussed above, identify the female figure as *qdš*.[20] Therefore, Pritchard's Type I is also known as the *qdš* type.[21]

Of interest in this connection is an image of a nude female figure found on scarabs of the Second Intermediate Period. She is often winged, has some features of the goddess Hathor, and frequently holds lotus blossoms or a branch in her hands. The representation is quite similar to the *qdš* type.[22] Yet the figure on the scarabs is for the most part certainly not in accord with typical Egyptian style.[23] Likewise, the *qdš* type itself, apart from particular points (e.g., the Hathor wig), is thoroughly un-Egyptian; full (nude) front-view representations were extremely rare in Egypt, in the case of divinities (if *qdš* is a goddess; more on this below) almost unknown.[24] It is undoubtedly best to regard the *qdš* type (and the figure on the scarabs) as being brought from Syria-Palestine, where it existed previously, into Egypt. In fact, a number of the features of this type seem to have been derived from Mesopotamian influences. As mentioned above, the inspiration for the slender spiral locks on some of the Palestinian plaques apparently came from third millennium Mesopotamia. Moreover, the element of a goddess (or a god) standing on a lion was utilized in the last half of the third millennium in Mesopotamia and later appears to have been widespread.[25] After reviewing the evidence, this writer feels that a *qdš*-like representation, and perhaps even the *qdš* type itself, was present in Palestine during the Middle Bronze Period, that the *qdš* type became firmly established in Palestine and Syria toward the end of the Middle Bronze Period or at the beginning of the Late Bronze Period, that its popularity continued through the Late Bronze Period, but that its production in Palestine and Syria for the most part was discontinued in the Iron I Period. Further, the *qdš* type (either in the Middle Bronze Period or at the very beginning of the Late Bronze Period) secondarily took on characteristics of the goddess Hathor (e.g., wig, face) as a result of Egyptian contacts/influence in Syria-Palestine, and in this form later was brought into Egypt (there are no *qdš* examples in Egypt before the Nineteenth Dynasty), where its firm position in the life of at least a portion of the population began to weaken and recede into the background after the Twentieth Dynasty.[26]

Thus far it is apparent that the *qdš* figure shows elements associated with Hathor,[27] and -- that which goes hand in hand with these externals, in the writer's opinion -- the type represented a goddess. The specific outer Hathoric characteristics of the various *qdš* examples have already been mentioned: for example, Hathor wig, face, ears, and abacus crown.[28] Also, epithets of *qdš* on the Egyptian reliefs illustrate that she was a goddess and was identified with Hathor in Egypt.[29] She is called the "Eye of Re [that is, the eye of the sun], whose like there is not," "Lover/Sweetheart of Re," "Eye of Atum," besides being designated as the one "whom Ptah loves," "Lady of Heaven," "Lady/Ruler of All [or "the"] Gods," "Lady of Both Lands," "Divine One," and "Child of Re."[30] Further, the divine nature of *qdš* is indicated by her standing on a lion.[31] She is, moreover, depicted as being worshipped either alone[32] or as part of the triad.[33] Prayers or invocations to *qdš* are preserved on one of these reliefs and on an Egyptian votive stele which is not in the *qdš* class (more on these prayers below). Finally, that *qdš* appears with two gods (being worshipped together with them) indicates that she was regarded as a goddess (at least in Egypt). *qdš* has the chief position in the triad, standing in the middle, a god on either side facing her, with her head higher than those of the gods (most often because she is standing on a lion); in some instances, *qdš* appears much larger in form than the two gods.[34]

If it is best to view the *qdš* type as representing a divinity,[35] it is at the same time clear what kind of deity is being pictured. Several factors point to the fact that *qdš* was a goddess of (to capture the various nuances of the evidence) the erotic, sexual vigor, love, grace and beauty, and fertility. Her (frontal) nudity, one could argue, signifies all these aspects, while the objects which are held by her or shown with her relate more precisely to certain of these features -- the serpents primarily symbolize fecundity,[36] the gazelles (?) gracefulness, the flowers (whether identified as lotus flowers or lilies) grace, beauty, and charm,[37] and the rams sexual vigor.[38]

The appearance of Min with *qdš* on a number of the Egyptian reliefs similarly implies that she was a goddess of eroticism, fertility, and sexual vigor.[39] An important deity in Egyptian religion, Min was a god of fertility and harvest, of the generative/reproductive power of nature. He personified the masculine principle, and is almost always shown ithyphallic, with his raised right arm waving a flail.[40] Portrayals of Min usually have a small naos and lettuce field (the lettuce was his sacred plant) in the background.

According to Helck, the *dahinstürmende* Rešep was included in the triad as another deity of sexual vigor.[41] Strictly speaking, however, the Canaanite god was probably originally pictured with *qdš* and Min mainly because his worshippers in Egypt regarded him as a god of welfare.[42] Stadelmann, noting Rešep's aspect in Syria-Palestine as a fire, plague, and epidemic god,[43] explains that in Eighteenth Dynasty Egypt Rešep was viewed as a war god, and belonged to the group of "royal divinities."[44] In the time of the Ramessides, though, Rešep as a war god receded conspicuously into the background; instead, he was worshipped on many stelai of "private people," mostly of the lower social classes. Rešep, Stadelmann observes, continued to show on these stelai his known warlike aspect,[45] but in spite of this appearance it was apparently not for purposes of warfare that the dedicators of the stelai petitioned Rešep, because they were prominently peaceful artisans (from the East Delta, Memphis, and Thebes West).[46]

Rešep's character on these stelai is best seen as, generally speaking, that of a god of welfare. Since he was the god who sent disasters and plagues, Rešep was also understood by his worshippers in Syria-Palestine, and evidently in Egypt, as being able to keep such misfortunes from them. Further, they believed he could help against and rescue them from these evils, with the result that they would have life, health, and well-being.[47] Stadelmann comments that the appearance of these Rešep stelai shortly after the Amarna period may not have been accidental, since the Near East and very likely also Egypt were at that time afflicted with a devastating plague lasting for decades. Rešep, the god who had sent the plague, was implored as deliverer from and succorer against it.[48] This conception of Rešep as a god of welfare, then, was probably originally the main reason for his being pictured with *qdš* and Min. Once in the triad (or perhaps even before), Rešep undoubtedly also took on more precisely aspects of a god of fertility and eroticism; indeed, such may have become the dominant understanding of the character of Rešep on the *qdš* reliefs.[49]

Prayers directed to *qdš* on one of the stelai[50] show that *qdš* was regarded by at least some of her worshippers not only as a goddess of fertility/eroticism/sexual vigor (certainly the dominant understanding), but, in a secondary sense, more broadly as a welfare- and life-giving goddess, and, according to one of the prayers, as a goddess of the dead.[51] This prayer is further evidence for her identification with Hathor in Egypt.[52] The front side of Louvre Stele C.86 (from Thebes West) shows on the top register the triad Min-*qdš*-Rešep, and on the lower register the necropolis *sḏm*-ᶜ*š* *Ḥwy*, dedicator of the stele, with his son, both kneeling in prayer. Unfortunately, their prayer(s) has not been preserved in legible form. On the back side of the stele are depicted the wife and four daughters of *Ḥwy*, also kneeling in supplication. Each speaks a short prayer to *qdš*, who evidently for the women was the principal person of the triad.[53] The wife:

> Praise *qdš*, Lady of Heaven, Mistress of All the Gods. May she grant life, welfare, and health for the *ka* of the lady of the house, the one praised by her mistress *tꜣ-ḫꜣrw* [The Syrian], justified.

First daughter:

> Praise to the Lady of Heaven, prostration before the Lady of the Two Lands. May she grant a good life joined with health to the *ka* of her daughter, the lady of the house *Dwꜣ-m-mrt.s*, justified.

Second daughter:

> Praise *qdš*, the divine. Prostration before the Lady of the Two Lands. May she grant a good life to those who are dedicated to her, to the *ka* of her daughter *Ḥmt-nṯr*, justified.

Third daughter:

> Praise the child of Re. Prostration before the Mistress of the Gods. May she grant an enduring name in her temple to the *ka* of her daughter *Mryt-ỉry*, justified.

Fourth daughter:

> Praise the Lady of the Two Lands. Prostration before the Mistress of the Gods. May she grant a beautiful burial after old age, burial in the desert, praise in the great West of Thebes, to the *ka* of the *sḏm-ʿš* of the necropolis, *Ḥwy* son of *Dwꜣ*, justified. His beloved daughter *Nfrt-ỉỉtỉ*, justified, says: Be thou greeted, beloved of Re, *wḏꜣt*-eye of Atum. Mayest thou grant that I behold thy beauty daily.[54]

Stadelmann comments that the five short prayers are petitions which could have been directed to any goddess, joined with the request (of the fourth daughter) for a beautiful burial. Outside of this request *qdš* was thus addressed as a "folk goddess" of the Theban area, with no reference being made to the special concern(s) on account of which she was petitioned.[55] As one who bestowed a beautiful burial, *qdš* was also a goddess of the dead, which again closely connects her to Hathor, who was in Thebes West, especially in Deir el-Bahri, likewise a goddess of the dead.[56]

So much can be said thus far about the *qdš* representations and about *qdš* herself. Yet, in the opinion of this writer, there is additional relevant information from Byblos and the Sinai peninsula which should also be brought into the discussion. Already in the Old Kingdom Egyptians identified the goddess of Byblos with Hathor, and in the Middle Kingdom "Hathor, Lady of Byblos," as she was called, was worshipped in Egypt.[57] Evidently similarities in cults and attributes led to this identification (even among Byblians themselves).[58] In Byblos the overriding influence of Hathor was demonstrated by the fact that the old city goddess was fully assimilated in her external form to the appearance of the Egyptian deity. On the stele of Yeḥawmilk (ca. fifth-fourth century) the "Lady of Byblos" is still represented in the Hathor type.[59]

Albright has noted this identification of Hathor with the Byblian goddess, having simultaneously observed the picturing of the Hathor wig on many *qdš* figurines. He concludes:

> . . . the Palestinian and Phoenician examples [of the *qdš* type] have substituted a Hathor coiffure for the slender braids of the Babylonian prototype . . . there can be no doubt that the Canaanite form of the spiral ringlets is derived from Twelfth-Dynasty Egypt, probably through Byblus, where [the goddess of Byblos] . . . had already been identified with Hathor. We are, therefore, justified in considering the bareheaded Qadesh as representing a cult-form of the Lady of Byblus.[60]

If the consideration of Albright is accepted, the obvious deduction is that *qdš* and the "Lady of Byblos" were the same goddess. This matter will presently be put aside, to be taken up again later in the chapter.

Attention should also be focused on the sixteenth-fifteenth century Proto-Sinaitic inscriptions from the Sinai peninsula,[61] which name a *bᶜlt*, "Baᶜlat" ("Lady"), and *d̲t bt̲n*, *d̲āt bat̲ni*, "One (f.) of the Serpent" or "Serpent Lady."[62] Most of these inscriptions come from Serabiṭ el-Ḫadem, where a Hathor temple was located.[63] Besides having a close connection with the mines and raw material regions in Egypt, Hathor was viewed by the Egyptians as the protecting goddess and Lady of all territories around Egypt from which came raw materials, including the mining area on the Sinai peninsula. The reason for this may be drawn from the epithets which she carried in relation to the various raw material areas. In the temple at Serabiṭ el-Ḫadem Hathor was worshipped as "Lady of the Turquoise." Another epithet of Hathor (not connected to the Sinai territory) was "Lady of the Lapis Lazuli" (a product obtained by the Egyptians in trade), in addition to "Lady of the Amethyst" (being called this in the crevices of Wadi el-Hudi), "Lady of the Gold," and "Lady of the Silver" (both costly metals were from the border districts of Egypt and from abroad).[64]

Apparently Hathor had, judging from her epithets, a marked affinity to the products of the lands of raw materials lying around Egypt, especially to precious stones, gold, and silver. Because she was goddess of the splendid ornament, her connection with precious stones, gold, and silver, out of which the ornament was made, seems natural. As *Resortgöttin* of these raw materials Hathor accompanied the Egyptian expeditions into the lands from which the materials were derived and thus became for the Egyptians the Lady of those lands. Closely linked with incense and myrrh (used for anointing) as goddess of festivals, Hathor was given the epithet "Lady of Punt" (from where incense and myrrh came). During the Middle and New Kingdoms Hathor had the title "Lady of the Turquoise" and then also that of "Lady of the Turquoise Land" (most frequently in the Sinai region). On the Sinai peninsula the cult of Hathor, "Lady of the Turquoise (Land)," showed no trace of influence from local divinities and differed in no respect from the cult of the Hathor forms localized in Egypt.[65]

Concerning "Serpent Lady"/"One (f.) of the Serpent," this epithet is strikingly reminiscent of the iconography of *qdš*; in fact, it is quite reasonable to assume that the "Serpent Lady" and *qdš* were closely related.[66] Apparently the miners called upon "Serpent Lady" because she was their chief goddess (more on this below). Since the inscriptions with this title were those of (forced ?) laborers[67] and were located at the entrance to a mine,[68] near a mine,[69] and at a burial cairn,[70] the miners in this location calling upon the goddess may have regarded her, in their particular circumstances, not so much as a sex and fertility deity. Rather, they may have seen her more as a goddess of protection and aid, who could, for example, keep them safe in the mines, provide animals for their sacrifices, and also watch over the dead.[71] The serpent aspect of the cult could have symbolized for her petitioners in the Sinai primarily the goddess's life-giving powers (a slightly different nuance than "fertility-giving powers"), complemented by her ability to guard them from danger and drive out sickness and poison.[72]

Having made these considerations, the writer is of the opinion that "Baᶜlat" in the texts designated Hathor.[73] Proof for this idea seems to come from the small female sphinx, which bears an Egyptian dedication to Hathor together with a Proto-Sinaitic dedication to Baᶜlat.[74] In calling the Egyptian goddess *bᶜlt*, "Lady," the miners could have been using an abbreviated form of the Egyptian epithets "Lady of the Turquoise"/"Lady of the Turquoise Land"[75] and/or simply using the general Semitic title which was applicable to any goddess.[76] Moreover, judging from the strong ties between *qdš* and Hathor evidenced elsewhere, it is possible (but not certain) that similar connections, at least in part, were made between the Serpent Lady and Hathor by the miners[77] and/or the Egyptians.

At this point, following the discussion of the *qdš* type (in Syria, Palestine, Egypt), of *qdš* herself, of her possible connection with the *bᶜlt gbl*, and of the close relationship which very likely existed between *qdš* and the "One (f.) of the Serpent" (named in the Proto-Sinaitic inscriptions), the question must now be asked, "Who, then, was *qdš*?" Chapter 1 already reviewed material the writer thinks provides the answer: *qudšu*, "Holiness," appears as an epithet of ʾAṯirat in the Ugaritic mythological texts.[78] On the basis of such evidence from the literature of Ras Shamra, the position taken here is that *qdš* on the Egyptian stelai is the same title referring to the same goddess. Hereafter, *qdš* is "Qudšu."[79]

Yet the indications for the equation *qdš*/Qudšu = ᵓAšerah are not limited to Ugarit. As already mentioned, the Winchester College relief, dating approximately from the time of Ramesses III (ca. 1182-1151),[80] clearly belongs to the Qudšu type. Still, two columns of hieroglyphs arranged vertically on each side of the figure read "Qudšu - ᶜAštart - ᶜAnat."[81] Whether or not the relief shows a confusion of the three goddesses of a conscious merging of them into one deity, of significance here is the indication that Qudšu was independently an important goddess who, by process of elimination, must have been ᵓAšerah.[82] This, of course, corresponds to the Ugaritic *qudšu* evidence.

Information complementing that from the Winchester College relief may be provided by Egyptian Papyrus Sallier IV. Enumerating Memphite deities of Egyptian origin, the papyrus (apparently) also lists next to them the names of Baᶜlat, Qudšu, ᶜAnat, and (the barque of) Baᶜl-Ṣapon.[83] Helck makes reference to another papyrus in which "Baᶜlat" appears:

> Der Papyrus Wilbour nennt im Fajjumgebiet Tempel und Weinberg der Baᶜalat (b-ᶜ-al-ja-t), wobei ersterer vielleicht identisch ist mit dem Heiligtum der Astarte im arsinoitischen Gau, den uns späte Papyri überliefern. Daraus kann wohl abgeleitet werden, daß es sich bei der "Herrin" nicht . . . um die Herrin von Byblos handelt oder überhaupt um eine syrische Lokalgöttin, sondern um die Astarte im allgemeinen.[84]

As Helck goes on to point out, the absence of the name of ᶜAštart from the list of Syro-Palestinian divinities in Papyrus Sallier IV is indeed conspicuous, for which he concludes that probably "Baᶜlat" was substituted. ᶜAštart could therefore, says Helck, be addressed also under this name in Memphis and the Faiyum,[85] a suggestion the present writer accepts. With such an understanding of "Baᶜlat" in the Sallier papyrus it may be concluded that again Qudšu is presented as a goddess in the "same category" as ᶜAnat and ᶜAštart (and Baᶜl) but distinct from them, who is best seen as ᵓAšerah.

Around the flat top of a stone bowl, probably originally coming from Memphis or its environs, appears a band of hieroglyphic text, written during the reign of Horemheb (ca. 1333-1303), which gives exactly the same impression concerning Qudšu.[86] The text reads:

> Regnal year 16 (1) under the Majesty of the Lord of the Two Lands, Ḥoremheb (2), the Ruler (3); at the time of (4) his first victorious campaign (5), from Byblos (6) as far as the land of the vile chief of Carchemish (7). An offering-which-the-king-gives (to) Ptah South-of-His Wall, Lord of the Life of the Two Lands, (to) Astarte lady of heaven, (to) ᶜAnat the daughter of Ptah, lady of truth, (to) Resheph lord of heaven, (to) Qodsha lady of the stars of heaven[87]; (8) that they may give life, prosperity and health to the *kꜣ* of the stablemaster of the Lord of the Two Lands (9) Sen-nefer (10), repeating life.[88]

Here the placement of the name "Rešep" in the list seemingly makes even clearer the veneration of Qudšu as an important goddess separate from ᶜAštart and ᶜAnat. Again, ᵓAšerah is the likeliest deity with whom Qudšu is to be identified.

BM 646 (191) partially supports the inferences concerning Qudšu derived from the Winchester College relief, Papyrus Sallier IV, and the text on the Egyptian stone bowl. Pictured in the top portion of the stele is the triad Min-Qudšu-Rešep; the annotation calls Qudšu "*knt*, Lady of Heaven."[89] The bottom portion shows ᶜAnat (in typically Egyptian side-view), seated, wearing the atef (or Osiris) crown,[90] clothed, holding in her upraised left hand a club or an ax, in her outstretched, lowered right hand a shield and spear.[91] Three worshippers (the dedicator of the stele, his wife and son)[92] stand before her. She is named "ᶜAnat, Lady of Heaven, Lady/Ruler of the Gods."[93] Behind ᶜAnat the text reads: "All protection, life, duration, and good fortune behind her."[94] The most natural understanding of the stele is that it portrays two goddesses who are addressed with a common epithet ("Lady of Heaven") and perhaps for similar reasons but whose representations are completely different. In other words, BM 646 exhibits Qudšu and ᶜAnat as separate divinities.[95]

A small votive stele of a Memphite official named Ptah-ankh[96] presents a similar distinction between Qudšu and ᶜAštart. Ptah-ankh calls upon both to grant him life and health. With regard to ᶜAštart the inscription reads:

> A royal (funerary) offering to [or "by"] Hurrian Astarte, the Lady of Heaven, Mistress of the Two Lands, Mistress of All the Gods. May she grant life, prosperity, and health and efficiency in the temple of Ptah for the *ka* of the *sḏm-ᶜš* of the high priest of Memphis Ptah-mose, Ptah-ankh.

With regard to Qudšu it reads: "May she grant a good life combined with health . . ."[97] Again, the most natural interpretation here is that individual goddesses are being invoked.[98]

Other considerations based on the Egyptian evidence tend to lead to the deduction that Qudšu was ᵓAšerah. The attestations of ᶜAnat[99] and ᶜAštart[100] are numerous and clear; the goddesses are referred to by their names "ᶜAnat" and "ᶜAštart" (in all their various aspects) and their representation types differ from each other and very noticeably from the Qudšu type. If Qudšu is not ᵓAšerah, the latter does not explicitly appear in any (preserved) Egyptian material (either in inscriptions or representations),[101] which this writer finds difficult to accept. Further, in Magical Papyrus Harris F (thirteenth century B.C.) ᶜAštart and ᶜAnat are mentioned as the "great goddesses who conceive but cannot bring forth."[102] Although such an understanding of the two goddesses may have been limited to only a small portion of the population of Egypt,[103] this information provided by the papyrus perhaps is a bit of evidence strengthening the identification of Qudšu with ᵓAšerah. The reason fertility was so highly desired in a woman was that she be able to bring forth children. Evidently some people in Egypt, based on their acquaintance with Near Eastern mythology,[104] thought that ᶜAnat and ᶜAštart had no offspring,[105] but there could never have been any question that ᵓAšerah gave birth (many times). Thus, although they recognized the fertility of ᶜAnat and ᶜAštart, these people might have regarded ᵓAšerah as the fertility goddess *par excellence.*

Additional support for the position that Qudšu = ᵓAšerah comes from the Proto-Sinaitic texts. Text no. 358 (inside Mine M) reads *ᵓdn d̲ ᶜlm*, *ᵓadānu d̲ū ᶜôlami*, "Lord of Eternity" or "Eternal Lord."[106] This title is reminiscent of a number of epithets and descriptions of ʾEl made known by the Ugaritic literature.[107] The name "ʾEl" may even occur at Serabiṭ el-Ḫadem.[108] Very likely, therefore, the mate of ʾAšerah was worshipped at this mining site in the western Sinai peninsula, which is noteworthy in itself, but in the present discussion especially because of the close relationship of Qudšu with *ḏt bṯn*, "Serpent Lady," whom the texts mention four times (according to Albright's decipherment). Further, *ḏ ṯb*, "Merciful One," of the Proto-Sinaitic inscriptions is quite similar to the Ugaritic appellation of ʾEl, *dū paʾidu*, "Compassionate One."[109] A reasonable assumption is that *ḏ ṯb* was a title of ʾEl at Serabiṭ el-Ḫadem. Texts nos. 360 and 361 have this epithet, where it appears with *ḏt bṯn* (no. 360: *ḏ ṯb ʾt ḏt bṯn* . . . , "O Merciful One with the Serpent Lady . . ."; 361: *ḏ ṯb ḏt bṯn* . . . , "O Merciful One, O Serpent Lady . . .").[110] These texts lead to the conclusion that the Merciful One and the Serpent Lady were considered to be a divine pair, a judgment bolstering the identification of Qudšu with ʾAšerah, since the latter was the chief consort of ʾEl and most probably addressed here under the designation *ḏt bṯn*.[111]

Two passages in the texts from Ras Shamra may be relevant to the equating of Qudšu with ʾAšerah. *CTA* 4.2.5-7 (Chapter 1, text no. 3) describes ʾAṯirat as carrying her robe "into the sea, her two garments into the river." Are these lines saying that ʾAṯirat was nude? If so, this passage is of interest for the present discussion because of the nudity so typical of the Qudšu type. In the lines following the goddess implores ʾEl. Is she asking the Bull to travel to where she was and be intimate with her? *CTA* 4.4.27-8, 38-9 (Chapter 1, text no. 9) can be taken as hinting at the sexuality of ʾAṯirat. ʾEl is delighted to see the goddess, the primary reason perhaps being revealed in the last of a series of questions he asks her: "'Or does the love/member [Ug. *yd*; surely a pun] of ʾEl, the King, move you, the love of Bull arouse you?'" No doubt ʾEl is speaking on the basis of past encounters with ʾAṯirat. More generally, the sexual appetite, potency, and virility of ʾEl are clearly presented in Ugaritic lore (e.g., his epithet "Bull," the passage just cited, and *CTA* 23.31-53) and in the *Phoenician History*. A supposition is not unwarranted, then, that the eroticism and fertility of ᵓAšerah/ᵓElat -- the "Creatress of the Gods," mother of "seventy sons," and female counterpart of ᵓEl -- would have been emphasized, one such method being the Qudšu type.[112]

As mentioned above,[113] Albright thought that the "bare-headed" Qudšu represented a cult form of the goddess of Byblos, because of the Hathor wig typical of the Qudšu type. This wig, he felt, had been derived through Byblos, where the city goddess had taken on the Hathor type. Albright's proposal, coupled with the previously stated position of the present chapter that Qudšu = ᵓAšerah, obviously brings one to the decision that the goddess of Byblos was ᵓAšerah. Outside of Byblos, however, Egypt had various other contacts with Syria-Palestine, already during the first quarter of the second millennium;[114] the Hathor wig conceivably could have become a part of the Qudšu type via a route(s) not passing through, or exclusively through, that city. Nevertheless, there is evidence of another sort suggesting that Byblos's goddess may have been ᵓAšerah. Because of the location of Byblos by the Mediterranean and its important harbor it is legitimate to assume that the Byblian goddess had close connections with the sea.[115] Such an idea is perhaps reinforced by the fact that Hathor was known as protectress of sea travelers, an attribute, Stadelmann explains, which she possibly received in the New Kingdom as a result of her being identified with the goddess of Byblos.[116] Likewise Montet, concerning the associating of Hathor with the city goddess, refers to a fragment of a vase from Byblos depicting Unas receiving a rudder from Hathor, the Lady of Byblos, who, according to Montet, was thought to guide the Pharaoh's ships.[117] These beliefs concerning Hathor may be interpreted as indicating (indirectly) that the goddess of Byblos had significant ties to the sea. A comparable situation to that of second millennium Byblos -- namely, a port city with its chief goddess, or at least a leading goddess, having "marine connections"[118]

-- was that of Ugarit. There the wife or main consort of the head of the pantheon was called *rbt ʾaṯrt ym*, "Lady ʾAṯirat of the Sea"; in addition, she had a servant named "Fisherman." Identifying the goddess of Byblos as ʾAšerah, in this writer's opinion, satisfactorily fits the best available evidence.[119] Therefore, while Albright's precise suggestion remains uncertain, some kind of a connection between Qudšu and the goddess of Byblos was very likely.

Finally, the reader will recall,[120] on the one hand, the *Phoenician History*'s report of Kronos's (ʾEl's) giving of Byblos to Baaltis/Dione (Dione = ʾElat), but on the other hand, Lucian's implying, in his *De Dea Syria*, that the goddess of Byblos was Aphrodite,[121] the Greek equivalent of ʿAštart.[122] Is the information from the *Phoenician History*, which agrees with the conclusion reached above (the city's goddess was ʾAšerah), not correct? Or is Lucian's account in error? This apparent conflict disappears with the following consideration. The Greeks (rightly or wrongly) identified Hathor with their Aphrodite;[123] the Byblian goddess was assimilated to Hathor; thus Lucian (especially as a foreigner in the city) would have viewed the "Lady of Byblos" as being Aphrodite.[124] The accuracy of the *Phoenician History*'s account here again demonstrates the antiquity of the sources (certainly pre-Hellenistic) behind the sections of the work dealing with Rhea/Dione (ʾAšerah/ʾElat).

tnt

Thanks to the recovery of a multitude of stelai from several sites of Punic civilization in the western Mediterranean, it is well known that the name *tnt*, "Tannit," which occurs on a great many of these stelai, belonged to a female deity, specifically, the consort of Punic *bʿl ḥmn*. Actually, the goddess's full name was *tnt pn bʿl* (*panê baʿl*), "Tannit face/presence of Baʿl," a title usually preceded by *rbt*, "Lady." In the opinion of this writer *tnt* is ʾAšerah/Qudšu, for the following reasons.[125]

1) Tannit was a Phoenicio-Punic goddess, thus a Semitic divinity.

Until the first quarter of the twentieth century only material (symbols, inscriptions) from the West, primarily from Carthage, had been published which attested the existence (and worship) of *tnt* in the centuries B.C.[126] As a result, some scholars concluded that she was distinctly Carthaginian, perhaps even representing originally a Libyan deity.[127] This belief was held despite the fact that an inscription, dating to ca. 400 B.C. and found at Athens already in 1795, mentions an *ᶜbdtnt*, "Servant of Tannit," who is said to be a Sidonian.[128] As Pritchard explains, it was long assumed that *ᶜbdtnt* was a Carthaginian who had migrated to Greece.[129] Similarly, a Carthaginian stele from ca. 200 B.C., found in 1898, has the phrase "*tnt* in *lbnn*," but scholars, finding it impossible to take *lbnn* as the Syrian Lebanon, generally understood the term as referring to a "white" hill on which the temple of Tannit, mentioned in the text, had been built.[130]

By now a steadily growing list of discoveries of the Tannit sign in the eastern Mediterranean region clearly shows that the goddess was known in this area well before the Christian Era.[131] For example, the sign appears on fourth century B.C. coins of Byblos, some published in 1910.[132] In 1973 Linder reported on the finding of more than 250 figurines (many whole and nicely preserved) at a site lying about a kilometer offshore from Shave-Ziyyon, a modern Israeli village just north of ᶜAkko.[133] Many of these figurines have the sign of Tannit on their bases.[134] The statuettes could have been made as early as the sixth century B.C., but more probably are to be dated to the end of the fifth century or the early fourth century B.C.[135] Pritchard, also in the previous decade, published the results of excavations (1969-74) at ancient Sarepta, a coastal town 13 km. south of Sidon; among the discoveries was a small molded disk of glass bearing the Tannit sign.[136] Presumably, the disk comes from sometime between the end of the Late Bronze Period to the fourth century B.C.[137]

While this list of discoveries of the Tannit sign in the East amply demonstrates that ʿ*bdtnt* probably lived in Sidon, and that *lbnn* of the Carthaginian stele certainly could be a reference to the Syrian Lebanon, the most convincing evidence is provided by the inscriptional material. In 1964-5 Maurice Dunand found, at the temple of ʾEšmun at Sidon, a fifth century Phoenician ostracon containing a list of names, among which was *grtnt*.[138] Also, a completely preserved Phoenician inscription of four lines from Sarepta, incised on an ivory plaque which had been attached to a statue, reads at the end: [3] . . . *l* [4] *tnt*ʿ*štrt*, "for TannitʿAštart."[139] Whether one understands here the blending of two goddesses and their cults, or interprets line 4 as "Tannit (and) ʿAštart,"[140] there can be no doubt that the plaque evidences the recognition of Tannit's divine nature and her worship in the Phoenician homeland. Certain letters in the inscription, explains Pritchard, display forms current in Phoenician writing in the seventh century, yet the early sixth century is not to be excluded for other forms. Therefore, he concludes that it "is perhaps safe to date the inscription somewhere around the end of the seventh or the beginning of the sixth century."[141] Perhaps more can be said: the ivory plaque was found within a shrine -- specifically, within the *favissa* of the earlier of two shrines identified at this location[142] -- which Pritchard estimates to have been in use beginning with the eighth century.[143] The shrine was likely that of Tannit-ʿAštart[144] (either a compound deity or two goddesses); thus the supposition is possible, based on both the inscriptional and archaeological evidence, that already in the eighth century Tannit was venerated at Sarepta. Whatever the situation might have been, the inscription on the ivory label is the earliest evidence (aside from the glass disk, the precise date of which is uncertain) for the goddess's cult in Phoenicia and -- even more striking -- it is the earliest preserved mention of *tnt*.[145]

In summary, it is misleading to think that Tannit was distinctly Carthaginian (/Punic), and there is no need to posit a Libyan (or African) origin for the deity. Recent finds in the East have provided Tannit material not only contemporary with the earliest such material from Punic civilization, but older. These discoveries indicate, in the opinion of the writer, that Tannit certainly was a Phoenicio-Punic goddess, and further -- taking into consideration the direction of the expansion of Phoenician culture -- that Tannit was first worshipped in the Phoenician homeland, whence her cult was carried westward.

2) Convincing arguments for identifying Tannit with ᵓAšerah have already been given.[146]

Briefly, Cross points out that Philo Byblius, other classical sources, and inscriptions in Greek and Latin all establish the formula that *bᶜl ḥmn* (of Zincirli and the Punic colonies) on the one hand, and Canaanite ᵓEl on the other, are Greek Kronos, Latin Saturn.[147] Tannit's partner, then, was ᵓEl, "Lord of the Amanus."

Cross proceeds to treat proposals identifying the goddess with ᶜAštart, ᶜAnat, and ᵓAšerah, bringing into the discussion Tannit's alternate Greek and Latin titles.[148] A decisive argument against equating ᶜAštart and Tannit comes from a Carthaginian inscription (mentioned above). The text initially reads *lrbt lᶜštrt wltnt blbnn*, "To the Ladies, ᶜAštart and Tannit in Lebanon," and goes on to talk about their new temples (in the plural).[149] As Cross says, there "is not the slightest reason to doubt the identity of *tnt pn bᶜl* and *tnt blbnn*."[150]

Albright has made the best case for the identification of Tannit with ᶜAnat.[151] He combines Tannit's identification as *Virgo Caelestis* with ᶜAnat's title at Ugarit, *batultu ᶜanatu*, "Virgin ᶜAnat." Further, after noting ᶜAnat's epithets *baᶜlatu šamêmi rāmīma*, "Lady of the High Heavens" and *baᶜlatu darkati*, "Lady of Dominion" in a Ugaritic text,[152] Albright compares the former with Tannit's alternate title *Caelestis*,[153] and the latter with *Derketō*, the name of a goddess of Ascalon preserved by Diodorus Siculus.[154] The divinity of Ascalon named *Phanēbalos* is also identified with ᶜAnat by Albright, who relates this *Phanēbalos* (appearing on the coin beside a Tannit sign; n. 132 above) to the Carthaginian Tannit *panê baᶜl*. Thus, Albright essentially makes the equation *Phanēbalos* (Ascalon) = *Derketō* (Ascalon) = Tannit (Carthage) = ᶜAnat.

The position of Cross and of this chapter (see next section) agrees with all but the last portion of Albright's analysis ("ᶜAnat" is replaced with "ᵓAšerah"). There are problems in identifying Derketo/Tannit with ᶜAnat, mainly because in separate sources of information Derketo and Tannit are portrayed as sea goddesses, a characterization not well suited to ᶜAnat.[155]

After an examination of the Ugaritic literature, complemented by a study of Philo Byblius's *Phoenician History*, it is not at all surprising that Punic ᵓEl had as his consort ᵓAšerah/ᵓElat. Understanding Tannit to be ᵓAšerah nicely fits Tannit's being identified with Ops (consort of Saturn), the Latin counterpart of Greek Rhea (consort of Kronos),[156] and Tannit's being called *Nutrix*, "Nurse" and ᵓ*m*, "Mother."[157] In other literature, Cross points out, especially in biblical notices, ᵓAšerah is the consort of Baᶜl, which can provide an explanation for the identification of Tannit in the West with Hera (Latin Juno), Zeus's consort. Hera, too, was "a mother goddess, and as participant in the *hieros gamos* called *parthenos*."[158]

Cross presents the likeliest derivation of the goddess's name,[159] Punic *Tennit* (Greek ΘENNEIΘ, ΘIN(N)IΘ): from Canaanite **tannintu* > **tannittu* > **tannit* (hence the spelling "Tannit" used throughout this dissertation). Her name, deriving from *tannīn*, "serpent," is the feminine of a *qattīl* pattern which in Phoenician regularly becomes *qattiltu*. Thus *tannit* means "the One/Lady of the Serpent," or "Serpent Lady," and is a precise parallel to *ḏt bṯn* of the Proto-Sinaitic inscriptions. Both *tnt* and *bᶜl ḥmn* are epithets surviving for the most part on the peripheries of the spread of Canaanite and Phoenician culture.[160]

3) The "sign of Tannit" is a later, abstract continuation of the Qudšu type.

The question concerning this well-known pattern is not so much whether it should be associated with Tannit -- today the great majority of scholars agree that it is indeed Tannit's "sign"[161]-- but what the design actually represents. A number of suggestions have been offered.[162] For example, some regard it as being the Egyptian ankh sign; but the vertical piece of the ankh, even when widened toward the base, does not have sides inclined as those of the Tannit sign,[163] and the latter's disk/circle seems to be proportionately smaller and a different shape than the loop at the top of the ankh. Others think the design represents an anchor, yet there is no proof for their proposal.[164]

It is most satisfactory to view the pattern as an abstract stylization of a standing, clothed, female figure, who must be the goddess herself. In 1920 Gsell, despite having a completely different understanding of the Tannit sign (n. 162), admitted: "L'image tout entière fait penser à une femme, qui serait vêtue d'une longue robe et lèverait les bras."[165] Recent scholars have expressed similar sentiments, particularly after newly discovered material demonstrates that the circle/disk and triangle very probably represent the head and garment of a standing female figure facing the viewer.[166] For example, Oden rightly concludes that the sign "originated in a schematization of a clothed female figure,"[167] that it "is a schematized female figure,"[168] and that it "represented Tannit . . ."[169]

An important part of the complete Tannit sign[170] is the horizontal element, which may be a simple line or narrow rectangle (shaped like a narrow board) of somewhat varying length, appearing between the circle and triangle (which, with the "board" shape, often has a flat rather than a pointed top). Frequently at the ends of the horizontal element are shorter pieces (single lines; or continuations of the narrow rectangle, thus double lines) which bend straight upward or at a (normally) slight angle. These upper portions may be curved, with the ends (coming together to form a tip in the case of the double lines) pointing outward.

The logical deduction is that the horizontal element represents the arms of the goddess, which she is holding out from her sides, bent upward (judging from the more "complete" Tannit signs) at the elbows. This view is confirmed by the fact that the Tannit image not uncommonly is "grasping" an object at the end of one or both "arms."[171]

Therefore, the "Tannit sign" is a schematized, abstract representation of a standing female figure (the goddess herself), viewed from the front, who is clothed in a long garment that widens as it descends to her feet, and who is holding her arms out at her sides, bent upward at the elbows.[172] In the writer's opinion this same figure must be seen behind all the Tannit signs, which fall into a classification spectrum ranging from the more complete, "realistic"[173] to the more simple and/or abstract (even occasionally lacking the horizontal element),[174] with many varieties falling between the two types.

Moreover, what is being signified closely matches the Qudšu type, described earlier as a standing female figure (Qudšu), facing the viewer, holding her arms -- bent upward at the elbows -- out from her sides, and usually grasping serpents and/or vegetation of some sort (lilies, lotuses, papyrus stalks). The writer suggests that the Tannit sign actually is a continuation of the Qudšu type; it is a later, schematized version of essentially the same form representing the same goddess (thus, Tannit = Qudšu/ʾAšerah). In examining "complete" Tannit signs one does notice readily that the horizontal element, the "arms," goes straight out from the torso before bending upward at both ends, never duplicating precisely the V shape prominent in the Qudšu type (upper arm in a downward position, lower arm pointing upward). As a result, the "upper arms" are regularly higher in relation to the "head" and "torso" than are the upper arms in the examples of the Qudšu type. Such a relatively minor difference, however, is not to be unexpected between a realistic representation and an abstract schematization of essentially identical figures.[175] The immediate overall impression or concept produced by the portion between the circle (head) and triangle (torso and garment) is what matters, and that impression or concept clearly corresponds to the Qudšu type's extended, bent arms. This concept entered the knowledgeable viewer's mind, one may assume, also when the horizontal part was a simple line or "board" shape (or absent altogether).

A weightier objection to taking the Tannit sign as a later version of the Qudšu type (more precisely, a schematization of a figure understood to be a continuation of the Qudšu type) quickly arises: on the plaques of Syria-Palestine and the stelai of Egypt, Qudšu is nude. Yet the preceding paragraphs have stated repeatedly that the triangular shape of the sign stands for Tannit's long garment. There are indications, though, that nudity may have ceased being a characteristic of the Qudšu figure, which, with the passage of time and under various influences, could have been shown and/or conceived of as clothed. It was this possible later conception of the type (the western Phoenicians choosing to use the designation "Tannit" rather than "Qudšu" or "ʾAšerah" for the figure) that stood behind the Tannit sign.

One indication derives from seventh century Egypt. After the time of the Ramessides Qudšu disappeared to a large extent from the evident manifestations of Egyptian religious life, perhaps, as Helck thinks, "wegen der zunehmenden Prüderie des ägyptischen Lebens."[176] But she was never completely forgotten, and this is shown by the

> Darstellung eines Amulettanhängers mit der Triade durch Monthemhet im Schatz des Muttempels; Qadschu ist jetzt aber bekleidet (und das Gesicht von der Seite gesehen) dargestellt![177]

Various Mediterranean, non-Semitic cultures may have caused, or helped cause, the nude Qudšu type to evolve into a clothed figure. A hint of such potential influences comes from the representation on the fourteenth-thirteenth century ivory piece found at Minet el-Beida, previously said[178] to be a blend form exhibiting traits both typical and atypical of the Late Bronze Period Qudšu type. The female figure, nude from the waist up, particularly evidenced Cretan-Mycenaean influence, since she wore a full Cretan-Mycenaean skirt.

Assuming a change from a nude to a clothed figure in the artistic rendering of a type, then, is not unreasonable. Furthermore, numerous images of clothed females appear on the Punic monuments.[179] Also, the figurines stamped with the Tannit sign, discovered offshore from Shave-Ziyyon, are standing female figures wearing either a chiton or peplos.[180]

However, the strongest indications that such a change could have taken place -- and, more specifically, that the Tannit sign had its origins in the Qudšu type -- may be seen on a group of remarkable stelai from the Ghorfa region in northern Africa.[181] Before going into a description of these stelai dating from the second century of the modern era a small amount of background information is necessary. In the Hellenistic period, Bisi explains, there was a flourishing of Greek culture on Punic land (beginning especially with the third century B.C.), as shown, for example, by emblems of Dionysiac religion on the Punic stelai and the temples inspired by the Doric style of Sicily. The fall of Carthage (146 B.C.) did not interrupt the production of stelai or this network of cultural influence, as seen in the monuments of the Numidians, who wished to consider themselves the material and spiritual heirs of Carthage. Punic theology had exerted a great influence on the Numidians; the stelai of the child sacrifice precinct of El-Hofra (Constantine, ancient Cirta), written in good Punic and having symbols inspired by Carthaginian iconography, are excellent examples of the continuity and force of the Phoenician cultural tradition. Nevertheless, besides having elements of Phoenicio-Punic origin Numidian religious beliefs also showed Greek influence and allowed ample room for Greek deities and rites. Dionysius, Aphrodite, Demeter, and Core, in fact, are the divine figures now prevalent on the African stelai.[182]

Beginning with the early second century of the modern era, Rome, which had been on the North African stage especially since the time of the last Punic War, deeply imposed its culture on the local people. The Romanization of the entire territory took place with great rapidity. From this time onward many traditional iconographic elements of the

Punic type became lost, while others, characteristically Roman, took their place. Yet some images and motifs connected with Punic prototypes survived. Even in this period of the irrepairable decline of the Semitic cultural element, the Phoenicio-Punic tradition at times remained so strong that it was still evidenced side by side with the new styles and iconographic elements -- seen especially on the stelai -- imported from the classical world.[183]

The stelai from the Ghorfa region exemplify this continuation of motifs from Punic theology in a substantially Greco-Roman religious environment.[184] On them can be observed the process of anthropomorphization undergone by the deities of the Semitic pantheon, due to the influence of the typically anthropomorphic iconography with which the Greek and Roman gods were pictured.[185]

Focusing attention now on pls. 30.2 and 31 of Bisi's *Le Stele Puniche* (see drawings nos. 3 and 4 below), it is observed, first of all, that each stele represents the figure of a dedicator standing inside a temple and a divine figure or symbol in the pediment of the temple.[186] Concerning the upper part of the monuments, at the top center of the stele of pl. 31 is an upward-turned crescent, largely worn away (perhaps originally above the crescent was a rosette -- cf. pl. 30.1), and at the top center of the stele of pl. 30.2 is a human head surrounded by a wreath or two snakes intertwined at the lower portions of their bodies.[187] Directly below the crescent (pl. 31) and snakes (pl. 30.2) is a figure in a triangularly-shaped garment which extends from the shoulders downward so as to cover completely the legs and feet.[188] The figure has its arms at its sides, bent upward and outward at the elbows, and is holding in each hand a cornucopia (?),[189] out of which come a pomegranate (on the figure's left) and a bunch of grapes (on the figure's right). On each side of the figure, below her waist and arms, is a dove. Further down, Dionysius (crowned with ivy, wearing the *exomis* which leaves one shoulder bare, and holding the thyrsus in his hand) stands to one side of the figure, a nude Aphrodite to the other.[190] Together, the three figures are positioned according to a pyramidal scheme.[191]

Without question, the figure wearing the triangularly-shaped garment and holding the cornucopiae dominates the upper portion of the stelai. Because two deities (Dionysius, Aphrodite) are placed in a lower position, this figure also must be a divinity and, judging from the garment, undoubtedly a goddess. The viewer is immediately struck by two aspects of her representation. First, her complete form (head, garment, arms) is strongly reminiscent of the Tannit sign. Given the background of these stelai the double conclusion is surely warranted that a) the figure is an anthropomorphization of the Tannit sign,[192] and b) it was understood to be an image of Tannit herself.[193] Earlier the assertion was made that the most satisfactory way to take the Tannit sign was as the schematization of a standing female figure (the goddess herself), viewed from the front, who is clothed in a long garment that widens as it descends to her feet, and who is holding her arms out at her sides, bent upward at the elbows. Proof for the preceding, in the opinion of this writer, is provided by the stelai of the Ghorfa. The memory of what really stood behind the Tannit sign -- what it signified -- was preserved into the second century of the modern era. Rather than presenting the abstract, schematized version (the Tannit sign) of that reality the makers of the stelai, under the influence of the anthropomorphism characteristic of Greco-Roman religion, gave the actual, human form.

The second aspect of the representation of the Tannit figure which immediately strikes the viewer is how similar it is to the Qudšu type. She is standing and seen from the front; her arms are identically positioned,[194] and she is holding symbols of fruitfulness/fertility.[195] Basically, the only difference is, again, the distinctive garment worn by the figure of the second century representations. That the female figure behind the Tannit sign is indeed the clothed form of the earlier Qudšu type seems to be shown, rather amazingly, by another stele from the Ghorfa -- pl. 30.1 of Bisi's *Le Stele Puniche* (see drawing no. 5 below). On this monument, instead of the gowned Tannit, appears a nude female figure,[196] standing with her legs together. Everything else remains the same as on the other stelai -- the placement of her arms, the objects held, the general arrangement of the upper part of the stele (with Dionysius and the nude Aphrodite standing farther down and on either side of the central image). Moreover, the nude figure corresponds almost exactly to the Qudšu representations examined in the first portion of this chapter;[197] it would, objectively speaking, have to be classified as the latest preserved example of the Qudšu type. Apparently, therefore, the memory was retained into the modern era, despite the passage of many centuries, that an alternate -- more precisely, earlier -- form of the clothed female figure schematized in the Tannit sign was the same figure without the long garment, that is, nude. In short, the stelai of the Ghorfa, in the opinion of this writer, support the suggestion that the Tannit sign was a later, abstract continuation of the Qudšu type.[198]

4) Symbols associated with the sign of Tannit are in accord with understanding the goddess to be ʾAšerah/Qudšu.[199]

Fish are pictured with the sign,[200] as are dolphins,[201] thereby evidencing the marine character of Tannit and linking her with ʾAšerah.[202] Other objects associated with the Tannit sign symbolize ideas connected with ʾAšerah and vividly portrayed by the Qudšu type: fertility, beauty, and/or eroticism. They include the lotus or lily (in various stages of blossoming),[203] the female date palm (most often shown bearing clusters of dates),[204] the dove,[205] and the rabbit.[206]

A common motif on the Punic stelai is the crescent (which can point upward or downward) and disk. Often the pair is in the upper portion, and a Tannit sign in the lower portion, of a stele. In the writer's opinion the motif should be traced back ultimately to the second millennium Egyptian Qudšu reliefs, which exhibit the headpiece with the crescent and disk (most likely solar). Originating in Egypt, the motif may have been interpreted in different ways as it was handed down over the centuries. How the Punic worshippers regarded the crescent and disk on the stelai is uncertain; they themselves may not have completely understood the pair's meaning. Probably the crescent-disk was used on a number of stelai merely as a "conventional decoration."[207] Certain stelai do show, however, a close connection between the crescent(-disk) and the Tannit sign:[208] the sign enclosing the crescent and disk,[209] the sign grasping the ends of the downward-turned crescent and holding the lunar symbol over its head,[210] the disk and crescent right above the sign's left "hand,"[211] the crescent just above the head of the sign (the circle, still attached to the rest of the Tannit sign, may serve as both head and solar disk),[212] and instances where the circle definitely serves "double duty," since it is separated from the horizontal piece of the Tannit sign and situated between this and the crescent.[213] Infrequently a stele lacks the circle, showing simply the rounded crescent pointed downward, a little above the horizontal element and triangle.[214]

Discoveries made at the ruins of a first century B.C. temple dedicated to Baᶜl-Saturn and Tannit-Caelestis, located about a kilometer northeast of ancient Siagu,[215] demonstrate the persistence of additional elements in Qudšu's tradition.[216] A figurine, unfortunately poorly preserved, has the goddess, clothed in a long garment (only the torso and leg area remain), standing on a lion.[217] Also among the finds[218] was an image representing Tannit as a lion-headed female figure, clothed in a long garment which, widening at the bottom, almost completely covers her feet.[219] This rather startling type derived from the relationship between ᵓAšerah/Qudšu and the lion-headed Sakhmet, who was at Memphis the wife of Ptah.[220] The Astarte Papyrus, mentioned earlier,[221] may imply that ᵓAšerah was regarded by the Egyptians as the wife of Ptah (since Ptah in the papyrus corresponds to the Canaanite deity ᵓEl). Conceivably, then, she could have been connected by them with Sakhmet (although Nut is Ptah's wife/consort in the papyrus). More importantly, Qudšu was identified with Hathor, and Hathor, as the "eye of the sun," was identified with Sakhmet. Further, Qudšu's title at Memphis, "whom Ptah loves," perhaps suggests her being viewed there as the god's wife/consort.

Appropriate here are a few words about another symbol frequently seen on the Punic monuments, although the object is not part of the preserved ʾAšerah/Qudšu iconography of the Late Bronze and Iron I Periods: the upraised right hand (usually with upper arm). The motif, surely an appropriate symbol for Baʿl Ḥamon,[222] likely was also used to signify Tannit (and perhaps occasionally both deities).[223] Evidence for this suggestion includes the female figures with upraised right arm and hand recovered offshore from Shave-Ziyyon.[224] A Carthaginian stele, moreover, shows an apparently hooded figure wearing a longish garment reaching to the ground, whose right arm is in the same position, standing between two caducei and two Tannit signs.[225] On a second Carthaginian stele a standing figure, wearing a garment resembling that of the previous form but without the hood, with raised right arm and hand, is flanked by two palm trees and two caducei; at the top of the monument is a Tannit sign.[226] It is easiest, in the opinion of this writer, to take both figures as representations of Tannit. Thus the upraised right (arm and) hand probably should be associated with Tannit on several of the Punic stelai.[227]

Finally, as the reader no doubt realizes, an examination of the Punic monuments makes obvious the fact that the western Phoenicians loved not only to show the Tannit sign, caduceus (discussed next), palm tree, upraised right hand (and arm), and, to a lesser extent, the lotus, as separate, free-standing forms (usually having two or three types in symmetrical arrangement), but also joined together. Practically every possible combination of two or three of these emblems into a single unified image is witnessed in the preserved material, fascinating testimony to the creativity and abstract thinking ability of the people responsible for these depictions.

5) The so-called caduceus, another symbol connected with the Tannit sign, was indeed made up of two serpents on a pole, therefore fitting well with the iconography of Qudšu.

That the caduceus was a symbol of Tannit may be stated with little hesitancy, because of the frequency with which the caduceus and Tannit sign are paired on the Punic stelai -- the caduceus usually at the side(s) of the sign, sometimes held by the sign or united with it.[228] The challenge with regard to the caduceus is how to interpret the image, that is, determining what is being signified. An explanation often put forward defines the form as a disk surmounted by a crescent, on top of a staff which is in many instances "be-ribboned." The lengthy vertical piece, free-standing and supporting the rest of the emblem, may indeed be called a "staff" or "pole." Yet there are objections to seeing the uppermost part as a disk and crescent. In the first place, there is sometimes a gap where the "crescent" meets the "disk": the lower section of the "crescent" and the top section of the "disk" are not completely closed, with the result that the two elements hardly resemble a crescent and disk.[229] Secondly, there are representations where the curves of the "crescent" cross each other and continue downward to form the circular element. The impression is not of a disk topped by a crescent, but of one continuous curved line formed by the left half of the "crescent" element and the right half of the "disk" element, and so also for the other halves.[230] Thirdly, the "tips" of the topmost element are in many cases curved outward, or, less frequently, inward (almost touching), so that it cannot be called, objectively speaking, a crescent.[231]

An intriguing theory concerning the symbol has been skillfully presented by Oden: he proposes that the "caduceus" was a stylized palm tree.[232] Still, the ample evidence which he cites to support his theory is, in the opinion of this writer, open to other interpretations. Herewith is a summary of, and a response to, Oden's key arguments.

a) Oden points out that at Carthage, El-Hofra, and elsewhere in the West the caduceus is represented often with long "strings" or "ribbons," which descend from the point where the "staff" of the caduceus meets the circle-like element immediately above it. To Oden

> these cannot be simply ribbons, since the caducei of many Punic stelae have blossoms or fruit-pods at the ends of these "strings," which suggests that the "strings" are the flower- and fruit-bearing spadices of the date palm.[233]

Later Oden writes:

> In those cases where the "strings" bear no flowers or fruit, they may be ropes rather than spadices, and probably represent the ropes . . . used in climbing up the palm tree for the purpose of shaking a bag of pollen over the female flowers to aid in the pollination of the flowers.[234]

In response it may be said that there are reasons for deciding that the "ribbons"/"strings" shown without the blossoms[235] probably did not represent the flower- and fruit-bearing spadices of the date palm. Most importantly, these spadices do not hang down from the top of the tree until there are clusters of ripening dates at their ends.[236] Also, when they do so, they hang out from the trunk in a semi-arch-like shape, nothing at all as the rippling/waving/undulating appearance characteristic of the great majority of the caducei "strings." Moreover, the "strings"/"ribbons" are often proportionately too long (and/or too thick) to be easily taken as representing spadices of the date palm.[237]

As for those "strings" having blossoms at their ends,[238] they are rather lengthy and curve outward and upward from the caduceus (forming a shallow or deeper U shape); further, the blossoms are not date palm flowers but lotuses (or, perhaps, lilies). In the opinion of this writer, the more likely interpretation here is to regard these "strings" as the stylized means of connecting two motifs into one image, or as lotus stalks (there are other possibilities -- see n. 275 below), than to regard them as spadices of the date palm. Similar "strings" join lotus flowers to the upraised hand, and to the Tannit sign.[239] It should be noted, too, that the caduceus "strings" with flowers, in fact nearly all the caduceus "strings" pictured on the Punic stelai, come from beneath or from the lower part of the form often resembling a disk at the top of the staff/pole. This "disk," Oden explains, probably "grew out of the disk-shaped bulb beneath the fronds of the palm tree."[240] Yet the spadices of the date palm come out from above, not beneath or from the lower part of, this bulb.

With regard to taking the "strings" (bearing no flowers) as representing the ropes used in climbing up the palm tree, one observes that they are usually proportionately too short to be readily understood in such a manner.[241] Occasionally they are apparently an integral part (continuations) of the upper curved lines of the symbol, which does not lead to the impression that they signify ropes hanging from a tree.[242]

b) Oden mentions Carthaginian stelai portraying a caduceus, with two Tannit signs at the ends of the "descending spadices, whose base is plainly the trunk of a palm tree . . ."[243] Other stelai, Oden points out, have a similar scene, except that "the caduceus is replaced by a more realistically portrayed palm tree, again with the cross-hatched bark and again with two Tannit signs at the ends of the spadices . . ."[244] The former type, though, may simply be a "combination" image (of which the western Phoenicians were so fond), bringing together the Tannit sign, the caduceus, and the palm tree. One recalls that the top of a caduceus could appear as the head of a Tannit sign (n. 228). Conversely, assimilating the staff of the caduceus to the trunk of a palm tree was a relatively easy transition. The second scene, then, need not be viewed as a more realistic version of the first; in other words, the two scenes taken together do not necessarily indicate that the caduceus was a stylized palm tree.

c) Oden, referring to the fact that a typical arrangement on Punic monuments is two caducei flanking a central symbol, cites stelai on which a central symbol is flanked by a caduceus and a realistically portrayed palm tree.[245] This, however, is not decisive evidence, for there are numerous scenes which have a central image flanked by a caduceus and a symbol other than the palm tree.[246]

d) Oden calls attention to a Carthaginian representation[247] showing a central palm, realistically portrayed, with a bulb directly underneath the fronds and two "'strings'" descending from below the bulb. To the palm's right is a "typical caduceus," with "a ring which recalls the palm's bulb, and again with two 'strings' descending from below the bulb . . ." Oden concludes that the "juxtaposition seems designed to demonstrate the caduceus' origin in a palm tree."[248] Again, the palm and caduceus here could be regarded as two different symbols for the same goddess. The caduceus is in the background, next to a pillar, whereas the palm is in the foreground; the "strings" of the caduceus are not attached immediately below the "ring," but at a point farther down the staff/pole, and may actually have stood for ribbons or decorative streamers. Stelai show the caduceus and an image other than the palm tree, such as the caduceus next to the Tannit sign,[249] next to a dove,[250] or above a disk and crescent.[251] There are examples, moreover, of two symbols -- not including the caduceus or palm -- situated closely together, both of which conceivably signify Tannit but are otherwise unrelated: for example, the upraised hand next to a fish,[252] and the hand next to a dove.[253]

Indeed, the theory that the caduceus is a stylized female date palm tree may be correct; but on the basis of the presently available evidence this writer prefers an alternate proposal, namely, that the symbol actually consists of two serpents (/snakes) on a pole.[254] Regarding the upper portion of the emblem as two snakes which are most often, but not always, intertwined, fits well all the data brought into the discussion of the two previous theories. The snakes' heads could be pictured as pointing outward or toward each other; the bodies of the reptile images could have various lengths, their tails meeting at the top of the pole,[255] or their bodies crossing at that point and dropping down the pole in a waving manner imitating the shape of a snake's undulations.[256]

Of great importance, too, is the fact that on a number of the stelai the top part of the caduceus definitely resembles two snakes.[257] Whether or not the non-intertwined and intertwined (forming a circular shape immediately above the pole) types were understood to be of equal antiquity, or the latter was seen to be a development of the former (or vice versa),[258] the intertwined version predominated. The lines of connection are clear between the differing forms of this type, which include, generally speaking:[259] a) the "full" representations, with a portion of the serpents' bodies falling alongside the pole, and varying from the realistic[260] to the abstract and/or simplified (a characteristic of which is the serpents' heads not being evident or clear);[261] b) representations having the ends of the serpents' tails meet at the tip of the pole,[262] and the portion of the representation above the "circle"/"ring" still fairly open at the top, with heads either being pictured[263] or not evident or clear;[264] c) the same type as the previous, only, when heads are pictured, those heads touching or crossing each other, with the result that another "circle"/"ring" is formed,[265] and, when the heads are not evident or clear, the "ends" touching (or almost touching), with the same result;[266] and d) representations simply showing two circles/disks/rings.[267] This double-disk form could develop into three or more disks.[268] There could also be a disk within a disk(s) of a highly stylized caduceus.[269] The conclusion is warranted, therefore, that the Hieropolitan σημήιον, described by Lucian in his *De Syria Dea*[270] and pictured on coins of Hierapolis,[271] was essentially the same object as the Punic caduceus, a symbol of Tannit.[272]

On some stelai portrayals the undulating elements beside the pole do seem to be strings or streamers attached at the tip of the pole or a little bit higher, on the serpents' bodies (on the under-sections of the "circle").[273] Perhaps these in real life were decorative adornments on the caduceus being depicted.[274] It is possible, though, that at times the wooden and/or metal part of a caduceus consisted of the vertical pole topped by or opening out into the upper bodies of the serpents (depicted in a realistic or stylized fashion), to which were added strings/ribbons to represent the remaining portions of the serpents and to give "life" and movement to the otherwise motionless symbolical object. Each streamer would wave in the breeze, resembling closely the undulating lower body of a serpent.[275]

That serpents/snakes be associated with Tannit is only appropriate, for she was the "Serpent Lady." The western Phoenicians loved to focus on the symbolic elements of their religion, and the caduceus would have been a convenient method (soon becoming the standard method) of representing serpents/snakes and having them "present" and visible at cultic ceremonies. If the theory proposed here is correct -- that the symbol depicted on the Punic stelai and labeled a "caduceus" should be interpreted as two serpents on a pole/vertical support -- this would strengthen the identification of the goddess with Qudšu/ᵓAšerah. The remarkable conservatism of Punic religion thus is evidenced by the caduceus itself, and by various of its pairings with the Tannit sign on the monuments. For example, a typical scene -- the Tannit sign between two caducei -- was essentially the later, Punic version of the second millennium B.C. Qudšu figures holding serpents.[276] The stele from El-Hofra showing a large Tannit sign right above a standing lion, with a caduceus to the sign's right,[277] may be viewed as nearly a virtual equivalent of the Egyptian stele depicting Qudšu, standing on a lion, holding a serpent in each hand.[278]

Having so identified Tannit,[279] what new information is to be gained from the Punic material leading to a fuller understanding of ᵓAšerah? Her designation *pn bᶜl*, "face/presence of Baᶜl," shows that ᵓAšerah/Tannit was believed to be the hypostasis of Baᶜl Ḥamon.[280] Also, by the time *tnt* appeared in the inscriptions of Carthage, the goddess was regarded as the chief divinity of the city, since she is named before her consort. Elsewhere (e.g., at Hadrumetum and Cirta) Baᶜl Ḥamon is named before Tannit, suggesting that the phenomenon of Tannit's dominance as attested by the Carthaginian stelai was not typical of other Punic sites.[281]

Both "Baᶜl Ḥamon" and "Tannit" appear in inscriptions on stelai found in Punic precincts of child sacrifice.[282] The largest of these is the Carthaginian precinct, which has, since its discovery in 1921, yielded thousands of burial urns and monuments marking those urns.[283] Nine stratified levels of burials in the precinct have been excavated, which are usually fitted into three larger general "strata" (actually "periods"): Tannit I (ca. 750/25-600 B.C.), Tannit II (ca. 600-third century B.C.), and Tannit III (third century-146 B.C.).[284]

The contents of 130 burial urns from this site in Carthage have been systematically examined by Jeffrey Schwartz. Eighty of the urns fall into a chronological group dating mainly to the seventh century B.C., fifty into a group dating to the fourth century B.C.[285] In both groups the majority of urns contained the charred remains of children (see below); the remainder had the charred remains of animals (usually lambs or kids), with very few urns containing both human and animal remains.[286] Approximately two-thirds of the "human only" urns from the fourth century contained the remains of a single child, usually between one and three years old, sometimes a premature or newborn infant. A number of urns, however, contained two or three children (in the latter, two of the three children were twins). These double and triple interments invariably include a very young infant or twins, either premature or neonatal, and a child two to four years old.[287] The "human only" urns from the seventh century differed from those in the later group in that they ordinarily contained the remains of premature or newborn infants. The fourth century group, as just indicated, included such infants but a greater number of children one year and older.[288]

Furthermore, in the seventh century group, about six out of ten urns were "human only," whereas in the later group nearly nine out of ten were of this type.[289] It is also noteworthy that during the fourth century B.C. the density of burials in the site was much higher than at any earlier period, and the precinct reached its greatest extent, perhaps as large as 64,800 square feet (6,000 square meters).[290] Extrapolating from the density of urns in an area of the precinct he excavated, Stager estimates that perhaps as many as 20,000 urns were deposited during the years 400-200 B.C. This averages out to slightly fewer than one urn burial every three days, although there is no clear information concerning the interval between interments.[291] Mass sacrifice was unlikely or exceptional, however, since the preserved skeletal evidence indicates a conscious effort made by the dedicators and/or priests to collect from the pyre or altar the particular remains of the victims (when humans, one to three individuals) and deposit them in an urn.[292] Likewise, there is no evidence for mass burials: throughout the nine levels of precinct interments the typical burial pattern involved the careful placement of usually one, sometimes two, and rarely three urns in a single pit.[293] Taking all this evidence into consideration, the conclusion seems unavoidable that child sacrifice at Carthage was hardly a casual or sporadic occurrence,[294] but rather an important and commonly practiced component in the cult of Baᶜl Ḥamon and Tannit, a rite more frequently performed in the time of Carthage's heyday than in the early period of the colony.[295]

Besides Carthage, child sacrifice was practiced at Cirta, Hadrumetum (modern Sousse), in Sicily (Motya) and Sardinia (Monte Sirai, Nora, Sulcis, Tharros), and undoubtedly at other locations of Punic civilization.[296] The western precincts of child sacrifice, firmly established in North Africa, Sicily, Sardinia, and probably Malta by the seventh century B.C., reveal by their antiquity, geographical distribution, and temporal continuity both that the rite was an integral part of the religious life of the western Phoenicians, and that it originated in Phoenicia.[297] Mosca concludes, correctly in the opinion of this writer, that although no evidence of child sacrifice has been found in Phoenicia, the western precincts were founded by Phoenician colonists and modelled on mainland prototypes.[298] Child sacrifice continued after the fall of Carthage, as shown by evidence from Hadrumetum, Cirta, Guelma, and Ngaous, albeit in increasingly attenuated form. Only the *molchomor* (an animal substitution sacrifice) is attested by the second-early third centuries of the modern era.[299] Tertullian asserts that children were still being offered -- in secret -- as late as 200 A.D. His report may be accurate, but there is no confirming evidence.[300]

It is somewhat ironic, from the twentieth century point of view, that Tannit's/Qudšu's/ʾAšerah's typical emblems -- serpents, sea animals, palm trees, doves, lotuses -- symbols of fertility, beauty, and sexuality, appeared for the most part on stelai coming from such a grim environment. For the Punic worshippers, having the representations on monuments in a precinct of child sacrifice was, on the contrary, quite natural, for they obviously had an attitude toward the rite which is almost completely incomprehensible to modern man. Nevertheless, the possibility remains that the goddess's symbols, particularly in the precinct setting, may have had additional (secondary) connotations which are presently unclear or unknown. Concerning the serpents, however, it might be suggested that these creatures were also regarded as having a chthonic character, an aspect already implied to a certain extent by the Serpent Lady inscriptions from Serabiṭ el-Ḫadem and the Qudšu stele from Thebes West.[301]

To sum up: the worship of Tannit (ʾAšerah/Qudšu) was carried on in the Phoenician homeland and, especially, in the areas of Phoenician expansion in the West (North Africa, Malta, Sicily, Sardinia, and Spain[302]), at sites of which her cult persisted up to and well into the Christian Era.

Derketo/Phanebalos[303]

Diodorus Siculus (fl. ca. 60-30 B.C.) in his *History* writes about a goddess of Ascalon named "Derketo" (Δερκετώ). Roman era coins from the same city portray a warrior goddess with the name "Phanebalos" (ΦΑΝΗΒΑΛΟΣ). The proposal of this section of Chapter 3 is that both Derketo and Phanebalos should be identified with ʾAšerah/Tannit; hence, Derketo = Phanebalos.

Near Ascalon, on the shore of a large and deep lake full of fish, Diodorus tells his readers, is the precinct of a "famous" goddess called Derketo.[304] Of extraordinary form, she "has the head of a woman but all the rest of her body is that of a fish . . ."[305] After giving the reason for her duality, Diodorus tells how her baby daughter, whom she had exposed in the wilderness, was miraculously rescued by a great multitude of doves having their nests in the region where the infant was abandoned.

Initially there is a temptation, perhaps, to argue that Derketo was simply a local city goddess, but her undeniable identification with the Syrian Goddess, Atargatis (n. 305), rules out such an attempt. After a critical analysis of Diodorus's account the marine nature of Derketo remains clear,[306] especially when Lucian's description of an image of the goddess (n. 305) is taken into consideration. Derketo, then, is best identified with ᵓAšerah of the Sea, who had the Fisherman as a servant, and with Tannit, who was associated with fish and dolphins. The doves in Diodorus's story, though indirectly connected with the Ascalonite goddess, recall the representations of doves which were part of Tannit's iconography.[307]

Derketo's being worshipped at Ascalon in semi-piscine form does not absolutely exclude the possibility she could also have been depicted there as a normal female figure. In fact, the goddess appearing constantly on Ascalonite coins from the time of Augustus (4/3 B.C.) to Geta (198/9 A.D.),[308] wearing a turreted crown, standing on a prow, holding a standard (in her right hand) and aphlaston (in her left hand), and regularly accompanied by a dove and an altar, is in all probability Derketo.[309] Obviously, the female deity on the coins is a marine goddess, and thus the relative certainty of her being identified as Derketo, with the dove pictured beside her enhancing this identification. For the same reasons, naturally, one may understand the divinity on the coins to be ᵓAšerah. Moreover, the standard held by the goddess consists of a staff at times having a cross bar toward the top, often having a triangle at the top.[310] The latter may be a sign of Tannit.[311] In addition, the altar depicted on the coins, described by Hill as "of somewhat peculiar form, with three projections at the top,"[312] is an incense altar. Incense burners or altars are connected with Tannit on the Punic stelai.[313]

Another series of Ascalonite coins dating from 149/50 A.D. to 217/8 A.D.[314] presents a scene closely related to that of the previous series. A goddess, wearing a crescent or crescent and disk, holding a long scepter in her left hand and a dove in her right, stands on a Triton, who raises a cornucopia.[315] It is undoubtedly correct to identify this goddess simultaneously with Derketo and ᵓAšerah/Tannit.

Ascalonite coins of a third type, dating from 6/7 A.D. to 230/1 A.D., portray Phanebalos, whose name is inscribed on some of the monetary pieces.[316] She[317] wears a cuirass, and usually a helmet; on a number of the coins pteryges are clearly visible, while other coins show her wearing a long skirt. The standing goddess (at times on a pedestal) wields a sword in her right hand and holds a small round shield and long palm branch in her left.[318] ΦΑΝΗΒΑΛΟΣ, transparently the Greek for *panê baᶜl*, ties the goddess to Tannit/ᵓAšerah, an identification fortified by the appearance of what is surely a Tannit sign beside the representation of Phanebalos on one of the coins.[319] The palm branch likewise points to the equation Phanebalos = Tannit, not only because the palm tree as a symbol of Tannit was frequently pictured on the Punic stelai, but also because palm branches specifically were at times associated with the goddess.[320]

If Phanebalos should be identified with Tannit/ᵓAšerah, it is equally clear that this goddess portrayed on the Ascalonite coins was a martial divinity. Are these representations evidence for seeing a new, late development in the way Tannit/ᵓAšerah was perceived by her worshippers, a conception perhaps peculiar to Ascalon? In response, it may be said that the city goddess was not only considered a warrior, judging from the scenes on other contemporary monetary pieces. Also, though such an emphasis on Tannit/ᵓAšerah as war goddess may have been unique to Ascalon, the characteristic itself is indicated elsewhere, and was not necessarily a relatively new feature in the goddess's veneration. For example, the arms and the chariot of Juno, according to Virgil,[321] were located at Carthage, indirect testimony to Tannit being (in part) a martial goddess.[322] *Caelestis* (Tannit) was a warlike divinity: an inscription from Tunisia mentions her cuirass.[323] The bust of a helmeted woman appears on the obverse of a coin with neo-Punic inscription from the old Phoenician colony of Oea (Tripoli);[324] this very possibly is a representation of Tannit. The coin's reverse shows a tripod on which is suspended a bow and a quiver. Two stelai from El-Hofra are relevant here: one presents a Tannit sign enclosing a bow and arrow (with the arrow notched to the bow string),[325] the other a Tannit sign between a dagger and a staff.[326] As already mentioned, Qudšu was closely connected with Hathor, who had a fierce aspect to her character (Appendix C), and there is evidence pointing to an associating of ʾAšerah/Qudšu/Tannit with Sakhmet, a warlike goddess. Finally, the reader will recall that Kirta, advancing at the head of a huge army with which he would fight against and besiege ʾUdm (that he might obtain Ḥurriya), petitioned ʾAṯirat of Tyre and ʾElat of Sidon to grant success to his mission.[327]

In conclusion, it is the opinion of this writer that on the basis of the presently available evidence a reasonable case can be made for seeing the same goddess behind *qdš*, *ḏt bṯn*, *bʿlt gbl*, *tnt*, "Derketo," and "Phanebalos" -- that goddess being ʾAšerah.

NOTES TO CHAPTER III

1. Hereafter *PF*.

2. Pictures of these objects may be found in *PF*, 100-1; in Pritchard's *The Ancient Near East in Pictures Relating to the Old Testament* (Princeton: Princeton University, 1954; hereafter *ANEP*) 161 fig. 467 and 162 fig. 469; and in Albright's "Astarte Plaques and Figurines from Tell Beit Mirsim.," in *Mélanges syriens*: offerts à monsieur René Dussaud, secrétaire perpétuel de l'Académie des Inscriptions et Belles-lettres, par ses amis et ses élèves (vol. 1; Paris: Paul Geuthner, 1939) 111, 113, 115-6.

3. *PF*, 6-8, and 100 figs. 1 and 2. The figure on Pritchard's plaque no. 17 (p. 7), which incidentally is clothed (although lines would indicate female genital organs), holds with the right arm papyrus stalks, with the left a lotus blossom.

4. *PF*, 8, and 100 figs. 3 and 4. However, Pritchard's assigning figs. 3 and 4 to this subcategory under Type I is questionable. In fig. 3 something, perhaps a papyrus stalk, clearly is held in the left hand (cf. Albright, "Astarte Plaques," 113 fig. 4). Concerning fig. 4, it seems especially after a comparison with the larger representation of the same plaque in Albright's "Astarte Plaques" (113 fig. 1) that objects of some sort are being held, which are either too small to identify or perhaps have been partially rubbed off the plaque.

5. *PF*, 9-10, 36. Pritchard gives two examples: his first (no. 36) is debatable, since only the top portion of the (broken) plaque remains. The raised upper bodies of two serpents border the plaque. However, the position of the female figure's arms cannot be determined (only the upper arms are visible, and these hang straight down). It is uncertain if she originally held the serpents. See Robert A.S. Macalister, *The Excavation of Gezer, 1902-1905 and 1907-1909* (3 vols.; London: John Murray, 1912) 3: pl. 221.9. In Pritchard's second example (no. 37), the nude female figure holds with her left hand a stalk or serpent; coiled around her neck is a serpent with its head at her left thigh.

6. *PF*, 32. Pritchard considers the Late Bronze Period to be 1500-1200 B.C. (his complete dating scheme is given on p. 4 of *PF*). I understand the Middle Bronze Period to be 2000-1550, the Late Bronze Period to be 1550-1200, and the Iron I Period to be 1200-930. This is the dating framework I have in mind in the following discussion of the main body.

7. *PF*, 9 and 32. One example of the figure with arms extended to the sides holding stalks comes from a stratum at Ain Shems dated 1200-1000 B.C. (*PF*, 7 no. 14, and 32).

8. *PF*, 41; Stadelmann, 110-1; and Albright, "Astarte Plaques," 117-8. Albright mentions that it is not clear whether the goddess borrowed this headdress from a fashionable coiffure of the period, best illustrated by the spiral locks of Nefert, queen of Sesostris II (ca. 1897-1878), or whether the reverse is true. See *ANEP*, 184 fig. 547 for a good example of the Hathor wig.

9. Recent information provided by Ora Negbi may indicate that the Hathor wig dates already from the Eleventh Dynasty (*Canaanite Gods in Metal* [Tel Aviv University Institute of Archaeology 5; Tel Aviv: Peli, 1976] 78-9, 82). Marie-Thérèse Barrelet discusses the evolution in Mesopotamia, beginning from the Isin-Larsa period, of the coiffure of certain goddesses (especially of the "nude goddess") toward a form very similar to the Hathor wig, concluding that the "Hathor wig" seen on many Syro-Palestinian figurines does not necessarily indicate a direct borrowing from the iconography of Egypt. However, Barrelet admits that this evolution of the coiffure in Mesopotamia could have been created by an Egyptian influence ("Deux déesses syro-phéniciennes sur un bronze du Louvre," *Syria* 35 [1958] 31-4). In my opinion the headdress in question appearing on many of the Type I figurines is the Hathor wig, and to me the most reasonable supposition is that it was taken over directly from Egypt rather than indirectly (through Mesopotamia).

10. *PF*, 40-1. In his discussion Pritchard cites work done by Albright. See Albright, "Astarte Plaques," 114-7. Two of Pritchard's Type I figurines wear a feather headdress (7, nos. 15 and 16; 38-40; 100, fig. 2); cf. the photo in the report of Paul F. Jacobs, "Tell Halif/Lahav 1983 Season," *ASOR Newsletter* 36 (1985) 4. Related to the Type I examples is a terra cotta plaque from Alalakh; see Leonard Woolley, *Alalakh* (Reports of the Research Committee of the Society of Antiquaries of London 18; Oxford: University Press, 1955) 247-8 (AT/39/240), pl. 54 o, and Barrelet, 42 and 42 fig. 9. It comes from Level III, originally dated to ca. 1358-1285, but later dated by Woolley to ca. 1370-1350 (384-99). The representation on the plaque should perhaps be viewed as basically a Type I figure which has come under Hittite influence (note the high, conical cap/crown worn by the figure).

11. Negbi, 98-100, 103, nos. 1678, 1680, 1683-92, 1697-1702; see 98 figs. 114-6; 99 figs. 117-8; 100 fig. 119; 113 fig. 128; 119 fig. 134; pls. 52-4; *PF*, 34-5, except for Pritchard's second example (35), a fourteenth-thirteenth century ivory plaque from Tomb III of Minet el-Beida, a picture of which may be seen in *ANEP* (160 fig. 464) and F.-A. Schaeffer's "Les fouilles de Minet-el-Beida et de Ras Shamra," *Syria* 10 (1929) pl. 56; beautiful color photos are provided by James M. Robinson, "Claude Frederic-Armand Schaeffer-Forrer (1898-1982)," *BAR* 9 (1983) 57 (see also p. 58) and Seibert, pl. 47. While exhibiting some of the characteristics of Type I, it is not a true representative of this type. The figure on the piece (actually the cover of an oval ivory cosmetic box) wears a skirt; her face is seen in profile; from the elbow to the wrist her arms are bent almost straight up (the Type I examples have the lower arms bent more at an outward angle); the figure is seated on an altar (Schaeffer, 292) or a throne (*ANEP*, 160 fig. 464; Robinson, 58); and finally, Cretan-Mycenaean influence is evident (note especially the full skirt). Probably the engraving is a blend form, combining Type I traits with features drawn from a different type(s).

To be added to this group of Type I metal pieces listed by Negbi and Pritchard is the bronze head of an ax (used for display purposes?), which is decorated on one of its faces with the standing, frontally-viewed nude figure. She apparently wears a Hathor wig and, holding her arms out at her sides in the V shape, grasps two stalks/stems at the top of which are flowers. The axhead, found at ᶜAinjarr, dates from the period between 1400 and 1200 B.C. See Barrelet, 27-9, 36-44, pl. 1 b.

It should be stated that the Type I terra cotta figurines and metal pieces listed by Pritchard, Negbi, and the other scholars cited here, while a substantial portion of such discoveries, do not constitute a complete "list" of these finds. See, e.g., Joe D. Seger's review of Negbi's *Canaanite Gods in Metal* (*BASOR* 249 [1983] 95-6).

12. Despite the symbolic or "representational" (Negbi, 98) character of these plaques they should be classified with Pritchard's Type I figurines. Pritchard writes: "These pendants belong by their evident symbolism to this grouping of . . . Type I figurines" (*PF*, 35). Negbi explains, concerning the same group of objects, that they "recall" those metal plaques which portray the full Type I female figure (98; see also 100; cf. 113, 118-9).

13. Negbi's no. 1706 (101, 103) is in her "unclassified" section. This Late Bronze metal piece from Hazor is unfortunately badly preserved in its central area. Nevertheless, my impression of the plaque is that it originally represented a standing Type I figure (her face is still visible) holding a serpent in each hand.

Above the figure is a long, slender crescent; above the crescent is an unidentifiable curled form. See pl. 24 in *Near Eastern Archaeology in the Twentieth Century* (ed. James A. Sanders; Garden City, N.Y.: Doubleday, 1970).

14. For example, the figure usually holds plants (mostly lotus and papyrus) in her hands, but on one plaque she grasps in each hand what appears to be a ram (Negbi, 99 fig. 118) and on another a gazelle (Negbi, 99-100, no. 1701 and fig. 119; pl. 53; = *PF*, 35 no. 3 -- however, Pritchard writes that the figure holds a "bouquet" in each hand, which is incorrect). In at least three cases she stands on the back of a lion (Negbi, 99 and 99 fig. 118, 100 fig. 119). More specifically, the Type I figure holding gazelles and standing on the back of a lion (striding to the viewer's left) is on an exquisite pendant of sheet gold from Minet el-Beida (see drawing no. 1 below). She has a Hathor wig and face with cow-like ears (typical of Hathor -- see App. C, and *ANEP*, 184 fig. 547) and is smiling, wearing a necklace, arm bands, wrist bands, Egyptian abacus headpiece, and perhaps a girdle around the hips. Behind her hips two serpents apparently cross over one another, so that beside each of her hips appear the upper body of one serpent and the lower body of the other. A color photo of this pendant may be found in Peter C. Craigie's "The Tablets from Ugarit and their Importance for Biblical Studies," *BAR* 9 (1983) 65 (Craigie recognizes the animals being held as ibexes) and Seibert's *Women in the Ancient Near East*, pl. 36. The latter reference has a large, exceptionally clear photo.

15. Negbi, 98-100, 103 and 103 Table 18; *PF*, 35. Negbi's no. 1683, from Megiddo, dates either to the thirteenth or the twelfth century, and so may overlap from the Late Bronze Period into Iron I (99); the date of another metal plaque from Megiddo is uncertain because it lacks in proper archaeological data (Negbi, 98 no. 1684); Negbi's no. 1702, from Zincirli, has no definite date, but it likely belongs to the Iron Period rather than the Late Bronze Period (100 and 100-1 n. 38).
Finally, before leaving the Syro-Palestinian realm, mention should also be made of representations, which are regarded as belonging to Type I, on cylinder seals of the Second Syrian Group. See Barrelet, 34-6 (and the references cited in n. 1 p. 35) and Negbi, 100 (and the reference cited thereat).

16. Lists of the Egyptian portrayals, with pertinent references, are given by Wolfgang Helck, *Die Beziehungen Ägyptens zu Vorderasien im 3. und 2. Jahrtausend v. Chr.* (Ägyptologische Abhandlungen 5; Wiesbaden: Otto Harrassowitz, 1962) 497-8; Pritchard, *PF*, 33-4; and Charles Boreux, "La stèle C.86 du Musée du Louvre et les stèles similaires," in *Mélanges syriens*: offerts

à monsieur René Dussaud, 2: 674-6. See also Edwards, 49 and 49 nn. 2 and 3. A composite list of the Egyptian examples, drawn from a comparison of the first three sources, would be that of Helck, plus Pritchard's nos. 8 and 9 (BM 650 and a slab from the Mut temple of Thebes; *PF*, 34) and the fragment of BM 702 (817; Boreux, 675).

17. Helck's fourth entry (Helck, 498) -- corresponding to Pritchard's no. 4 (*PF*, 33) -- is a relief now in Cairo, which dates after 1000 B.C.

18. For photos of the Egyptian representations see *ANEP*, 163 figs. 470 (in Cairo; listed: *PF*, 33 no. 3, and second entry of Helck, 497), 471 (Berlin stele; listed: *PF*, 33 no. 1, and first entry of Helck, 498), 472 (in Cairo; listed: *PF*, 33 no. 4, and fourth entry of Helck, 498), 473 (BM 646/191; listed: *PF*, 33 no. 2, and first entry of Helck, 497; another photo: Boreux, 685 fig. 4); Boreux, 674 fig. 1 and pl. facing p. 674 (Louvre Stele C.86; partially reproduced in *ANEP*, 164 fig. 474; listed: *PF*, 33-4 no. 5, and third entry of Helck, 497), 675 fig. 2 (in Vienna; listed: *PF*, 34 no. 6, and sixth entry of Helck, 497), 682 fig. 3 (Stele 1601 in Turin Museum; listed: *PF*, 34 no. 7, and fourth entry of Helck, 497); Edwards, pl. 3 (Winchester College collection; listed: second entry of Helck, 498) and pl. 4 (BM 60308; listed: third entry of Helck, 498). Among the noteworthy variations is the presence or absence of a headpiece, which itself has differing forms: e.g., the abacus (seen on the Hathor capital -- *ANEP*, 184 fig. 547), a sun disk resting on a crescent, the abacus topped by disk and crescent, or the abacus surmounted by a naos having volutes, with the naos being topped by the disk and crescent (Edwards, 49-50). Cross has pointed out that, with regard to the disk and crescent, the Egyptianizing headpiece on these reliefs "resembles more the Khonsu crown than that of Hathor," indicating that "there was evidently some confusion" on the part of the artisans (*CMHE*, 34). Or, possibly the crescent had become so much a part of the iconography of the Type I figure that it was depicted intentionally instead of the Hathor horns (see below, n. 28). The naos with volutes is undoubtedly the naos sistrum (without the lower handle), the sistrum being a cult symbol of Hathor (see Hans Bonnet, *Reallexikon der ägyptischen Religionsgeschichte* [Berlin: Walter de Gruyter, 1952] 362, 716-8). Bonnet, showing (716-7, and 717 fig. 171) how the lower grip of the naos sistrum ended in a head of Hathor (just below the naos), proposes that the two volutes rising from the base to the top of the naos were intentionally reminiscent of the goddess's cow horns.

Showing the most noticeable variation from the main pattern is the relief of fig. 472 in *ANEP* (p. 163), on which the female figure wears a crown of vegetation or feathers and stands facing to the right. Perhaps this is because the relief is dated to a later period than the bulk of the other Egyptian examples (see n. 17). For further discussion concerning variations in these reliefs see Edwards (49-50).

19. *ANEP*, 163 fig. 470 is one exception: in place of Min appears the Egyptian god Sutekh (according to Pritchard, *PF*, 33 no. 3), and in place of Rešep stands a clothed female figure. "Sutekh" was another name for Seth, the Egyptian deity with whom the Canaanite god Baᶜl was identified (and vice versa). See Bonnet, 77, 702, 705; E. A. Wallis Budge, *The Gods of the Egyptians* (2 vols.; New York: Dover Publications, 1969; a reprint of the 1904 work) 2: 250; Alan H. Gardiner, "Egypt: Ancient Religion," *The Encyclopaedia Britannica* 9 (11th ed., 1910-11) 53; and Alfred Wiedemann, *Religion of the Ancient Egyptians* (New York: G. P. Putnam's Sons, 1897) 220-3.

The other exception is a small stele in Copenhagen (Helck's fifth entry, p. 497), dating to about the Nineteenth Dynasty, which pictures in place of Min the Egyptian god Onuris (Stadelmann, 122 and 122 n. 2). A bronze amulet, probably coming from the beginning of the Nineteenth Dynasty, also shows the triad Onuris-Type I figure-Rešep, as does a late representation of such an amulet in the temple of Karnak (Stadelmann, 122-3; cf. Helck, 499). More will be said about this triad in n. 56 below.

20. Boreux, pl. facing p. 674; 675 fig. 2; 682 fig. 3; and *ANEP*, 163 fig. 471. One relief (*ANEP*, 163 fig. 473) calls her *knt*. Scholars usually conclude that this writing is inexplicable or propose alternate readings (see Helck, 498 and 513 n. 157; Edwards, 49). Perhaps the epithet is related to Akkadian *kanūtu* (verbal adjective from *kanû*), "the honored, estimable, cherished," a title of goddesses. Cf. *CTA* 4.4.54: *mô̱tabi kallāti kanyāti*, "the dwelling of the honored brides." Other translators render the Ugaritic adjective "perfect." See Chap. 1, text no. 10, n. m.

21. Albright thinks that the "absence" of the lion on the Syro-Palestinian plaques and pendants (absent when he wrote; but since then a few examples have been found with the lion -- see n. 14) is "accidental" (*YGC*, 122). Pritchard holds that while "the lion is not shown on any of the Palestinian [terra cotta] examples, the position of the feet is such that we are justified in supposing that at one time the lion was shown or understood as supporting the figure" (*PF*, 42). Stadelmann, perhaps correctly, views the gold pendant from Minet el-Beida (described in n. 14 above), on which the female figure stands on a lion, as an important connecting link between the stylized representations on other gold pendants (showing only the head and sex characteristics), the Type I Palestinian terra cotta plaques, and the

reliefs of Egypt providing the name *qdš*. According to Stadelmann, when the pendants made of gold are seen as depicting *qdš*, the terra cotta plaques must also be regarded in the same way (111-2).

22. Helck, 506; Stadelmann, 15 (citing references for illustrations of the scarabs), 20, 111-2. Stadelmann concludes that nothing definite can be stated about where these scarabs were made (southern Palestine? the Nile delta?).

23. Stadelmann, 15.

24. Stadelmann, 110-1.

25. *PF*, 37-8, 41-2. Cf. the photograph of the Akkadian cylinder seal in Marie-Henriette Gates's "Dura-Europos: A Fortress of Syro-Mesopotamian Art," *BA* 47 (1984) 171.

26. The fact that Rešep appears with *qdš* (and Min) in the Egyptian triad representations may also indicate that the *qdš* figure came to Egypt from Palestine-Syria.

27. See App. C for an extended discussion of Hathor.

28. A *qdš* relief in Berlin (*ANEP*, 163 fig. 471; see drawing 2 below) has small circles on both sides of the figure. Explaining that these represent the stars of the heavens, Stadelmann connects them with Hathor, the goddess of the heavens (115-6). There apparently are a lunar crescent and stars at the bottom of Negbi's plaque no. 1699 (99 and 99 fig. 117; see also Barrelet, pl. 2 c), and numerous stars on the sheet gold pendant from Minet el-Beida (n. 14 above). To me it seems probable that the crescent and stars on the plaque and pendant were a result of Egyptian influence, but the possibility exists that the crescent, at least, was shown with the *qdš* figure originally in Syria-Palestine and then brought to Egypt (resulting in the crescent and disk headpiece -- see n. 18 above).

29. On the *qdš* stelai Rešep is called "Lord of the Heavens" and "great god, Lord of the Eternity, Sovereign of the Duration, the very powerful, Sovereign of the Divine Nine" (Boreux, 680; Stadelmann, 119-20). Epithets of Min on these stelai are ordinary epithets of the god: "Min-Amen, great in strength on his great throne, the great god," "Min-Amen-Kamutef, Lord of the Heavens," "the bull of his mother, Lord of the Heavens," "the great god, with the high plumes/feathers, whose arm is raised" (Boreux, 680 n. 6; Stadelmann, 119-20).

30. Helck, 497-8; Stadelmann, 115-6, 120-2; Wiedemann, 152-3. In Egyptian references the epithets "Lady of the Heavens" and "Lady/Ruler of the Gods" are also applied to ᶜAnat (Černý, 127; Helck, 496; Stadelmann, 92, 95;

Wiedemann, 151-2) and ʿAštart (Černý, 127; Stadelmann, 104-9), probably because these epithets were more or less general titles used by the Egyptians for other female deities (undoubtedly due in part to the numerous assimilations/identifications of goddesses in Egyptian religion).

31. Pritchard states that the "motif of the Qadesh type standing upon the back of a lion (as seen in the Syrian and Egyptian examples) is a common method of indicating that the person is a super-human being" (*PF*, 42). Boreux (679; citing the opinion of another scholar) suggests that a picture of a divinity on a lion may express the power of the deity. Another consideration with regard to the lion is that it may have been *qdš*'s sacred animal.

32. E.g., *ANEP*, 163 fig. 472.

33. E.g., Boreux, pl. facing p. 674; 682 fig. 3. The triad of Min, *qdš*, and Rešep enjoyed a lively worship especially among the working class in Thebes West (Stadelmann, 139; cf. 117-8).

34. E.g., *ANEP*, 163 fig. 473 and Boreux, 675 fig. 2.

35. Cf. the horned emblem worn by the *qdš* figure on Negbi's plaque no. 1700 (99 and 99 fig. 118). The same figure appears in *ANEP* (161 fig. 465).

36. Indulging my curiosity, I did a little research concerning the reproductive habits of snakes, in order to learn why they are considered a symbol of fertility. I found in Herndon G. Dowling's article "Snake" in *The Encyclopedia Americana* (25 [1973] 90) that those species which are exposed to the hazards of living in view of other animals produce large numbers of eggs. A python may lay more than 100 eggs in a single clutch, and a garter snake may give birth to more than 80 young in a litter. The "average" number of young produced by a female snake in a season is probably between 8 and 15. In many snakes the production of eggs or young is biennial rather than annual. Also, a female can store sperm and produce young several times after a single mating. Additionally, the courtship habits of snakes may partly have led to their being pictured in the *qdš* scenes (relating to the erotic aspect). As a male courts a female he uses a stroking or rubbing technique to stimulate her; in some species a muscle ripple moving along the male's body will provide a lateral caress (Dowling, 90; James A. Peters, "Serpentes," *The New Encyclopaedia Britannica* Macropaedia 16 [1980] 561). Peters notes that there "are many descriptions in the literature of courtship dances done by snakes, in which the bodies are entwined and as much as one-third lifted off the ground, the coils ebbing and flowing with silent grace. Unfortunately,

in many of these reports, the snakes were not captured and sexed, and the observer simply assumed that a male and female were involved. Recent work, where the snakes have been sexed, tends to indicate that the dance often, if not always, involves two males and is of little or no significance in reproduction" (561).

Returning to the area of Near Eastern studies, it should be mentioned that Coote, in his dissertation "The Serpent and Sacred Marriage in Northwest Semitic Tradition," has argued skillfully that "images of serpents are a powerful adjunct to the rites of sacred marriage and their accompanying forms of potency ritual" (63; see additionally 55, 91). Coote also refers to the serpent's shedding its slough, by which act it was believed to grow young again (132 and 141 n. 67). For a brief discussion of images of serpents in Canaanite cults see John Gray, *I and II Kings* (2nd ed.; Old Testament Library; London: SCM, 1970) 670-1; cf. R. W. Hamilton, "*Beth-shan," *IDB* 1 (1962) 399.

37. To put it another way, the flowers indicate her "sex appeal" (Albright, *ARI*, 76). *qdš*'s holding what seem to be papyrus stalks in some of the representations possibly is another sign linking her with the Egyptian goddess Hathor.

38. The V shape of the arms, such an important characteristic of the *qdš* type, occurs because the female figure is holding objects (often in a rather restricted space), but I wonder whether the formation was secondarily viewed as symbolizing or emphasizing the V shape of the figure's genital area.

39. Helck explains that *qdš* was a goddess of the "folk faith," as opposed to being one of the royal divinities (those having a connection with the king), who had a prominent warlike aspect. There is no indication of *qdš* being joined with the *Königsmythos*, nor does she appear in the *Königsbilder*. Rather, she is represented on "private stelai" (498-9, 503-4, 506; see also Stadelmann, 117-8, 122, 135, 138). The dedicators of the stelai (either showing the goddess alone or in the triad) have Egyptian names (see Helck, 497-8), which is one reason for surmising that *qdš* was worshipped in Egypt not only by Syrians and Palestinians, but also by the Egyptians themselves (Helck, 499). Cf. Boreux, who understands the triad stelai he has examined as coming from a local cult of the Theban necropolis carried on by Semitic workers of the lower classes who had adopted Egyptian names (680-7; see esp. 684-7); cf. also Edwards, 51. In general, I understand the worshippers of *qdš* in Egypt as including both Semites and native Egyptians -- the latter particularly because of the appearance of Min on *qdš* stelai, the epithets taken from Egyptian religion, and, except for *qdš* herself, the Egyptian mode of representing the deities (including ᶜAnat, on the lower half

of BM 646) and worshippers (e.g., Louvre Stele C.86, BM 646, Turin Stele 1601).

Related to this understanding is the fact that *qdš*, according to Helck, may have had a chapel or temple in Memphis (499). Stadelmann's judgment is that the center of the worship of *qdš* by the Egyptians probably lay in Memphis, where she possessed a cult place in the temple of Ptah as a *Gastgöttin* (115). There, says Stadelmann, she was considered to be the daughter of Ptah and perhaps also his consort/wife, because a stele (*ANEP*, 163 fig. 471) names her: "*qdš*, whom Ptah loves."

40. Wiedemann, 127; "Min," *The New Encyclopaedia Britannica* Micropaedia 6 (1980) 905. Helck proposes that *qdš* filled a void in Egyptian religion: Min lacked a female counterpart (498-9). Stadelmann thinks that *qdš* was viewed among the Asians as wife/consort of Min in Thebes, an idea which was possibly strengthened under Egyptian influence (118). What is certain to me is that both Min and *qdš* were viewed as deities of fertility and sexual vigor, and so their appearing together on reliefs was entirely natural.

41. Helck, 498.

42. Stadelmann, 73-4.

43. Stadelmann, 49.

44. Stadelmann, 56-8, 135.

45. Most of the time Rešep holds in his extended left hand a shield, and frequently also a spear, while with his right he swings a club (or battle ax) overhead (see, e.g., *ANEP*, 164 fig. 476); sometimes the right hand with the club is shown in a lowered position (Stadelmann, 61). Stadelmann suggests that this warlike appearance of the god on private stelai was partly determined by the older method of representation of the Eighteenth Dynasty, but also partly by the idea that Rešep was defending against angry demons of sickness and evil (63; see main body).

46. The titles on the stelai give no specific information about what kind of god Rešep was understood to be, since he is called throughout "the great god" and "Lord of the Heavens" (Stadelmann, 61).

47. See, e.g., Albright, *YGC*, 139; Caquot and Sznycer, *Ugaritic Religion*, 15; and Stadelmann, 52-70. In his discussion, Stadelmann refers to two small Rešep monuments from the beginning of the Nineteenth Dynasty, both almost surely dedicated by the same person, *P3-šd*, a member of the worker settlement of Deir el-Medina (65-6). They indicate that the god was petitioned for and believed to grant life, health, and well-being;

the second mentions additional blessings. Moreover, Egyptian seals and scarabs represent Rešep in his aspect as a god of protection against sickness and disaster (Stadelmann, 74; see also 74 n. 3). I wish to express my thanks to Prof. Thomas Lambdin for his translations of the two Rešep monuments just mentioned and of other Egyptian texts, as will be noted below.

48. Stadelmann, 63.

49. Cf. Stadelmann, 56, 73-4, 117-8, who thinks that the erotic and fertility aspect was the strongest link connecting the deities in the triad. In addition, Stadelmann notes that on the *qdš* reliefs Rešep appears with weapons lowered -- the "peaceful" type (74 n. 1; 119). Cf. also Helck (505-6).

50. Boreux, 674 fig. 1 (back side of stele) and pl. facing 674 = Louvre Stele C.86.

51. Stadelmann, 121.

52. Egyptian worship of Near Eastern divinities occurred, according to Stadelmann, because the Egyptians recognized in them divine powers which in Egypt were either strange and new or represented in another form. He sees a distinction between this worship in the New Kingdom as opposed to the Middle Kingdom. During the earlier period, Stadelmann explains, their assimilation to related Egyptian deities was complete and included even their being named with Egyptian names (the prime example -- the identification of the goddess of Byblos with Hathor, which continued in the New Kingdom; more on this in the main body). However, during the New Kingdom the Near Eastern divinities (including *qdš*, who was closely assimilated to the Hathor type) consistently were designated as independent, foreign deities. Thus there was, comparatively speaking, no longer a total, but a partial, identification (141-2).

53. Stadelmann, 120-1.

54. These five translations of the prayers are Prof. Lambdin's; cf. Stadelmann, 121-2.

55. Stadelmann, 122.

56. Cf. Stadelmann, 122; also Helck, 498. A few more remarks concerning *qdš* in the Egyptian material are in order. First, Helck notes (in a magical context) that the sufferer of Papyrus 343 and 345 mentions *qdš* as "remover of poison" (499). Also, "*qdš*," according to Helck, does not appear as a component of names in Egypt (499). Finally, regarding the rarely attested triad of Onuris-*qdš*-Rešep (see n. 19 above), Stadelmann concludes -- correctly, in my opinion -- that since the style of

depicting this triad (with the exception of the late example from Karnak) is the same as that of the original Min-*qdš*-Rešep triad, the idea being expressed was essentially unchanged (123 and 123 n. 1). He reasons that Onuris could be substituted for Min-Amen because of the progressive identification of *qdš* with Hathor, especially as to the role of "eye of the sun," which resulted in the goddesses' becoming blended also in the myths of the "eye of the sun" going away and being brought back. Only in Coptos did Min-Amen secondarily become the "Bringer of the Eye of the Sun." Usually the responsibility of bringing back the "eye of the sun" from afar was ascribed to Onuris (Stadelmann, 122; see Bonnet, 546-7, for further discussion of this legend). Though celebrated in a text of the Eighteenth Dynasty as a creative solar power, Onuris essentially was regarded as a hunter and powerful warrior, with the result that he was frequently invoked against enemies and noxious animals (Bonnet, 545; Eberhard Otto, "Egyptian Religion," *The New Encyclopaedia Britannica* Macropaedia 6 (1980) 507 table 2; Adolf Erman, *A Handbook of Egyptian Religion* [trans. A. S. Griffith; London: Archibald Constable, 1907] 76, 161; Wiedemann, 77-8).

57. Stadelmann, 8, 10; Černý, 124-5; cf. Alan Gardiner, *Egypt of the Pharaohs* (Oxford: Oxford University, 1961) 88-9.

58. Stadelmann, 11. Stadelmann also thinks that this identification was made on the Egyptians' part for additional reasons, namely, because of Hathor's role as goddess of the raw materials and of their lands of origin, and because of her attributes as *Resortgöttin* (10).

59. Stadelmann, 11-2, 98 and 98 n. 4 (where Stadelmann gives an example of a representation of the Lady of Byblos not modelled after Hathor); Pierre Montet, *Eternal Egypt* (trans. Doreen Weightman; New York: Praeger, 1964) 111. See *ANEP*, 165 fig. 477. Up till now, of course, no evidence has been brought to light which furnishes the proper name (e.g., "ᵓAšerah," "ᶜAštart," "ᶜAnat," or something else) of the goddess of Byblos. In the Egyptian records of the Middle Kingdom and later she is named "(Hathor), Lady of Byblos," and the same holds true for the inscriptions of Byblian kings (see Chap. 2, n. 34), where she is addressed as the *bᶜlt gbl*, "Lady of Byblos." Assuming (rightly, in my opinion) that there was in Byblos a native city goddess with her own proper name, who was later identified with Hathor, Stadelmann puts forward the following interesting theory: "Ich möchte annehmen, daß Hathor in Byblos im Lauf des MR mit bewußter Förderung durch die nach Ägypten orientierte Oberschicht die alte Stadtgöttin überlagert und soweit verdrängt hat, daß sogar ihr Name gegenüber der ägyptischen Bezeichnung ‚Herrin von Byblos' zuerst zurücktrat und schließlich ganz in Vergessenheit

kam" (11 n. 2). Prof. Cross has advised me that it is unlikely the Byblians would have forgotten the identity of their city goddess, so I would modify Stadelmann's last phrase, proposing that her name was not entirely forgotten but rather that it fell into disuse.

60. "Astarte Plaques," 117-8. See n. 9 above. Cf. Albright, *ARI*, 76; also Stadelmann, 11-2.

61. Albright, in *The Proto-Sinaitic Inscriptions and their Decipherment* (HTS 22; Cambridge: Harvard University, 1966; hereafter *PSI*) 6 and 12, dates the texts to a maximum range of ca. 1550-1450, but more probably between ca. 1525 and ca. 1475. In the sections of the main body and the following footnotes dealing with these inscriptions I rely heavily on *PSI*.

62. For this translation of *ḏt bṯn* see *PSI*, 39.

63. See the excellent color photos of ruins of this temple, plus a plan and discussion of the structure in Itzhaq Beit-Arieh's "Fifteen Years in Sinai," *BAR* 10 (1984) 41-4, 47.

64. Stadelmann, 1-4. Cf. Helck, 482.

65. Stadelmann, 4.

66. Albright, *PSI*, 14 (see also 20), says that the Serpent Lady was "apparently identified with a Nubian serpent-goddess," but he at the same time cites a previous article of his ("The Early Alphabetic Inscriptions from Sinai and their Decipherment," *BASOR* 110 [1948] 17), in which he relates the Serpent Lady to *qdš* (as I read him). Gardiner, writing about Egyptian religion, comments that the "form of a snake, attributed to many local goddesses, especially in later times (e.g. Meresger of the Theban necropolis), was borrowed from the very ancient deity Outo (Buto); the semblance of a snake became so characteristic of female divinities that even the word 'goddess' was written with the hieroglyph of a snake" ("Egypt: Ancient Religion," 50). It is not totally impossible that the Serpent Lady was Buto (for information about her see Bonnet, 853-4; Budge, 1: 441-4; and Otto, 505), another Egyptian goddess (other Egyptian deities besides Hathor were patrons of the mines [Montet, 112]), or a local goddess peculiar to the area of Serabiṭ el-Ḫadem on the Sinai peninsula. However, the fact that these miners were Semites, plus the fact that *qdš* was the Semitic goddess having a clear connection with serpents, point strongly to a relationship between the Serpent Lady and *qdš*.

67. It seems likely that the group of people at the mines was made up of Semitic miners (perhaps Hyksos captives -- see Albright, *PSI*, 12-3, 20; cf. Beit-Arieh, 48), Egyptian

overseers and guards, and probably Egyptian slaves, craftsmen, and merchants.

68. These are texts nos. 351 and 353, both originally located at the entrance to Mine L (*PSI*, 19-22). For a (color) photo of Mine L, see Beit-Arieh, 45.

69. This is text no. 361, originally found near Mine N (*PSI*, 25).

70. This is text no. 360, originally located at a cairn on a ridge (*PSI*, 14, 24-5).

71. See Albright's translations of the inscriptions (*PSI*, 16-30), especially nos. 351, 353, 360, 361.

72. Cf. Albright's comment: "In view of the prevalence of venomous serpents in Sinai, it would be very strange if particular reverence were not paid to the serpent-goddess" ("Early Alphabetic Inscriptions," 17-8). Also, cf. the previous discussion (in the main body) of the prayers directed to *qdš* on Louvre Stele C.86, and Stadelmann's remarks (139-40).

73. The equation Baᶜlat = Hathor in the inscriptions is also made by Albright (*PSI*, 12). Cf. Beit-Arieh, 48.

74. *PSI*, 2, 16.

75. Of interest in this connection is where the inscriptions with *bᶜlt* were located: three were in the Hathor temple (nos. 345, 346 a-b; partially restored in 347 a; *PSI*, 16-7), one in the camp of the Egyptians (no. 365 a; *PSI*, 26), and only one near an entrance to a mine (L; no. 349, *bᶜlt* partially restored in line 3; *PSI*, 18-9). All the Serpent Lady inscriptions, as already mentioned, were situated outside of the temple and camp.

76. Thus, the "Lady" in Serabiṭ el-Ḫadem was not necessarily the Semitic city goddess of Byblos known as the "Lady of Byblos" (see n. 59 above). The miners may not have had any ties with Byblos, come into contact with the city, or had any reason to name the "Lady (of Byblos)" in their inscriptions (cf. n. 67 above).

77. A slight difference, though, is discernable in the general thrust of the inscriptions naming Baᶜlat and those naming the Serpent Lady. Regarding the former, *bᶜlt* is preceded by an adverb (*l*, "to, for" in nos. 345, 346 a-b, 347 a, 349; [ʾ?]*t*, ["wi]th" in no. 365 a), with the idea in the first four texts of presenting a gift or offering a sacrifice to the goddess (the reading in no. 365 a is only one possibility among several). Instead of speaking about something being done for the Serpent Lady, the inscriptions (nos. 351, 353, 361;

cf. 360) call upon her to do something for her petitioners -- namely, bring a sacrifice. Too much should not be made out of this distinction, however, due to the paucity of texts and data. Also, while I have been "assuming the general correctness" (Albright, *PSI*, 10) of Albright's decipherment, a definite understanding of every aspect of the Proto-Sinaitic inscriptions has yet to be attained.

78. See Chap. 1, text no. 17 and the last section of that chapter.

79. Albright already asked in 1939 "whether the vocalization of the appellative is not *Qudšu*" ("Astarte Plaques," 118 n. 2). Cf. the portion of the main body having n. 60.

80. Edwards, 51; he cites Černý, who "is of the opinion that some of the signs in the inscription betray peculiarities in formation which are characteristic of documents dating from the time of Ramesses III."

81. Edwards, 50. Edwards observes that some inconsistency in the direction of the signs is noticeable, and an inversion occurs in the spelling of "ᶜAnat" (50 n. 15).

82. See Albright, "Some Observations on the New Material for the History of the Alphabet," *BASOR* 134 (1954) 26; Cross, *CMHE*, 34; Edwards, 50-1 and 51 n. 20; Helck, 512-3 n. 145; and Oden, *Studies*, 96-7. Cf. Stadelmann, who holds that Qudšu should not be identified with any one goddess, but rather that she represented a (fertility) cult form of ʾAšerah, ᶜAnat, and ᶜAštart. He bases this conclusion, first of all, on *lqdš ʾaṯrt ṣrm* in *CTA* 14.4.197-8, which he translates "der Heiligkeit der Aṯirtu der Tyrier." Then Stadelmann refers to the "*qdš* goddess" of the Winchester College relief, which, he feels, must be translated in a similar manner. Explaining that the annotation should be understood as "Zeilenspaltung . . . die in Ägypten ja sehr häufig ist," he reads:

	ᶜn.t	Die „Heiligkeit der ᶜAnat"
Qdš		und die
	ᶜstr.t	„Heiligkeit der Astarte."

Thus, Stadelmann takes Qudšu on this relief (and on the other Egyptian reliefs) as the hypostasis of ᶜAnat and ᶜAštart. For Stadelmann, the names "Qudšu" and "ᶜAštart" in Egypt are only two different names for the same divinity; the same holds true for "Qudšu" and "ᶜAnat." This fact was generally known in Egypt, he says, even when Qudšu there seems to have become an independent goddess (112-6; see also 99, 119).

In my opinion, Stadelmann's translation of *CTA* 14.4.197-8 is incorrect (see Chap. 1, text no. 17).

Further, his handling of the Egyptian annotation strikes me as being somewhat forced. See the main body, where other evidence is discussed which can be seen as demonstrating directly or indirectly that in Egypt Qudšu was regarded as a distinct goddess, and not simply as a special form of ᶜAštart and/or ᶜAnat.

83. Černý, 127; also Helck, 499-500 and Stadelmann, 36, 147. Prof. Lambdin has advised me that the name of Baᶜlat is badly damaged, and ᶜAnat's name is oddly written.

84. Helck, 500.

85. Helck, 500. See also Stadelmann, 104-5. ᶜAštart was closely associated with Baᶜl in Egypt (see, e.g., Stadelmann, 43, 104).

86. See Donald B. Redford, "New Light on the Asiatic Campaigning of Ḥoremheb," *BASOR* 211 (1973) 37, 43-6. Redford has a good discussion of the worship of ᶜAštart, ᶜAnat, Rešep, and Qudšu in Egypt (43-6). He himself argues that the accession year of Horemheb was 1353 B.C. (49).

87. Redford comments that the title "'lady of the stars of heaven'" is unknown elsewhere as a designation of Qudšu, "but in view of the astral connexions of goddesses of this type, the epithet is appropriate. Qodsha is elsewhere called *ḥnwt nṯrw*, 'mistresss [*sic*] of the gods,' and the present title may simply be a variant of this" (46).

88. Redford, 37.

89. Helck, 497. See n. 20 above.

90. This is the White Crown with two plumes, from the side seen as one plume on the front and one on the back of the crown. Sometimes it also has a pair of horns at the base. See Budge, 2: 131 and the drawing on pl. facing 2: 136.

91. She is thus depicted as a war goddess.

92. Stadelmann, 119.

93. Helck, 496; Stadelmann, 95.

94. Stadelmann, 95.

95. Stadelmann, understanding Qudšu to be ᶜAnat's cult form as fertility goddess (n. 82 above), sees in this stele a conscious connection between ᶜAnat and Qudšu (119), an opinion with which I am in disagreement.

96. See and compare Stadelmann's treatment of this stele (108).

97. This and the preceding translation are Prof. Lambdin's.

98. For an Egyptian in Memphis, according to Stadelmann, "Qudšu" and "Hurrian ᶜAštart" were only different names for the same goddess; thus the parallel listing of Qudšu next to ᶜAštart on the stele (108). This explanation I find somewhat artificial. Why not simply understand the inscription as addressing two goddesses with essentially identical petitions? Stadelmann's supposition certainly involves an element of redundancy on the part of Ptah-ankh (twice requesting ᶜAštart for life and health).

99. See, conveniently, Stadelmann, 91-6, and Helck, 494-7; cf. the shorter description of Oden, *Studies*, 85-6. The earliest clear indications of the worship of ᶜAnat in Egypt date from the Nineteenth Dynasty, when as a war goddess she joined the group of "royal divinities" (Stadelmann, 91, 135; Helck, 494; however, see also Stadelmann, 20, where he mentions names with the element ᶜ*nt*, which were probably those of *Unterfürsten* of the Hyksos in southern Palestine and perhaps also in the East Delta). She, as ᶜAštart, too, was presented as a daughter of Re and mate of Seth-Baᶜl. Apparently Ramesses II had a special preference for ᶜAnat: not only did he call his mares and war dog after the goddess, and name his favorite daughter *bty* [*banti* ⟶ *batti*] -ᶜ*nt*, "Daughter of ᶜAnat," but he probably also built a temple or at least a small shrine for ᶜAnat in Pi-Ramesse (Černý, 127; Helck, 496; Stadelmann, 91-2, 94-5). There, two groups of statues of ᶜAnat and Ramesses have been found. In the first group, only the body of the goddess (without the head) to the knees is preserved. Still, one can recognize that she wore a long, transparent garment. In the second group ᶜAnat, wearing the atef crown and a long transparent garment, sits next to Ramesses, with her right hand on the shoulder of the king (Stadelmann, 91-2; Helck, 496). She is represented on a fragment of a relief wearing the atef crown, swinging a club in her raised hand, protecting the cartouche of Ramesses II (Stadelmann, 95). While Ramesses III fought against his enemies ᶜAnat and ᶜAštart were "a shield for the king," and parts of the royal chariot were compared to ᶜAnat (Stadelmann, 95, 106). ᶜAnat is a great war goddess in the Magical Texts, who repulses the angry demons in battle. Together with ᶜAštart she combats the sickness demon *smn* (Stadelmann, 95). On Egyptian "folk religion" ᶜAnat did not have a deep influence (Helck, 496); only a few monuments of private persons which attest the worship of ᶜAnat are preserved (Stadelmann, 95-6). One is the already-discussed BM 646. A small votive stele of an Egyptian official in Beth-šan dates from the time of Ramesses III. Again wearing the atef crown, the goddess in this representation holds a scepter and sign of life. In a short offering prayer the dedicator asks for "life,

welfare and health" (Stadelmann, 96). Stadelmann explains that the stele exemplifies the religious concept of the New Kingdom that the *Landesgottheiten* in their own region were able to give the most effective help. According to Helck, after the time of Ramesses IV (ca. 1151-1145) an assimilation of ᶜAnat to Hathor may be detected (496).

100. See, conveniently, Stadelmann, 101-10; Helck, 490-2 (cf. 492-4 with Stadelmann's discussion); and the briefer description of Oden, *Studies*, 75-6. The earliest evidence for the worship of ᶜAštart in Egypt dates to the Eighteenth Dynasty. As a war goddess, ᶜAštart was a "royal divinity" (Stadelmann, 135), being connected with the "new" weapon -- the chariot. In the reign of Amenophis II (ca. 1436-13) she was thought of as a riding goddess, and her epithets included "Lady of the Horse Teams," a conception which continued to the time of the Ptolemies, when she was regarded as "Lady of the Horses and Chariots" (Stadelmann, 101-2). Yet preserved representations of the riding ᶜAštart first come out of the time of Tuthmosis IV (ca. 1413-1405). Generally, the stelai picture ᶜAštart on horseback, either nude or clothed, wearing the atef crown, brandishing shield and club, spear, and/or bow and arrows (Stadelmann, 103-4). It is not always easy to distinguish between the riding ᶜAštart and the riding Rešep, who in Eighteenth Dynasty Egypt was also connected with horses (and chariots), especially when the representation is partially ruined and the annotation is missing. However, in the time of the Ramessides Rešep as a war god receded into the background, while Seth-Baᶜl, the god of the new dynasty, stepped into the foreground. Now the riding ᶜAštart displaced almost entirely the riding Rešep (Stadelmann, 57-8, 61). Ramesses II called at least one of his sons after the goddess, and several proper names compounded with her name were current (Wiedemann, 150-1; Stadelmann, 105). A number of stelai have her standing (often with weapons) (Stadelmann, 104, 109). On an Abu Simbel stele from the end of the Nineteenth Dynasty ᶜAštart -- wearing the atef crown, holding a scepter and the sign of life -- is shown with Amen-Re, Nut, Re-Harakhte, and Seth-(Baᶜl) (Stadelmann, 106). The goddess possessed a cult place in or very close to the temple of Ptah in Memphis, which led to her becoming the "daughter of Ptah"; elsewhere she was also known as the daughter of Re (Černý, 127; Helck, 490; Stadelmann, 69, 127-8). In the "Astarte Papyrus" ᶜAštart is designated as daughter of Ptah (Stadelmann, 127). She was, furthermore, a "folk divinity," because Amenophis III (ca. 1405-1367) was believed to have twice been wonderfully healed by "Ištar of Nineveh," undoubtedly a statue or cult picture sent to him by the King of Mitanni when he learned about the Pharaoh's grave illness. The report of this healing spread throughout Egypt, with the

result that the dwellers of the Nile Valley turned to ᶜAštart with petitions for healing from sickness or for a pleasant life with health, since "Ištar of Nineveh," generally called the "Hurrian ᶜAštart," was recognized as a local form of ᶜAštart (Černý, 128; Stadelmann, 106-7). ᶜAštart was assimilated to Sakhmet and represented in the form of a woman with the head of a lion (still being named "ᶜAštart") in Edfu (Stadelmann, 104; Budge, 2: 278-9).

101. I base this assertion on my reading of Helck and Stadelmann. In the "Astarte Papyrus" (see Stadelmann, 125-8), the Memphite god Ptah corresponds to the Canaanite deity ᵓEl, while Nut as the mother of the deities (i.e., Osiris, Horus, Seth, Isis, and Nephthys), is Ptah's wife/consort, paralleling ᵓAšerah (Stadelmann, 127). At Memphis, the chief center of his worship, Ptah's wife was Sakhmet. Both Nut and Hathor were considered to be the sky goddess; their personalities often were blended together. Likewise, during the course of the myriad assimilations in Egyptian religion, Hathor, as the "Eye of Re," was identified with Sakhmet. As already stated, Qudšu at Memphis (a center of her worship in Egypt) had as one of her titles "whom Ptah loves," which has led to the suggestion that Qudšu was viewed there not only as the daughter of Ptah but perhaps also as his wife/consort (see n. 39 above). I found no evidence of this epithet being applied to either ᶜAštart or ᶜAnat.

102. Albright, *ARI*, 75; *YGC*, 130; Helck, 495; Stadelmann, 108; Wiedemann, 150. The entire passage reads: ". . . the mouth of the wombs of ᶜAnat and ᶜAštart was closed, the two great goddesses who conceive, but cannot bring forth; they were closed by Horus, but opened [?] by Seth" (translation of Prof. Lambdin).

103. Helck thinks that this "knowledge" was limited only to a small circle of the magicians, having no place in the folk religion (496).

104. One recalls that in the extant Ugaritic mythological texts children are not attributed to ᶜAštart, and if ᶜAnat is described as having a child (*CTA* 5.5.18-22 is usually cited in this connection), the testimony is unclear at best (she is on occasion designated as a wet nurse). In the *Phoenician History* (see Chap. 2) ᶜAštart does produce offspring, but ᶜAnat (if "Athena" = ᶜAnat) is not reported as having given birth. Both the Ugaritic epics and the *Phoenician History* (assuming that "Rhea/Dione" = ᵓAšerah/ᵓElat), of course, make plain the fact that ᵓAserah had progeny.

105. Cf. Stadelmann, 108-9, who says, regarding the papyrus passage (n. 102), that the Egyptians were puzzled by the fact that ᶜAštart and ᶜAnat, although consorts of Seth (Baᶜl), had no children.

106. Anson F. Rainey, "Notes on Some Proto-Sinaitic Inscriptions," *IEJ* 25 (1975) 114-5, and pl. 12B; and Rainey, "Some Minor Points in Two Proto-Sinaitic Inscriptions," *IEJ* 31 (1981) 92, 93 fig. 1, and pl. 16A.

107. See Cross, *CMHE*, 15-6.

108. See the photo and discussion of Beit-Arieh, 46, 48. Note also Albright's decipherment and translation of text no. 363 (*PSI*, 26).

109. Cross, *CMHE*, 19; Albright, *PSI*, 13.

110. *PSI*, 24-5. Albright restores *ḏ ṯb* in text no. 351: [*ḏ ṯb ʾt*] *ḏt bṯn* . . . , "O Merciful One, with the Serpent Lady . . . " (*PSI*, 19-20).

111. Cross has proposed to read Proto-Sinaitic text no. 347, *tnt*, "Tannit," an epithet of ʾAšerah discussed in the next section (*CMHE*, 32). Presently, however, I lean toward the suggested translation "gift," understanding *tnt* to be either an infinitive of Canaanite *ytn/ntn* -- *tintu* (at Sinai there are both assimilated and unassimilated *nuns*) -- or the form *tinatu* from the same verbal root. See *CMHE*, 19 n. 41; 32 and 32 n. 119; also *PSI*, 17, 32.

112. Portraying the goddess as nude, of course, was for the ancient Near Eastern worshipper in no way a sign of disrespect, but rather a celebration of the deity's sexual aspects. See Seibert (33-40), who explains that, concerning anything related to coition and reproduction, there "was no prudishness because . . . everything concerning sex seemed natural and, therefore, decent to man in the ancient Orient" (40).

113. See the portion of the main body having n. 60.

114. E.g., see Michael C. Astour, "Ugarit and the Great Powers," in *Ugarit in Retrospect* (ed. Gordon D. Young; Winona Lake, In.: Eisenbrauns, 1981) 5-6; John Bright, *A History of Israel* (3rd ed.; Philadelphia: Westminster, 1981) 53, 82; Gardiner, *Egypt of the Pharaohs*, 132-3; Raphael Giveon, "Some Egyptological Considerations Concerning Ugarit," in *Ugarit in Retrospect*, 56-8; William W. Hallo and William Kelly Simpson, *The Ancient Near East* (New York: Harcourt Brace Jovanovich, 1971) 247; Stadelmann, 9-10.

115. Stadelmann makes basically the same assumption (10-1).

116. Stadelmann, 10-1, 143; see also Černý, 124-5.

117. Montet, 110.

118. The phrase is Cross's (*CMHE*, 31).

119. D. R. Ap-Thomas's comment is appropriate: ". . . [the Lady of Byblos] might even have been Asherah, who, as Asherat-yam, 'She who walks the sea', would obviously have a high claim on the veneration of a sailor community -- not to mention some of her other characteristics" ("The Phoenicians," in *Peoples of Old Testament Times* [ed. D. J. Wiseman; Oxford: Clarendon, 1973] 270).

120. See Chap. 2.

121. *De Dea Syria*, 6: "'I did see, however, in Byblos a great sanctuary of Aphrodite of Byblos . . . The market, however, is open to foreigners only and the payment becomes an offering to Aphrodite'" (*SGAL*, 12-5).

122. For ᶜAštart's frequent identification with Aphrodite see Oden, *Studies*, 80-1 and 80 n. 170.

123. See App. C.

124. Prof. Cross has reminded me of an alternate way to handle the "conflict": to point out that Lucian was writing at a late period, by which time there could have been a fusion of the deities (ᵓAšerah, ᶜAštart). Lucian simply may have gone to his main female deity, Aphrodite, to identify this (compound) goddess of Byblos.

125. Evidence coming from a number of Phoenicio-Punic sites and from different centuries will be examined in the discussion of the main body. It is, I think, highly probable that the knowledge of what the majority of religious signs stood for was widespread among those practicing Phoenicio-Punic religion, and that this knowledge was passed on to succeeding generations. In my opinion, most of these emblems (which appear so frequently on the stelai and other objects) thus consistently signified the same thing throughout the years and in the various localities.

126. *tnt* first appears in the Punic sphere on Carthaginian stelai which may date as early as the sixth century B.C., but more likely should be placed in the fifth century. Cf. *KAI* 2: 77, 90; Lawrence E. Stager and Samuel R. Wolff, "Child Sacrifice at Carthage -- Religious Rite or Population Control?," *BAR* 10 (1984) 35, 38; and Yigael Yadin, "Symbols of Deities at Zinjirli, Carthage and Hazor," in *Near Eastern Archaeology in the Twentieth Century* (ed. James A. Sanders; Garden City, N.Y.: Doubleday, 1970) 216-7. *bᶜl ḥmn* is attested as early as the seventh century B.C. (Stager and Wolff, 38). The famous "sign of Tannit" (to be discussed) is evidenced in the Punic world "possibly from the fifth century, but certainly from the fourth century B.C. onwards" (M. Dothan, "A Sign

of Tanit from Tel ᶜAkko," *IEJ* 24 [1974] 45 and 45 n. 5). Cf. Donald Harden, who says that the sign does not seem to occur in the West "much, if at all, before the fifth century B.C." (*The Phoenicians* [Harmondsworth, Middlesex, England: Pelican Books, 1971] 80).

127. See, e.g., the statement of Francis W. Kelsey (made in 1925), quoted by Pritchard, *Sarepta*, 106. Cf. Sabatino Moscati, who, while affirming that this goddess had possible Oriental antecedents (being, as he holds, the equivalent of ᶜAštart), allows for "noticeable local components, such as the name, which might be the result of the Libyan environment" (*The World of the Phoenicians* [trans. Alastair Hamilton; London: Weidenfeld and Nicolson, 1968] 138).

128. Pritchard, *Sarepta*, 20, 107; Yadin, 218. See *KAI* 2: no. 53.

129. *Sarepta*, 20.

130. Pritchard, *Sarepta*, 107. See *KAI* 2: no. 81.

131. For a good discussion of Tannit signs found in the East see, conveniently, Oden, *Studies*, 147-8; Oden in turn cites (146 n. 190) the excellent summary of Dothan, 46-7.

132. See John Wilson Betlyon, *The Coinage and Mints of Phoenicia* (HSM 26; Chico, Ca.: Scholars Press, 1980) 121 and the references cited by Betlyon. In 1914 George Francis Hill published a coin from Ascalon (*Catalogue of the Greek Coins of Palestine* [Catalogue of the Greek Coins in the British Museum 27; London: British Museum, 1914] lix-x, 129 no. 187; pl. 13.18) almost certainly exhibiting the sign of Tannit, with what is the image of a goddess and the name ΦΑΝΗΒΑΛΟΣ (Dothan, 46), the Greek equivalent of *pn bᶜl*. This coin, however, dates to 132/3 A.D.

133. Elisha Linder, "A Cargo of Phoenicio-Punic Figurines," *Archaeology* 26 (1973) 182-4, 186-7. The figurines are "standing, hooded female figures wearing either a chiton or peplos; the right arm is lifted in a gesture of benediction, while the left is held bent against the breast" (Linder, 184). Cf. photos of similar Carthaginian figurines in Jean Ferron's *Mort-Dieu de Carthage* (Text and Plates; Collection Cahiers de Byrsa Série Monographies 2; Paris: Librairie Orientaliste Paul Geuthner, 1975).

134. Linder, 184-6. Linder writes: "Now, for the first time, the sign appears stamped on the base of a female figure which, I strongly believe, represents Tanit herself, and which leaves little room to doubt that a direct connection exists between the goddess and the symbol" (186).

135. Linder, 186-7.

136. "Les fouilles de Sarepta," *Bible et terre sainte* 157 (1974) 7-9 and 7 fig. 7; *Sarepta*, 107-8, and 108 fig. 104. Pritchard comments that the molded disk could have been an insert for a ring or other ornament.

137. Pritchard assigns the glass object to no specific century(ies), but the general background of the pertinent portions of his discussion seems to be this rather lengthy period: *Sarepta*, 77, 147; cf. "Les fouilles," 7.

138. A. Vanel, "Six *ostraca* phéniciens trouvés au temple d'Echmoun, près de Saïda," *Bulletin du Musée de Beyrouth* 20 (1967) 45-8; 76; pl. 1; Dothan, 46 n. 12; Pritchard, *Sarepta*, 107 and 107 n. 12.

139. Pritchard, *Sarepta*, 104-6 and 104 fig. 103; Stager and Wolff, 50. See above, Chap. 2, n. 73. The inscription begins with *hsml*, "The statue/image . . ." Since in Phoenician there is a feminine form of the noun -- *smlt* -- which apparently was used when the statue was that of a female, Pritchard reasons that the image referred to by the ivory plaque represented a male (*Sarepta*, 105). Pritchard speculates that the material used for the statue had been wood, because of the well-documented fashion of inlaying wood with ivory, and because nothing of the image itself remains (*Sarepta*, 105).

140. As indicated in Chap. 2, I lean toward the first understanding of *tntʿštrt*. Pritchard holds out both interpretations as possibilities, but feels that the second "is more probable," because "there is an implied conjunction between the two divine names. The dedication is to Tanit (and) Ashtart, both of whom were served at the same shrine" (*Sarepta*, 107).

141. *Sarepta*, 147.

142. For some reason, explains Pritchard, the small original shrine was later replaced by a larger one (*Sarepta*, 139). The walls on the north and east sides were moved outward from the lines of the earlier building so as to enlarge considerably the area of the room of the shrine. Judging from the votive objects coming from the *favissa*, it seems that the cult at the shrine(s) was carried on principally by women, who performed their acts of devotion to the goddess or goddesses giving them the blessings of conception and successful parturition (see Pritchard, *Sarepta*, 139-46; cf. 148).

143. *Sarepta*, 147.

144. Pritchard, *Sarepta*, 147-8. Pritchard admits there is a remote possibility that the votive statue to which the ivory label was attached had been brought from elsewhere and deposited in the shrine (148). Nevertheless, he thinks it is more likely that the shrine in which the plaque was found was that of *tntʿštrt*, a deduction which is surely correct.

145. Pritchard, *Sarepta*, 107.

146. See Cross, *CMHE*, 24-36, especially 28-35, and the references provided thereat.

147. *CMHE*, 25. Having recognized in 1967 that the epithet *baʿl ḫamōn/ḫamān*, applied to ʾEl, meant "Lord of [Mount] Amanus," Cross equates the element *ḫmn* with *ḥmn* in the epithet *bʿl ḥmn*, due to the merging of *ḥ* and *ḫ* (> *ḥ*) (*CMHE*, 26-7).

148. *CMHE*, 29-34.

149. *KAI*, no. 81.

150. *CMHE*, 30. In addition, see above and in Chap. 2 concerning the Sarepta inscription reading at the end *l tntʿštrt*.

151. *YGC*, 42-3 n. 86, 129-30, 134-5; Cross, *CMHE*, 31.

152. RS 24.252, lines 6-7 (*Ug 5*, 551).

153. The usual name of Tannit in the first centuries of the modern era was *Caelestis*. It was by this adjective taken substantively that the Latins designated the goddess (of Phoenician origin) who was the principal divinity of the second Carthage and who received homage in all of North Africa, especially in the regions where the Carthaginian civilization was implanted. In the Roman epoch this *Caelestis* was also called *Virgo Caelestis* and *Iuno Caelestis* ("Juno" itself was another name by which Tannit was known). Several African dedications have been found addressed to *Iuno Caelestis* (Stéphane Gsell, *Histoire ancienne de l'Afrique du nord*, vol. 4, *La civilisation carthaginoise* [Paris: Hachette, 1920] 261-2; cf. Harden, 79).

154. II.4.2-6; cf. Herodotus I.105.

155. See Cross, *CMHE*, 31, and the discussion which comes subsequently in this chapter. Albright's comparing of epithets is not conclusive proof for equating Tannit with ʿAnat. *Caelestis*'s designation as *Virgo Caelestis* was relatively rare (Gsell, 261-2). There is, furthermore, a way to reconcile Tannit's being identified as ʾAšerah with *Caelestis*'s (Tannit's) being called *Virgo Caelestis* (explained in the next paragraph of main body). Objectively speaking, *darkatu*, "dominion" (see n. 307

below), could apply to ᶜAnat, ᶜAštart, or ᵓAšerah (Cross, *CMHE*, 31), as could *baᶜlatu šamêmi rāmīma* and *Caelestis*, "[lit.] Heavenly." The lunar crescent, solar disk, and stars, for example, were very much a part of the iconography of Qudšu. One also recalls that in Egypt all three goddesses were called "Lady of Heaven."

156. "Rhea" was one of ᵓAšerah's designations in the *Phoenician History* (Chap. 2).

157. Cross, *CMHE*, 32 and the references cited.

158. Cross, *CMHE*, 32 and the reference cited.

159. *CMHE*, 32-3.

160. Cross, *CMHE*, 24; 33.

161. This matter will be taken up again in n. 198 below.

162. Among the least satisfactory are that the sign is a deformed ax, or an altar topped by a star (Gsell, 381, 387; Gsell himself stands behind the latter proposal).

163. Gsell, 381.

164. For more viewpoints, see Magdeleine Hours-Miedan, "Les représentations figurées sur les stèles de Carthage," *Cahiers de Byrsa* 1 (1951) 26-31 and Colette Picard, "Genèse et évolution des signes de la bouteille et de Tanit à Carthage," *Studi Magrebini* 2 (1968) 77-80, 84-7. Also note the additional references and comment in Oden, *Studies*, 141 n. 162.

165. Gsell, 378.

166. Cf. Moscati's "L'origine del 'segno di Tanit,'" *Atti della Accademia Nazionale dei Lincei* (Rendiconti della classe di scienze morali, storiche e filologiche) series 8, vol. 27 (1972) 371-4 and pls. 1-3.

167. *Studies*, 141.

168. *Studies*, 141 n. 164.

169. *Studies*, 141. Oden's fig. 3 (*Studies*, 160) is apparently holding her breasts; however, I see the Tannit sign figure as holding her arms and hands out from her sides, as will be explained in the main body.

170. Tannit signs may be seen throughout the figures and plates of Anna Maria Bisi's outstanding *Le Stele Puniche* (Studi Semitici 27; Rome: Istituto di Studi del Vicino Oriente, Università di Roma, 1967), but see, conveniently, fig. 7. Another superb collection of photographs of Punic stelai exhibiting Tannit signs (and other Punic

religious symbols) is contained in the Plates volume of André Berthier and René Charlier's *Le sanctuaire punique d'El-Hofra à Constantine* (Plates and Text; Paris: Arts et Métiers Graphiques, 1952, 1955).

171. E.g., a caduceus: Bisi, pls. 26.2,3; 27.3; 29; Berthier and Charlier, pls. 4.A; 6.A; 25.D; 42.D (arm lowered); 43.B; two caducei: Bisi, pl. 26.1; two caducei "tops": Bisi, fig. 7.1. Other objects which are held include a wreath (Bisi, pl. 34), crescent (Berthier and Charlier, pls. 5.C; 9.A), caduceus and palm branch (Berthier and Charlier, pl. 12.A), and caduceus and trident-like object (Berthier and Charlier, pl. 25.A; see Bisi, p. 109 and fig. 73).

172. Cf. Bisi, pls. 25.1, 27.2, and 28: the figures, which show a neck, are midway between a lifelike representation of a clothed standing female and the more schematized Tannit sign.

173. E.g., Bisi, fig. 7.e, f, k; pls. 26.2,3; 29.

174. E.g., Bisi, figs. 40 (central portion of stele), 7.b, c, d, n, p.

175. The Qudšu type certainly has the natural, comfortable position for arms held out at the sides, especially when the hands are grasping objects.

176. Helck, 499.

177. Helck, 499.

178. N. 11 above.

179. Bisi points out that nudity of divine female figures is almost completely absent on the African stelai, but, of course, customary in the Syro-Palestinian and Near Eastern area in general (129-30). Note, however, her discussion of a nude Qudšu-like figure from Saint-Leu (the ancient Portus Magnus).

180. Linder's assessment (n. 134 above) that the figurines represent Tannit herself is, in my opinion, correct. I understand these hooded figures, with the right arm raised in a gesture of benediction and the left held against the breast, as another (perhaps later) "type" commonly used for representing the goddess.

181. The region is located in central Tunisia, between Dougga (or Thugga), Kef (Sicca), and Maktar (Bisi, 117), south and west of ancient Carthage (see the map of Gilbert Picard, *Carthage* [trans. Miriam and Lionel Kochan; New York: Frederick Ungar, 1964] 181). In the following discussion, which relies heavily on Bisi's *Le Stele Puniche*, 113-8, attention will be directed initially

to two stelai, pls. 30.2 and 31 of that work, which are very typical of the stelai from the Ghorfa. Cf. the drawings of twelve stelai of the Ghorfa (including the stelai seen in Bisi, pls. 30.1,2 and 31, and Moscati, *Phoenicians*, pl. 25) in F. Du Coudray La Blanchère and P. Gauckler, *Musée Alaoui* (Catalogue des Musées et Collections Archéologiques de l'Algérie et de la Tunisie 7; Paris: 1897) pls. 18-19. For further information concerning stelai from the Ghorfa region see the reference in Bisi, 117 n. 292. All these stelai are now in various museums of Europe and Africa (Bisi, 117).

182. Bisi, 113-5. Cf. Moscati, *Phoenicians*, 130.

183. Bisi, 115-6. Cf. Moscati, *Phoenicians*, 130-1.

184. Bisi points out that these stelai offer "the most evident example of the *interpretatio graeca* of Punic theology" (116).

185. Bisi, 116-7. Cf. Moscati, *Phoenicians*, 158-61.

186. Bisi, 117. There apparently is a bust of Tannit Caelestis in one pediment (pl. 30.2), an eagle (the bird connected with the chief god) in the other (pl. 31); cf. the pediment in pl. 30.1, which seems to have a dove (Bisi, 117 n. 293). Another stele has in the pediment, according to Bisi, a human head with cow ears, "a distant reminiscence of . . . Hathoric typology" (Bisi, 117 n. 293).

187. Cf. Bisi, 117. The head of the sun, sending out rays, is to the (viewer's) right of the intertwined snakes and head, a head surmounted with a crescent (= the head of the moon) to the left (Bisi, 117).

188. Bisi describes the image as "a figure with a legless triangular body but with a perfectly human head" (117).

189. Bisi, 117-8.

190. Bisi, 118. On the stele of pl. 30.2 Aphrodite is accompanied by a winged Eros; both hold an arm on a lit altar which presumably indicates the necessity of sacrifice in order to promote natural fecundity (Bisi, 118).

191. Cf. Bisi, 117-8. The circular indentations in the upper portion of the stelai may have been inserted with gilded studs, symbolizing stars (Gilbert Picard, *Le Monde de Carthage* [Paris: Buchet/Chastel, 1956] 185 pl. 77; see also pl. 78, and cf. his discussion of the stelai of the Ghorfa, p. 79).

192. The close relationship between this figure on the stelai of the Ghorfa and, e.g., the figures mentioned in n. 172 above and those seen on the stelai of Bisi, pl. 26.2, 3 and pl. 29 (n. 173) is easily seen. Picard also

recognizes the Ghorfa figure as the "sign of Tannit" (*Monde de Carthage*, 79).

193. Bisi is of like judgment, stating that "this strange image . . . must be considered as a hypostasis of Tanit, and . . . evidently derives from an anthropomorphization of the homonymous idol, according to that process of transformation already in progress on certain Punic stelai" (118).

194. Cf., e.g., *ANEP*, 162 fig. 469 (first two figurines); 163 fig. 473; and 164 fig. 474. Two stelai of the Ghorfa -- nos. 744 and 745 of La Blanchère and Gauckler, pls. 18-19 -- have more abstract representations of the Tannit figure (the image of no. 744 is very similar to the one on the stele seen in Bisi, pl. 25.1). Their figures have arms in a position resembling the horizontal piece of the Tannit signs. Cf. also no. 748 (Moscati, *Phoenicians*, pl. 25). These two stelai (nos. 744 and 745) indicate, in my opinion, that the horizontal element of the Tannit sign is in fact a schematization of the more natural, realistic position (V shape) seen in the other Ghorfa stelai and the Qudsu type.

195. The triad arrangement of these stelai (Dionysius, Tannit, Aphrodite) is somewhat reminiscent of the triad scenes (Min, Qudšu, Rešep) of the Egyptian monuments, older by more than a millennium.

196. To my surprise, Bisi regards this figure as Mercury with the petasus and wings at his feet ("Mercurio con petaso e ali ai piedi"; 118). I disagree completely. The figure is definitely that of a female: she has feminine breasts, hips, and genital area (no phallus). Further, according to my observations of the photo, she is standing on a small, rectangular platform, and beside each of her lower legs is a dove, although these are quite faint in the photograph, especially the one beside her right leg (cf. pls. 30.2 and 31). I do not see the "petaso e ali ai piedi."

197. The figure (as also the clothed Tannit figures on the other two stelai) does not have the Hathor wig or slender braids which were noted previously, but a change in hair style is to be expected after so long a period of time and due to various cultural influences. She does not wear a headpiece (as did Qudšu in several Egyptian depictions); however, right above her head is a lunar crescent turned upward around a rosette, which certainly recalls the crescent and disk headpiece of some of the Egyptian examples. Finally, although the grapes and pomegranate were not seen on the Qudšu plaques, pendants, and stelai of the Late Bronze and Iron Periods, the concept they express, as already mentioned, is identical to a number of the objects held by the goddess in the older representations.

198. Gsell, with his understanding of the sign (n. 162 above), holds that it did not appertain exclusively to Tannit but also to Baᶜl (389-90). Hours-Miedan is of a similar opinion (27, 30). Gsell refers to: a) a Carthaginian stele (*CIS*, Pars Prima, no. 435) on which the circle of the sign is replaced by the word *bᶜl*; b) another stele (*CIS*, Pars Prima, no. 436) where the sign is flanked by a *tav* on one side and a *bet* on the other; and c) stelai with the sign and dedications addressed only to Baᶜl Ḥamon or to *Saturnus*. None of these examples convince me that the sign necessarily pertained also to Baᶜl. Concerning the first stele, the scene may simply have been an attempt to illustrate the goddess's full title, "Tannit face of Baᶜl." The artist of the second stele, in planning to present the divine pair, perhaps chose to take the main emblem of the dominant deity, placing at its sides the *tav* and the *bet*. The stelai showing the goddess's sign and dedications to the male deity could be interpreted as including the emblem for the sake of completeness (/inclusiveness): while attention was directed chiefly to Baᶜl, Tannit was not to be ignored altogether.

199. The caduceus, one such symbol, will be discussed fully in the next section.

200. E.g., *CIS*, Pars Prima, nos. 2086, 2734, 3406; Moscati, *Phoenicians*, pl. 37.

201. E.g., Moscati, *Phoenicians*, pl. 18 (stylized; also Bisi, pl. 26.3); *CIS*, Pars Prima, no. 3252.

202. Hours-Miedan mentions stelai of Carthage having representations of ships or barques (whose real-life counterparts were probably used for religious functions); a number of these vessels carry the Tannit sign (67-8). There are Carthaginian coins which show on one side the head of a goddess with dolphins (see, e.g., L. Müller, *Numismatique de l'ancienne Afrique* [3 vols.; Copenhague: Bianco Luno, 1860-2] 2: 78 no. 40), with dolphins and Tannit sign (Müller, 2: 77 no. 32), with a dolphin and a caduceus (Müller, 2: 76 no. 26), and with dolphins and a scallop shell (Müller, 2: 76 no. 14). Müller thinks that the goddess is Ceres (the goddess has corn ears in her hair), but it is more probable, in my opinion, that Tannit, the chief deity of Carthage, is being pictured. See G. K. Jenkins and R. B. Lewis, *Carthaginian Gold and Electrum Coins* (London: Royal Numismatic Society, 1963) 11-2. On one side of another Carthaginian coin (Müller, 2: 76 no. 17) appears the head of a goddess wearing a cap shaped as a sea shell, who very possibly is Tannit (Müller identifies her as Venus [2: 75]).

203. E.g., *CIS*, Pars Prima, nos. 240, 363, 1261, 1573, 1737, 3029.

204. E.g., *CIS*, Pars Prima, nos. 335, 797, 968, 974, 2485, 3333. Oden puts the matter nicely: ". . . a fruitful tree is an ideal symbol of the mother goddess ᵓAšerah/Tannit. Hours-Miedan's study ["Les représentations," 45] of the Punic palm tree concludes that the palm carries a clear 'allusion à la fécondité' because it almost always bears bunches of fruit; and there is no more appropriate candidate for this allusion than the 'Creatress of the gods' ᵓAšerah" (*Studies*, 154).

205. E.g., Bisi, pls. 30.2 and 31 (stelai of the Ghorfa); fig. 44.

206. E.g., Moscati, *Phoenicians*, pl. 55 (*CIS*, Pars Prima, no. 3000); Picard, *Carthage*, 158 pl. 81 (a stele from the Ghorfa).

207. Cross, *CMHE*, 35.

208. See also Cross, *CMHE*, 34-5 and 34-5 nn. 133-4.

209. E.g., *CIS*, Pars Prima, no. 2122, and the stele to the left of no. 3029.

210. E.g., Berthier and Charlier, pls. 5.C; 9.A (a small disk is atop the head of the Tannit sign, just below the crescent); cf. Hours-Miedan, pl. 6.e (the circle of the sign perhaps serves as both head and solar disk).

211. Berthier and Charlier, pl. 25.C.

212. E.g., Hours-Miedan, pl. 6.b, c (head and crescent actually touching), f, g, j.

213. E.g., Hours-Miedan, pl. 6.a, h.

214. E.g., Bisi, pl. 15.1. See also pl. 32.1. Perhaps the inscription found at Athens, containing the name ᶜ*bdtnt*, relates in part to these stelai (nn. 209-214). Actually a bilingual inscription, the Greek translation renders the Semitic name Ἀρτεμιδώρος (Gsell, 248; Yadin, 218). This substitution of "Artemis" for "Tannit" may indicate that the latter was regarded as a moon goddess. It should also be remembered that an alternate title of Tannit was *Caelestis*.

215. The reference work used here is that of Alfred Merlin, *Le Sanctuaire de Baal et de Tanit près de Siagu* (Notes et Documents 4; Paris: Direction des Antiquités et Arts, 1910).

216. As noted by Cross, *CMHE*, 35. See especially 35 n. 136.

217. Merlin, pl. 6.2.

218. One figurine is that of a woman nursing a child (Merlin, pl. 4).

219. Merlin, pl. 3.1 (a color photo of the statue is provided by Stager and Wolff, 48). Pl. 3.2 shows a very similar lion-headed figure without the lower legs.

220. Always in the background, too, is ʾAšerah's/ʾElat's designation as the mother of a "pride of lions" in the Ugaritic literature.

221. N. 101 above.

222. Oden makes a good case for understanding the upraised hand to signify Baʿl Ḥamon (*Studies*, 142 and 142 nn. 168-9), but I would modify his proposal somewhat by not limiting the symbol only to that god.

223. Thus the arm-hand could be described as a "flexible" symbol. Oden mentions stelai on which the emblem could reasonably be assigned to Baʿl (see previous note) and below (n. 227) examples will be given where I think Tannit is the natural choice. Yet one should not try to be overly precise, and without specific written explanations from the original worshippers themselves a certain interpretation regarding the arm-hand motif on many (if not all) the stelai is impossible.

224. On two of the terra cotta figures the Tannit sign "was replaced by a beautiful representation of a dolphin" (Linder, 186), strengthening the association of these statuettes with Tannit.

225. Bisi, fig. 39.

226. Bisi, fig. 36.

227. Possible examples for such an interpretation are the upraised hand from which come two lotuses (Bisi, fig. 49; *CIS*, Pars Prima, no. 861); the arm-hand on one side of a Tannit sign, a caduceus on the other (Bisi, pls. 19.2, 20.1; Berthier and Charlier, pls. 21.A, C, D; 22.A; 24.C; and many other stelai); the Tannit sign in the hand (*CIS*, Pars Prima, nos. 300, 618); the upraised hand flanked by two Tannit signs and two caducei (*CIS*, Pars Prima, no. 620); the hand flanked by two caducei (*CIS*, Pars Prima, nos. 756, 779, 2204); the upraised hand in the trunk of a palm tree bearing date clusters and flanked by two caducei (*CIS*, Pars Prima, no. 2465); the hand flanked by a caduceus on one side and a Tannit sign on the other (*CIS*, Pars Prima, nos. 3273, 3282, 3312); the hand flanked by two doves (*CIS*, Pars Prima, no. 3320); the hand in a Tannit sign (*CIS*, Pars Prima, nos. 2633, 3687); etc.

228. Examples of this unification include the top of a caduceus appearing as the head of a sign (*CIS*, Pars Prima, nos. 523, 712, 943, 2578) and the sign's triangle enclosing a caduceus (*CIS*, Pars Prima, nos. 2118, 2228,

3009). On *CIS*, Pars Prima, no. 3083 the top of a caduceus appears as a sign's head, while the caduceus's vertical support is enclosed by the sign's triangle. See also Oden, *Studies*, 143 and 143 nn. 173-4; in n. 174 are listed scenes of two Tannit signs atop the ends of "strings" coming from the caduceus.

229. E.g., Berthier and Charlier, pls. 5.B; 15.A; 21.A, C; Bisi, pl. 29.

230. E.g., Berthier and Charlier, pls. 3.B; 4.A; 6.A; Bisi, pl. 19.2.

231. E.g., Berthier and Charlier, pls. 3.B; 4.A; 6.A; 9.A; 14.B; 21.A; 22.A, B; 24.A; 41.A; Bisi, pls. 19.2; 20.1; 21.2.

232. *Studies*, 143-4, 149-155.

233. *Studies*, 152.

234. *Studies*, 152 n. 212.

235. I did not see any fruit pods in the examples cited by Oden, nor in my examination of the Punic stelai. *CIS*, Pars Prima, no. 823 does show two pod-like shapes () coming from a caduceus (and not at the end of the "ribbons"/"strings" which are also shown), which I understand to be unopened lotus blossoms.

236. Helpful sources of information about the date palm (*Phoenix dactylifera*), used in this and the following paragraphs of the main body, are V. H. W. Dowson's *Dates and Date Cultivation of the ʾIraq* (3 parts; Agricultural Directorate, Ministry of Interior, Mesopotamia, Memoir 3; Cambridge, England: Heffer, for The Agricultural Directorate of Mesopotamia, 1921-3); see esp. pt. 1, 1-3; James C. McCurrach's *Palms of the World* (New York: Harper and Brothers, 1960); see esp. xxxii-xxxiv, 162-4; Paul B. Popenoe's *Date Growing in the Old World and the New* (Altadena, Ca.: West India Gardens, 1913); see esp. pl. opposite title page, and pp. 110-3; Popenoe's *The Date Palm* (ed. Henry Field; Miami, Fla.: Field Research Projects, 1973); see esp. 92-3, 239-41; and Hilda Simon's *The Date Palm* (New York: Dodd and Mead, 1978); see esp. 62-3.

237. The flowerstalks (spadices) of *P. dactylifera* can grow to four feet in length, but the trunk can grow to one hundred feet (McCurrach, 163). Several plates in Dowson's *Dates and Date Cultivation of the ʾIraq* show date clusters hanging from palms, as does the title page of Simon's book. A number of Assyrian reliefs have quite realistic depictions of date palms with hanging clusters of dates (e.g., *ANEP*, 128 fig. 367; Simon, 28, 31, 34); so, too, do many Carthaginian coins (see, e.g., Müller, 2: 75, nos. 8, 11; 76, nos. 17, 26; 77, nos. 27, 28,

30-32; 78, nos. 38, 40, 41, 43, 44). Realistic and semi-realistic representations of date palms are, of course, encountered regularly on the Punic stelai: Bisi, figs. 36, 51, 132; *CIS*, Pars Prima, nos. 797, 968, 2119, 2465, 2485, 3318, 3325, 3332, 3333, 3397, etc. Concerning "ribbons" that are too thick, see, e.g., *CIS*, Pars Prima, no. 4569 = Hours-Miedan, pl. 12.f (drawing no. 7 below).

238. E.g., *CIS*, Pars Prima, nos. 3363, 3508, 3555.

239. E.g., Bisi, figs. 49, 53; *CIS*, Pars Prima, nos. 861, 1261, 3163.

240. *Studies*, 154 n. 219.

241. It would be expected that the "strings" would hang past the mid-way point (the date palm has a tall trunk) or to the bottom of the caduceus pole, yet this is most often not the case.

242. E.g., Berthier and Charlier, pls. 9.A; 22.A; 24.C.

243. *Studies*, 153.

244. *Studies*, 153.

245. *Studies*, 153.

246. E.g., a Tannit sign flanked by an upraised hand and caduceus (*CIS*, Pars Prima, nos. 3041, 3042, 3272, 3285); a disk and crescent on one side of a Tannit sign, a caduceus on the other (*CIS*, Pars Prima, no. 3054); the upraised hand flanked by a Tannit sign and caduceus (*CIS*, Pars Prima, nos. 3282, 3312); etc.

247. Bisi, fig. 13.

248. *Studies*, 153.

249. Bisi, pl. 27.2; Berthier and Charlier, pls. 5.C (sign holding crescent); 27.C (a lion below); 37.C; 41.C (a crescent above). Cf. Berthier and Charlier, pls. 11.B (a caduceus above a Tannit sign) and 14.C (a caduceus below a Tannit sign).

250. *CIS*, Pars Prima, no. 2166.

251. Berthier and Charlier, pl. 26.A.

252. *CIS*, Pars Prima, no. 1308.

253. *CIS*, Pars Prima, no. 1441. One notices that the upper portion of the caduceus is quite unlike the top of a palm tree. Oden explains, as already noted, that it "seems likely . . . the caduceus' 'disks,' which can

number from one to five, grew out of the disk-shaped bulb beneath the fronds of the palm tree" (*Studies*, 154 n. 219). Yet this "bulb" is not seen, or is not obvious on many realistic and semi-realistic representations of the palm on Punic monuments. I question why this was the feature chosen for emphasis on the caduceus, if the caduceus is a stylized palm tree. Also, the topmost element of the symbol is too often "open" (not completely closed), with the tips of both curves frequently turned outward, to be readily taken as a "disk." It might have been expected that the palm branches (technically leaves), such a dominant and beautiful aspect of the tree, would somehow have been represented in the symbol. These branches, however, except for a few which are vertical, curve outward from the trunk in a shape which is just opposite that of the upward curves of the topmost element of the caduceus. In my opinion, images which could more easily be labeled as stylized palm trees are seen on two stelai from El-Hofra (Berthier and Charlier, pls. 20.A and 22.C) and especially on a Carthaginian coin (Müller, 2: 98 no. 220). Cf. Bisi, fig. 12; also André Lemaire, "Who or What Was Yahweh's Asherah?," *BAR* 10 (1984) 48 (central drawings).

254. Such is also the opinion of Berthier and Charlier (Text, 184-5) and Bisi (204). I do not agree with Harden, who states that the caduceus "has nothing in common except the name with the Greek and Roman symbol of Hermes/Mercury" (80). Besides also showing two serpents on a staff, representations of the god's caduceus, except for the wings, at times noticeably resembled some forms of the caduceus appearing on the Punic stelai. See, e.g., the caduceus beside Mercury on a Roman era coin from Sabrata (Müller, 2: 29 no. 62) and from Leptis Minor (Müller, 2: 49 no. 15). The caduceus did not appear in Carthage before the fifth (Berthier and Charlier, 184, citing Gilbert Charles Picard) or fourth (Bisi, 204) century B.C.; Bisi argues that it was derived from the Greek caduceus at the beginning of the Hellenistic period in the Punic world (204). This is unlikely in my opinion, especially since Bisi also thinks that once the caduceus was adopted in the Punic realm it became the emblem of Baᶜl Ḥamon. The earliest mention of Tannit in the West, after all, is on stelai which probably do not date before the fifth century. Further, although some Greek influence on the form of the Punic caduceus cannot be theoretically ruled out altogether, such influence is far from certain. Near Eastern examples of emblems consisting of a staff- or pole-like object topped by a symbol are well known in the first half of the first millennium. Cf., e.g., "the weapon of Aššur" (see Morton Cogan, *Imperialism and Religion: Assyria, Judah and Israel in the Eighth and Seventh Centuries B.C.E.* [SBLMS 19; Missoula, Mont.: Scholars Press, 1974] 53 and 62-3 figs. 1-2). Bisi herself notes the resemblance between the Carthaginian caducei

and images appearing on Assyro-Babylonian *kudurrū* and seals already in the second millennium (204). At least by that same millennium, moreover, serpents/snakes as symbolic creatures had an important role in Near Eastern religion.

255. Perhaps this is more accurately described as an "abbreviated" form, one showing only the upper bodies of the serpents, and not the portions which would have fallen alongside the staff/pole.

256. Interestingly, the Late Bronze pendant from Minet el-Beida (n. 14 above; drawing no. 1 below) shows two serpents, with raised upper bodies on each side of Qudšu (and heads pointing in opposite directions), "crossing" behind the goddess's hips, so that their lower bodies descend in an undulating manner, each along the side of Qudšu opposite the one flanked by the upper body.

257. Several striking examples may conveniently be found among the photographs of stelai from El-Hofra provided by Berthier and Charlier; the reader is invited to page through these plates and see for himself/herself. In addition, see Bisi, pl. 34 and especially pl. 29, where not only does the upper side of the caduceus to the viewer's right particularly resemble a serpent, but also undulating serpents' bodies apparently are emerging from behind the "shoulders" of the Tannit sign and descending, one along each side of the sign. Berthier and Charlier's plates volume, it should be mentioned, is a handy reference for noting the differing forms the caduceus could take, from the realistic to the more abstract and/or simplified.

258. Cf. the intertwined necks of the mythical creatures on the side of a slate palette from Hierakonpolis depicting the triumph of King Narmer (*ANEP*, 93 fig. 297). The palette dates to ca. 3100 B.C.

259. The following is only a brief description of four of the main forms as I see them. Not every "intertwined" caduceus pictured on the recovered Punic stelai would, of course, match precisely one of these four, and a number appear to be a blend of two of the forms.

260. E.g., Berthier and Charlier, pls. 3.B; 9.A; 22.A (drawing no. 6 below); 24.C.

261. E.g., Berthier and Charlier, pl. 7.A; *CIS*, Pars Prima, nos. 463, 4351, 4569 = Hours-Miedan, pl. 12.b, e, f. For Hours-Miedan, pl. 12.f, see drawing no. 7 below. Cf., e.g., pl. 9.A of Berthier and Charlier and no. 463 of *CIS* (Pars Prima).

262. Perhaps these are better understood, as explained in n. 255, as showing only the upper bodies of the serpents.

263. E.g., Berthier and Charlier, pls. 4.A; 6.A; 25.A, D; 37.C; Bisi, pls. 26.2, 27.3 (drawing no. 8 below).

264. E.g., Berthier and Charlier, pls. 20.A; 24.B (drawing no. 9a below); Bisi, pl. 20.1 (drawing no. 9b below); *CIS*, Pars Prima, no. 4363 = Hours-Miedan, pl. 12.h. Cf. Bisi, pl. 43.2.

265. E.g., Berthier and Charlier, pls. 5.C (drawing no. 10a below); 24.A; Bisi, pls. 21.2; 26.3 (drawing no. 10b below); 27.2.

266. E.g., Berthier and Charlier, pl. 17.C (drawing no. 11a below); *CIS*, Pars Prima, nos. 689 (drawing no. 11b below), 3285 (cf. no. 3265), 3432 (caduceus to viewer's left). Cf. Berthier and Charlier, pl. 40.C; also Bisi, pl. 44 (caduceus to viewer's right).

267. E.g., Berthier and Charlier, pls. 7.D; 27.C (drawing no. 12 below); 38.A; cf. Bisi, pl. 32.2.

268. E.g., *CIS*, Pars Prima, no. 2235 (drawing no. 13 below).

269. E.g., Bisi, pl. 25.1 (drawing no. 14 below). Cf. Berthier and Charlier, pl. 6.C; also *CIS*, Pars Prima, no. 463 = Hours-Miedan, pl. 12.b. For a caduceus which exemplifies both the previous note and this note, see Bisi, fig. 94.

270. Par. 33 (*SGAL*, 44-5).

271. See Stocks, pl. 1.1, 5 (Oden, *Studies*, 160 figs. 2 and 1), and Oden, *Studies*, 110-5. Cf. the caduceus in Bisi, pl. 25.1 (drawing no. 14 below) and the σημήιον pictured in Stocks, pl. 1.5.

272. Such is the conclusion of Oden (*Studies*, 149-55), although he interprets the Punic emblem in a different manner.

273. E.g., Berthier and Charlier, pls. 13.C; 21.A, C; Bisi, pl. 19.2. Cf. Berthier and Charlier, pl. 15.A.

274. As was surely the case for those strings/streamers which were tied on at a point farther down the pole. See, e.g., Bisi, fig. 36; *CIS*, Pars Prima, nos. 554, 4266 = Hours-Miedan, pl. 12.i, d.

275. Concerning those portrayals of the caduceus with "strings" having blossoms (or, e.g., Tannit signs: Bisi, fig. 52) at their ends, these are "combination" images, and it is possible that the "strings" were understood to be strings/streamers (as those just discussed), the stylistic means of connecting emblems, lotus stalks, or even the lower bodies of the serpents.

276. A similar comparison could be made between images of two lotus blossoms connected with the Tannit sign and Qudšu figurines having the goddess holding lotus stalks.

277. Berthier and Charlier, pl. 27.C (drawing no. 12 below). Cf. pl. 27.A, where an animal, apparently either a lion or a ram, is beneath a Tannit sign and a caduceus (to the sign's left). Toward the top of the stele is a crescent and disk. Conceivably, the "anvil" shape which is occasionally pictured beneath the triangle of the Tannit sign (e.g., Bisi, fig. 7.a, c, d, e, j, o, s) may stand for a lion; on the other hand, it may represent a pedestal.

278. *ANEP*, 163 fig. 471 (drawing no. 2 below).

279. One recalls that Tannit's full title (used continually on stelai at Carthage) was "Lady (*rbt*) Tannit, face of Baᶜl." At Ugarit, the title "Lady" was used almost exclusively of ᵓAṯirat: "Lady ᵓAṯirat of the Sea" (an exception is *CTA* 16.1.36-7, *rbt špš*, "Lady Šapaš"). From Carthage comes an inscription mentioning the ". . . priestess of our *rbt*," two stelai designating Tannit simply by her epithet *rbt*, and the theophoric name *ᶜbdrbt* (Gsell, 239 and 239 nn. 7-8). However, at Carthage ᶜAštart, too, was called a *rbt* (n. 149 above). Cf. also Gsell (235-6) for occurrences in the Punic inscriptions of *ᵓlt*, which may be references to ᵓElat. One of these (*CIS*, Pars Prima, no. 149; *KAI*, no. 172), discovered at Sulcis in Sardinia, speaks of a temple being built *lhrbt lᵓlt*, perhaps "for the Lady, for ᵓElat." The principal goddess at Sulcis was Tannit; thus Tannit may have also been called "ᵓElat."

The Punic names with *tnt* as an element, coming from Carthage and Sardinia, occur relatively rarely in the extant inscriptions. They are: *ᵓštnt*, *bdtnt*, *ᶜbdtnt*, and *ᶜztnt*. See Benz, 429-31; Gsell, 241 n. 9, 264; and Harden, 79 and 226 n. 92.

280. Cross has noted that an epithet of ᶜAštart found at Ugarit in the fourteenth century and Sidon in the fifth, *šm bᶜl* (*CTA* 16.6.56; restored in 2.1.8; *KAI*, no. 14, line 18), "name of Baᶜl," is "semantically equivalent" to the *panê baᶜl* used of Tannit. These epithets, he explains, "belong to a general development of hypostases of deity in Canaanite religion" (*CMHE*, 30).

281. Cf. Moscati, *Phoenicians*, 138-9.

282. Paul G. Mosca, in his dissertation "Child Sacrifice in Canaanite and Israelite Religion" (Ph.D. diss., Harvard University, 1975), states that Baᶜl Ḥamon is mentioned in virtually every complete Punic inscription discovered in a sacrificial precinct, from the seventh century B.C. to the Neo-Punic era. Tannit, the Carthaginian (as opposed to Punic) deity *par excellence*,

appears in the Punic sacrificial inscriptions at a time corresponding exactly to the period of Carthaginian supremacy (fifth-third centuries B.C.). The goddess "is completely absent from the earliest inscribed stelae -- even those from Carthage -- and is mentioned only sporadically in the latest [Christian Era] inscriptions. It was Baal Hamon who was and remained the great Punic god, the head of the Punic pantheon, and it was primarily to him that children were sacrificed" ("Child Sacrifice," 99).

283. Stager and Wolff, 33-4. Not every urn had a marker (Stager and Wolff, 36).

284. Stager and Wolff, 35. A full treatment of child sacrifice at Carthage is beyond the scope of the present discussion. For such, see Mosca, "Child Sacrifice," esp. 36-116 (Mosca deals with all the Phoenicio-Punic evidence); Lawrence E. Stager, "I. The Rite of Child Sacrifice at Carthage," *New Light on Ancient Carthage* (ed. John Griffiths Pedley; Ann Arbor: University of Michigan, 1980) 1-11; and Stager and Wolff, esp. 38-51.

285. Stager, "Rite," 4; Stager and Wolff, 40.

286. The exact numbers and percentages are given by Stager, "Rite," 5 table 1.

287. Stager, "Rite," 4-5. Stager adds that when inscribed stelai were set up to mark the urn burials, they recorded the genealogy (often at some length) of the dedicants, who likely were the parents of the interred child or children found in association with the stone ("Rite," 5).

288. Stager, "Rite," 7.

289. Stager, "Rite," 5 table 1; Stager and Wolff, 40.

290. Stager, "Rite," 3; Stager and Wolff, 32.

291. Stager, "Rite," 3.

292. Cf. Stager, "Rite," 4; also Stager and Wolff, 44.

293. Stager and Wolff, 44.

294. Stager, "Rite," 3.

295. Stager and Wolff, 40-1. Inscriptions on the Carthaginian precinct's monuments demonstrate that the most frequent reason for child sacrifice was the fulfillment of a vow (Stager and Wolff, 44). A typical inscription is provided by Stager and Wolff: "'[1] To our lady, to Tanit, the face of Baᶜal [2] and to our lord, to Baᶜal Hammon [3] that which was vowed (by) [4] PN

son of PN, son of PN [5] Because he [the deity] heard his [the dedicant's] [6] voice and blessed him'" (45). Aside from the religious context, Stager and Wolff plausibly suggest that child sacrifice at Carthage may have served a less obvious function: regulating population growth (50-1; also Stager, "Rite," 7).

296. Mosca, "Child Sacrifice," 37-48; Moscati, *Phoenicians*, 142; Pritchard, *Sarepta*, 106-7.

297. Mosca, "Child Sacrifice," 54, 97-8.

298. Mosca, "Child Sacrifice," 98. Mosca notes that the author Quintus Curtius (fl. ca. 50 A.D.) reports that child sacrifice, performed in ancient Tyre, had by 332 B.C. been discontinued there for many years and was rejected by the elders; also, that the founders of Carthage had imported the rite directly from the mother country ("Child Sacrifice," 8-9, 27). Indirect evidence for child sacrifice in Phoenicia is provided by passages throughout the Hebrew Bible: see Mosca, "Child Sacrifice," 117-240, and Stager and Wolff, 31-2. Cf. also the *Praeparatio evangelica*, 1.10.44 (*PBPH*, 60-3).

299. Mosca, "Child Sacrifice," 98.

300. Mosca, "Child Sacrifice," 27, 98.

301. Louvre Stele C.86; see above.

302. Tannit is mentioned at Ibiza, where she had a rock shrine according to a Neo-Punic inscription of the second century B.C. (*KAI*, no. 72 B; Moscati, *Phoenicians*, 241; cf. Harden, 39). Votive half-length figures of a deity identified by Spanish archaeologists as Tannit were discovered at the location of this sanctuary (Harden, 192). The figures, according to Harden, "are not only Punic in dress and attributes, but basically so in physiognomy as well." Tannit, as Juno Caelestis, was worshipped in mainland Spain, where she had a wide-spread cult (Moscati, *Phoenicians*, 241). Under the Roman emperor Septimius Severus (193-211 A.D.), who came from North Africa, Tannit was given a temple on the Capitoline Hill in Rome (*KAI*, 2: 90).

303. The following basically builds on the discussion of Cross, *CMHE*, 30-1.

304. The pertinent passage is II.4.2-6. I use here the translation of C. H. Oldfather (*Diodorus of Sicily I* [LCL; London: William Heinemann, 1933] 358-61).

305. Lucian mentions the goddess in his *De Dea Syria* (14): "I saw a likeness of Derketo in Phoenicia, a strange sight! It is a woman for half its length, but from the

thighs to the tips of the feet a fish's tail stretches out" (*SGAL*, 20-1). See Oden, *Studies*, 69-72; on pp. 69-70 Oden provides the sources making certain the identification of Atargatis with Derketo. Ovid, too (*Metamorphoses* 4.44-7), relates a tale of a goddess *Derceti* who becomes a fish (Oden, *Studies*, 72).

306. Diodorus says, regarding Derketo's body changing into that of a fish: ". . . it is for this reason that the Syrians to this day abstain from this animal and honour their fish as gods" (II.4.3). That Derketo was so firmly linked to water and fish is not surprising, since Ascalon was a seacoast city.

307. "Derketo" is most likely to be derived from the Ugaritic *darkatu*, "dominion" ($\sqrt{drk}$, "to tread"). Credit for the Semitic etymology goes to Albright (see Oden, *Studies*, 71, and the references cited thereat). "Dominion" also occurs in connection with ʿAnat (see main text above and n. 155). Another abstract term used as an epithet of ʾAšerah is, of course, *qudšu*, "holiness." William H. Propp ("The Goddess ʾ*Aṯiratu* and the Israelite Asherah" [Senior Honors thesis, Harvard University, 1979] 13) makes a noteworthy alternate proposal, suggesting that the name, taken from *drk*, "to step, tread," could have been parallel to ʾ*aṯiratu* (from ʾ*ṯr*, "to step, tread, advance"; see Conclusions section below).

308. Hill, *Coins of Palestine*, lviii, 114-37.

309. Hill, *Coins of Palestine*, pl. 13.6, 9, 13, 14, etc.

310. Cf. Hill, *Coins of Palestine*, lviii; see pls. 13.17, 14.3.

311. Cf. Berthier and Charlier, pl. 22.B. The stele shows a triangularly-shaped Tannit sign (the "head" and "dress" are one unit, the "head" being more narrow and pointed), with "arms" extended horizontally at the sides, atop a staff. The triangle standard on the Ascalonite coins could be regarded as a simpler version of the standard represented here. Cf. Bisi, fig. 6 (central image).

312. *Coins of Palestine*, lviii.

313. E.g., Bisi, fig. 112 (*CIS*, Pars Prima, no. 138): a thymiaterion, to the (viewer's) left of which is a Tannit sign and caduceus; pl. 43.1: a female worshipper placing incense in a thymiaterion, above which is a Tannit sign; *CIS*, Pars Prima, no. 3407 (partially preserved): a Tannit sign flanked by two tall thymiateria and two caducei (see Hours-Miedan, 59). *CIS*, Pars Prima, no. 3659 (also broken), shows from (the viewer's) left to right a tall thymiaterion, an upraised hand, a Tannit sign, and a caduceus.

314. Hill, *Coins of Palestine*, lviii, 130-7.

315. Hill, *Coins of Palestine*, lviii; pls. 13.21; 14.8, 12; etc.

316. Hill, *Coins of Palestine*, lix, 115-39.

317. Hill thinks that the figure is probably male, "in spite of the curiously feminine appearance which it assumes on some coins, which show a long skirt and broad hips (e.g., no. 225, Pl. XIV.6)" (*Coins of Palestine*, lx). The feminine appearance is not so curious if Phanebalos is simply admitted to have been a goddess. Albright regards the figure on the coins as "a man-like goddess, with slender uncurved body . . . ," explaining that the "broad hips" mentioned by Hill "seem to indicate a robe caught up at the hips, not the hips themselves" (*YGC*, 129 and 129 n. 48). After examining photos of the coins provided by Hill, Albright's explanation strikes me as being a bit forced.

318. Hill, *Coins of Palestine*, lx-lxi; pls. 13.7, 12, 15; 14.4, 5, 14; etc.

319. Hill, *Coins of Palestine*, lx, 129 (no. 187); pl. 13.18. See n. 132 above. A lead weight has been discovered south of Ashdod-Yam in the Ascalon region, on one side of which is a Tannit sign (Yadin, 229 n. 85).

320. E.g., Bisi, fig. 93 (a Tannit sign flanked by two palm branches); cf. fig. 75, which shows a central image flanked on one side by a caduceus and on the other by a palm branch; Berthier and Charlier, pl. 12.A (a Tannit sign holding in its left "hand" a caduceus, in the right a palm branch); cf. pl. 40.C (apparently a palm branch next to a caduceus).

321. *Aeneid*, I.16-7.

322. See Cross, *CMHE*, 30 n. 100, and Gsell, 256-7.

323. Gsell, 263.

324. Gsell, 277; Müller, 2: 15 no. 30.

325. Berthier and Charlier, pl. 43.B.

326. Berthier and Charlier, pl. 26.B. Cf. the images of battle equipment on stelai from El-Hofra (e.g., Berthier and Charlier, pls. 17.A; 18.A, B, C, D).

327. *CTA* 14 (see above, Chap. 1, text no. 17).

Chapter IV

MISCELLANEOUS WRITTEN AND REPRESENTATIONAL MATERIALS

Chapter 4 will deal with miscellaneous written and representational materials which are, or have been suggested as being, pertinent to a study of ᵓAšerah. The chapter is subdivided according to the geographical locations from which the materials were derived.

Amarna

As is well known, the prince of Amurru named Abdi-Aširta (-Aširti[te], -Ašratum[ti, ta]) is mentioned several times in the Amarna Letters.[1] Such a name, narrowly speaking, evidences the worship of ᵓAšerah in the central Syrian territory during the last half of the fifteenth and first half of the fourteenth centuries B.C. The alternate "Abdi-Ašratum" may be due to the scribe(s) perhaps being under Babylonian influence. Interestingly, the same prince is also called in the letters "Abdi-Ašta(r)ti" and "Adra-Aštarti" (probably "Adra" is a mistake for "Arda" = "Abda"). These variants could again stem from the fact that the scribe(s) possibly was under Babylonian influence (confusing or replacing "Aširtu" with "Aštartu," which corresponded to Babylonian "Ištar").[2] However, they may indicate a confusion or blending of ᵓAšerah with ᶜAštart in the Syrian territory already during the period of the Amarna Letters.

Lachish

The Lachish Ewer, well preserved and dating to the second half of the thirteenth century or first half of the twelfth century (or perhaps slightly later), has the longest and most legible Proto-Canaanite inscription from the period between the Proto-Sinaitic inscriptions (Chapter 3) and the ᵓEl-Khaḍr Arrowheads (to be discussed next).[3] Cross has, in the writer's opinion, put forward the definitive decipherment and translation of the dipinto (which reads from left to right):[4]

mtn . šy[5] l [6][rb][7]ty ᵓlt

"'Mattan.[8] An offering/tribute[9] to my Lady ᵓElat.'"

Presumably the offering or tribute was the decorated ewer itself and perhaps what was contained therein, presented by the Canaanite Mattan to the temple.[10] Thus the inscription not only testifies to the worship of ᵓElat/ᵓAšerah in southern Palestine during the thirteenth/twelfth century B.C., but also apparently indicates that this small temple at Lachish (n. 3), which was possibly founded in the first half of the fifteenth century B.C.,[11] was dedicated in part to the goddess.[12]

ᵓEl-Khaḍr

In 1953 a large hoard of arrowheads was uncovered in a field of ᵓEl-Khaḍr (five km. west of Bethlehem) and scattered among a number of antiquities dealers in Jerusalem and ᶜAmman. Since that time twenty-seven arrowheads belonging to the ᵓEl-Khaḍr hoard have been examined, including five which are inscribed.[13] Based on their type and script the bronze pieces are dated to ca. 1100 B.C.[14] Four of the five inscribed arrowheads bear essentially the same inscription: *ḥṣ ᶜbdlbᵓt*, *ḥiṣṣ ᶜabdlabiᵓt*, "arrow(head) of ᶜAbdlabiᵓt."[15] The fifth reads on the obverse *ᶜbdlbᵓt*, on the reverse ᶜAbdlabiᵓt's patronymic, *bn ᶜnt*, *bin ᶜanat*, "Bin-ᶜAnat."[16] Certain men surnamed Bin-ᶜAnat ("Son of ᶜAnat") are known to have had military connections,[17] and thus it is not surprising that ᶜAbdlabiᵓt ("Servant of the Lion Lady"), probably a member of a company or guild of archers, carried this patronymic.[18]

The Lion Lady is best identified with a war goddess, and Milik understands her to be either ᶜAštart or ᶜAnat,[19] while Cross holds that *labiᵓt(u)* was an old epithet of ᵓAšerah.[20] The reading of *bn ᶜnt* on the fifth inscribed arrowhead (in 1979), one could argue, supports the position that the deity in question was ᶜAnat.[21] However, although ᶜAnat is graphically portrayed as a war goddess in the Ugaritic literature, and her intense interest in the (composite) bow and arrows of the hero ᵓAqhat depicted in *CTA* 17.6 - 19.1, her connection with lions in the Syro-Palestinian realm is rather weak, as is likewise the case with ᶜAštart.[22] Concerning the latter, Milik has mentioned a) ᶜAštart's being assimilated to Sakhmet in Egypt and represented as lion-headed, and b) the fact that lions were associated with Babylonian Ištar (often shown with a bow and spear), who was called *la-ba-tu Ištar*.[23] Yet the goddess having the strongest links with lions in Syria-Palestine was ᵓAšerah/ᵓElat/Qudšu. In the Ugaritic Baᶜl Epic the sons of ᵓAṯirat/ᵓElat are repeatedly called her "pride of lions" (Chapter 1); metal plaques show Qudšu standing on the back of a lion; and the Taanach cultic stand (discussed next) represents Qudšu between two lions.[24] Moreover, Qudšu was pictured standing on a lion's back in Egypt, besides being identified there directly and/or indirectly with Sakhmet. Images of a lion-headed female figure -- Tannit/ᵓAšerah -- have been recovered near the Punic settlement of Siagu in North Africa (Chapter 3). As observed in the previous chapter, there is evidence from various localities and time periods which apparently indicates that ᵓAšerah, too, was regarded as a war goddess. Further, *labiᵓt(u)* parallels *tannittu* > *tannit*, "Serpent Lady."[25] Thus, the Lion Lady could very likely have been ᵓAšerah, and the ᵓEl-Khaḍr arrowheads are probably additional evidence for viewing her in part as a martial divinity, an aspect of ᵓAšerah's character which seems undeniable.

Taanach[26]

In 1968 the Concordia-ASOR excavation at Tell Taᶜannek (ancient Taanach) recovered the pieces of a cultic stand. The pieces were found in a tenth century B.C. silt layer of a collapsed cistern.[27] In reconstructed form, the stand, of poorly fired clay, stands less than two feet high (about 50 cm.).[28] Built up of four superimposed hollow squares, it is open at the base and capped at the top by a shallow basin.[29] The front panels of the squares are in high relief; from each of the lower three protrude the heads of a pair of creatures (at the top corners), whose bodies are shown in relief on the side panels of the square.[30] Of significance is the lowest square's front, which shows a standing nude female figure, perhaps wearing the Hathor wig, whose arms are held out from her sides, seemingly bent downward from the shoulders to the elbows, and upward from the elbows to the hands. In the writer's opinion the representation definitely belongs to the Qudšu type. Flanking Qudšu are two lions: on the front panel appear their heads (teeth bared) and fore-legs, while the side panels have their bodies with hind legs and "flying"[31] tails. This scene on the lowest square therefore evidences both the continued existence of the Qudšu type in northern Palestine into the early first millennium B.C., and probably also the worship of ᵓAšerah at Taanach.

Kuntillet ᶜAjrud

Excavations conducted at Kuntillet ᶜAjrud in 1975-76 (under the supervision of Zeᵓev Meshel) and subsequent publication of findings have shown that this site in the northern Sinai (about 50 km. southeast of Kadesh-barnea) was an Israelite religious center.[32] The remains of only two structures still exist: a main building at the site's western extremity, and a smaller building on the east (of which almost nothing is left).[33] In the west building were discovered Hebrew and Phoenicianizing inscriptions on plaster, pottery vessels, and stone vessels. Furthermore, two large pithoi, besides having inscriptions, were covered with several pictures. Similar decorative elements indicate that the east building was contemporary with the main structure. The pottery and epigraphic evidence suggest that both belonged to a short period dating approximately from the mid-ninth to the mid-eighth centuries B.C.

Although incomplete and difficult to decipher, the inscriptions for the most part seem to be religious in nature.[34] They apparently indicate a syncretistic environment at Kuntillet ᶜAjrud, mentioning, for example, the divine names "ᵓEl," "Baᶜl," and "Yahweh."[35] Of special interest for this study of ᵓAšerah is a Hebrew inscription on the first of the large pithoi having several pictures:

> ᵓmr.ᵓ...h..k.ᵓmr.lyhl...wlywᶜśh.w[l-PN] brkt.ᵓtkm.lyhwh. šmrn.wlᵓšrth.[36]

Apparently, the initial portion is to be translated "X says: Say to *yhl*... and to Yawᶜaśah and [to PN]: . . . "[37] The second portion contains a crux: "I bless you by Yahweh of Samaria [*šomron*] and by his *ᵓšrh*."[38] Proposed translations for *ᵓšrh*[39] include "consort,"[40] "ᵓašerah" (cult object, as many, including this writer, have interpreted *ᵓăšērāh* in certain passages from the Hebrew Bible),[41] "(holy) place," "cella," or "shrine,"[42] and "ᵓAšerah" (the goddess).[43]

Taking *ᵓšrh* here[44] as "(divine) consort" seems to be an ad hoc interpretation (due to the connection with *yhwh*). There is no clear indication in the material examined thus far that the word (= Ugaritic *ᵓaṯrt*) could have this generic meaning, neither does any definite proof come from biblical sources for translating *ᵓšrh* at ᶜAjrud as "consort." Likewise, the writer is of the opinion that there is no biblical backing for the suggested rendering "(holy) place," "cella," or "shrine."[45] However, *aširtu*, "sanctuary," or one of its variants (*ešertu*, *iširtu*, *išertum*) is not uncommon in Akkadian. *ᵓšrt*(/*ᵓšrh*), "(holy) place," "sanctuary" is also attested in Phoenician and probably Aramaic (it does not definitely occur in Ugaritic or Arabic).[46] With regard to viewing *ᵓšrth* as "his [Yahweh's] ᵓAšerah" (= the goddess ᵓAšerah), such an understanding goes against Hebrew syntax, which prohibits the use of the possessive suffix on a personal/proper name.[47]

A number of scholars, it should be mentioned, have referred to the pictures immediately below the inscription on the first pithos, arguing that one, or a combination, of the drawings is evidence for a particular translation. Dever holds that the image on the right -- a seated woman playing the lyre (?)[48] -- is a portrayal of ᵓAšerah, which, he feels, points to the "his ᵓAšerah [= the goddess]" interpretation (despite the syntactical problem).[49] Some view the two standing figures on the left as bovine-like creatures; since the calf may have had a sacred significance in Israel (/Northern Kingdom),[50] they suggest that the figures are linked to the reading "Yahweh of Samaria."[51] Another proposal is that a standing figure paired with the seated woman, or the two standing figures taken together,[52] illustrates "Yahweh (of Samaria) and his consort [or "his ᵓAšerah"]."[53]

In the writer's opinion, making a connection between one or more of the drawings and the inscription is precarious. Such a connection may not, in fact, have existed. These pictures possibly were only "doodlings," or perhaps practice sketches by artists.[54] Also, the larger standing figure, at least, does not seem to have been put on the pithos at the same time as the inscription, since its headpiece is overlapped by the writing in rather ugly fashion. A thin brush was used by the scribe of the inscription (who wrote in fine cursive style), in contrast to the thick brush employed for the awkwardly drawn standing figures.[55] After viewing all the pithoi drawings and inscriptions, the general impression of Beck concerning the latter,

> based mainly on the "stratigraphy" and placement of the inscriptions rather than any analysis of their contents . . . is that they were drawn by different hands than those that applied the drawings to the pithoi and at different times.[56]

Further, two or more artists were responsible for the drawings on the first pithos of the (larger) standing figure on the left (L), the standing figure on the right (R), and the seated lyre player. For example, the elbows of R are sharply angular, whereas those of L are fairly straight.[57]

The legs of R show more definition and "skill" in execution than the corresponding appendages of L. Moreover, R's legs, with feet pointing in opposite directions, join the body in a V shape; L's legs, with both feet pointing to the (viewer's) left, are attached to the body "like an upturned U."[58] Apparently L, overlapping not only R but also the pictures of a cow (L's right foot) and a garland (L's face, neck, right shoulder), was added to the pithos after these drawings.[59] Though Beck thinks certain details reveal the same hand for the drawing of R and the lyre player,[60] the present writer is not totally convinced by the particulars she refers to and is of the opinion that separate artists could have been involved.

In addition, one cannot be sure how to interpret L, R, and the picture of the seated woman playing the lyre. The last perhaps was supposed to represent ᶜAnat,[61] ᶜAštart, a sacred prostitute, a priestess, a queen, or simply a lyre player.[62] The image may or may not have been associated with either of the standing figures. If such an association did exist, its nature remains uncertain.[63] Concerning the drawings of the two standing creatures, is R to be regarded as female, or are both male? Beck has made a good case for understanding L and R as Bes figures.[64] However, as she admits, "the ᶜAjrud representations of the Bes figures is unlike anything known so far in the Levant."[65] Possibly L in particular is an image combining Bes and non-Bes features.[66] Finally, should L's head be regarded as that of a lion(ess)?

The position taken here, then, is that little can be said with assurance about the drawings beneath the inscription, and so they will not be used to help determine the translation of ᵓ*šrth*. There is, accordingly, no decisive reason for, and weighty arguments against, adopting the "his ᵓAšerah [= the goddess]" proposal. The remaining three suggestions are all theoretically possible,[67] but on the basis of the available evidence "his consort" seems to be the least likely. Forced to select either "his (holy) place" or "his ᵓašerah" (cult object), the writer would take the latter (for this and the other ᶜAjrud inscriptions). Aside from the general biblical testimony for choosing such an understanding of the word, certain passages may shed light on the ʾšrh mentioned in the phrase "I bless you by Yahweh of Samaria and by his ʾšrh" at ʿAjrud.[68] ʾAšerahs, as 1 Kgs 14:15 seems to imply, were made in the Northern Kingdom during the reign of Jeroboam.[69] Later, 1 Kgs 16:33 reports: *wayyaʿaś ʾaḥʾāb ʾet-hāʾăšērāh*. One might infer from the verse that this cult symbol was a special, outstanding, and/or well known ʾašerah, undoubtedly because it was made by the king, but perhaps also because it was of particularly splendid appearance, and/or was placed in an important location. Concerning the last inference, a reasonable assumption is that Ahab's ʾašerah was situated in his capital city, Samaria.[70] 2 Kgs 10:25-28 tells about Jehu's attempting to rid Israel of Baʿl worship by slaughtering the Baʿl worshippers who had been lured to the god's temple in Samaria, and by destroying that temple and what was contained therein. Nevertheless Jehu, verses 29 and 31 relate, did not turn away from the sins of Jeroboam; moreover, no specific mention is made of Ahab's ʾašerah being demolished. The cult symbol, conceivably, still remained standing. In fact, 2 Kgs 13:6 could be viewed as giving support to the preceding assumptions (about the ʾašerah's location and preservation), for the verse, in a context describing the reign of Jehoahaz, son of Jehu, states: *wĕgam hāʾăšērāh* [surely Ahab's] *ʿāmĕdāh bĕšōmrôn*.[71] Was ʾšrh of the inscription from the first ʿAjrud pithos a reference to this Samarian ʾašerah?[72]

In conclusion, it is the writer's opinion that ʾAšerah is not mentioned in the material from Kuntillet ʿAjrud. Hence, these inscriptions at most provide only indirect information about the goddess.

Khirbet el-Kom

A few words are in order about Inscription No. 3[73] from Tomb 2 at Khirbet el-Kom,[74] especially the second and third lines. The second line for the most part is clear and usually rendered: *brk . ʾryhu . lyhwh*, "Blessed be ʾUriyahu[75] by Yahweh."[76] The third, unhappily, bristles with problems, and has eluded a completely satisfying decipherment. Indeed, after careful examination, Dever,[77] Lemaire,[78] Naveh,[79] Mittmann,[80] and Zevit[81] each suggest a different solution for this frustrating line. Of interest here is the fact that Lemaire, Naveh, and Zevit, despite disagreeing in their treatment of the initial portion of line 3, read in the central section *lʾšrth*, Lemaire and Naveh translating "by his *ʾšrh*" (thus: "May ʾUriyahu be blessed by Yahweh . . . and by his *ʾšrh*"), Zevit "O Asherata" (thus: "I blessed ʾUriyahu to Yahweh and from his enemies, O Asherata [= ʾAšerah], save him").

The *l*, *ʾ*, *š*, *r*, *t*, and *h* are fairly certain,[82] but exactly how they are to be combined (with each other and/or what precedes and follows in the line) and interpreted is open to question. Suffice it to say that if one would choose the rendering of either Lemaire or Naveh (and the writer does not),[83] what was said about *ʾšrh* in the Kuntillet ʿAjrud material could arguably apply also to the same word so read in this inscription from Khirbet el-Kom. With regard to Zevit's rendering of line 3, the writer, aside from having a different reading for the first portion of the line (n. 83), is not convinced by Zevit's explanation of *lʾšrth*. Zevit proposes that the *h* of *lʾšrth* should be taken "as a *mater lectionis* for a final vowel *ā* marking, in this case, the double feminization of the name *ʾšrt*: **ʾašērátā*."[84] This, however, involves two suppositions which are debatable: first, that the "archaic" or "dialectal"[85] form *ʾšrt* appears here (and at Kuntillet ʿAjrud) instead of the expected *ʾšrh*, and second, that this archaic or dialectal form would have added to it another feminine ending.[86] Thus, while Zevit's proposal is theoretically possible, in the opinion of this writer it is unlikely.

Arslan Tash

A small limestone or gypsum plaque, bearing a main inscription engraved around and between three figures in relief, and three short inscriptions (legends), one on each of the figures, was discovered in 1933 near Arslan Tash[87] by Count du Mesnil du Buisson, who published his find in 1939.[88] Subsequently the plaque has been the object of not a little scholarly interest.[89] Although written in a typical Aramaic script of the early seventh century B.C.,[90] the text's orthography regularly follows its language, which is Phoenician.[91] As Cross and Saley have shown, the inscriptions are Canaanite[92] incantations against demons who go abroad in darkness.[93]

The main inscription, after naming three types of demons (lines 1-5), tells them not to enter the house (lines 5-8), proceeding to give the reason for this command:

(8) ... k{r}
(9) rt. ln. ʾlt
(10) ʿlm ʾšr. krt
(11) ln. wkl bn ʾlm.
(12) wrb. dr kl. qdšn[94]

Albright translates this section of the main inscription, "(for?) the goddess of eternity, Asher(at?), hath made a covenant with us, hath made a covenant with us, and (so have?) all the gods and the chief . . . (?) and all the holy one(s?)";[95] Gaster, "for there hath been made with us a bond everlasting! Ašur hath made (it) with us, governor of the beings divine, and burgomaster of all the holy being[s]";[96] and Cross and Saley, "(9) The Eternal One has made a covenant with us, (10) Asherah has made (a pact) (11) with us, And all of the sons of El, (12) And the great of the council of all the Holy Ones."[97]

The best translation is that of Cross and Saley, for they use prosody to aid in the interpretation of the text.[98] Thus, *ʿlm* parallels *ʾšr* (contra Albright and Gaster), and *wkl* ("and all"; contra Gaster) parallels *wrb* ("and the great"). Of importance for this study is the fact that *ʾšr* most probably is a Hebrew(/Aramaic) isogloss.[99] One would expect in this sort of text the naming of the divine consort of ʾEl (the "Eternal One"),[100] especially since Heaven and Earth (line 13), and Ḥawran/Baʿl Qudš and his wives (lines

16-18),[101] are mentioned. ʾAšerah was, according to Ugaritic mythology, the "Creatress of the Gods," the mother of "seventy [divine] sons" -- and lines 11 and 12 refer to these gods. In sum, the plaque from Arslan Tash may be regarded as testifying to the retention of the memory and worship of ʾAšerah in Upper Syria of the seventh century B.C.

Tyre[102]

A Tyrian coin dating from the reign of Gordianus III (238-244 A.D.) depicts on its reverse a clothed female figure standing in a galley, holding a cornucopia in her left hand, a short scepter in her extended right hand. In the forward part of the ship is a sailor, at the stern a helmsman bends over the rudder, and below the galley is a murex shell. The inscription, in Phoenician, reads *ʾlt ṣr*.[103] The female figure has been identified as Dido,[104] but this is not definite. Since the coin could be showing an ancient Tyrian divinity (cf. n. 104), the writer thinks another interpretation of the inscription is possible, based especially on two phrases parallel to each other from the Kirta Epic (*CTA* 14.4.198-9, 201-2; Chapter 1, text no. 17): *ʾaṯiratu ṣurri-mi* and *ʾilatu ṣidyāni-mi*, "ʾAṯirat of Tyre" and "ʾElat of Sidon."[105] The coin's *ʾlt ṣr*, then, could mean "ʾElat of Tyre"; in any case, there is reason to suppose, in light of the Ugaritic passage and other evidence previously discussed, that the female figure standing in the galley is ʾAšerah.[106] Interpreted in such a manner, the Tyrian monetary piece bears witness to the preservation of the memory (if not the worship) of ʾAšerah in Tyre well into the third century of the Christian Era.[107] Further, the coin, judging from the cornucopia, testifies to her being remembered as a deity of fruitfulness/fertility.[108]

NOTES TO CHAPTER IV

1. *EA* 2: 1555 lists the occurrences.

2. See *EA* 2: 1128-30, 1555.

3. Cross, "The Evolution of the Proto-Canaanite Alphabet," *BASOR* 134 (1954) 17, 19; "The Origin and Early Evolution of the Alphabet," *Eretz-Israel* 8 (1967) 10*. The ewer has been published in Olga Tufnell's, Charles H. Inge's, and Lankester Harding's *Lachish II: The Fosse Temple* (The Wellcome-Marston Archaeological Research Expedition to the Near East Publications 2; London: Oxford University, 1940; hereafter *Lachish II*) 47-54; frontispiece; pls. 51A.287, 51B fig. 287, and 60 fig. 3. Forty-two fragments of the decorated ewer were recovered from the great deposit of rubbish outside the east wall of the temple. A fragment of the ewer's shoulder, though, came from a collection of sherds found on the plastered temple floor. The sherds had been blackened by the fire in the sanctuary, which seems to indicate that the vessel was used in the sanctuary and then thrown onto the rubbish pit not long before the destruction of the temple (*Lachish II*, 47, quoting James L. Starkey). Further, the great accumulation of pottery and especially of broken bowls in and around the temple makes it probable that once the vessels had been used (mainly for purposes of offering) they had to be demolished (*Lachish II*, 25). The temple is estimated to have been destroyed in the second half of the thirteenth century (*Lachish II*, 22-4; cf. David Ussishkin, *Excavations at Tel Lachish 1978-1983: Second Preliminary Report* [Tel Aviv University Institute of Archaeology Reprint Series 6; Tel Aviv: "Achdut" Press, 1983] 169) or first half of the twelfth century (or perhaps slightly later) (Ussishkin, 168-70).

4. Cross, "The Evolution," 19-21; "The Origin," 16*. A summary of previous attempts at decipherment may be found in *Lachish II*, 49-54.

5. The initial sign of the word is *ṯann*, the composite bow. In the fifteenth century *ṯann* was used for *ṯ* and *ś*; by the thirteenth century the shift to *š* had taken place in south Canaanite (Cross, "The Origin," 16* n. 48).

yodh is the only acceptable reading for the second letter of the word (see Cross, "The Evolution," 19 fig. 2, 20).

6. Crcss notes that the "trace is perfect for *lamedh*. The form would be slightly more curved, perhaps, than the one in the text, closer to the Beth-shemesh form" ("The Evolution," 20 n. 16).

7. In "The Evolution," 20 n. 17, Cross convincingly argues for his proposed *rb* (based in part on the Ugaritic literature; see Chap. 1 for *rbt*, "Lady," as a title of ʾAṯirat, who is also called *ʾilt*, "ʾElat"), and suggests vocalizing *rbty* as *rabbōtay* (the so-called plural of majesty, as in Phoenician) or *rabbatiya* (singular, as in Ugaritic). To the reading *lrbty ʾlt* cf. the Punic inscription from Sulcis, mentioned in Chap. 3, n. 279.

8. An alternate rendering could be "A gift" (Cross, "The Evolution," 21).

9. Cf. Hebrew *šay*, "gift, tribute." See Cross, "The Origin," 16* n. 48, and "The Evolution," 21 n. 19; cf. "The Evolution," 20 n. 13 and 21 n. 20.

10. Cross, "The Origin," 16*. Or, Mattan may have only been the maker of the ewer, while the actual presenter of the piece to the goddess remains unknown ("The Evolution," 21).

11. *Lachish II*, 19-22, 24.

12. See *Lachish II*, 24-5. A Qudšu plaque was found in the vicinity of the temple (*Lachish II*, pl. 28.6).

13. Cross, "Newly Found Inscriptions in Old Canaanite and Early Phoenician Scripts," *BASOR* 238 (1980) 4; see also J. T. Milik and Cross, "Inscribed Javelin-heads from the Period of the Judges: A Recent Discovery in Palestine," *BASOR* 134 (1954) 5, and Cross, "The Origin," 13*. The preferred term for the pointed objects is "arrowhead(s)," rather than "javelin-head(s)" (as explained by Cross, "Newly Found Inscriptions," 18 n. 8). Cross theorizes that the arrowheads were the contents of the quiver of a Canaanite archer ("The Origin," 13* n. 33).

14. Milik and Cross, 5-6, 9-15; Cross, "The Origin," 13*-4*, and "Newly Found Inscriptions," 1, 4-7.

15. The second inscribed arrowhead does not have the *ʾaleph*, and the fourth lacks the second *bet* (*ʿbdl<b>ʾt*). For detailed discussion of these variations, and the decipherment, vocalization, and translation of the inscriptions, consult Milik and Cross, 6-8, 11-5; Cross, "The Origin," 13*-4*, and "Newly Found Inscriptions," 4-6.

16. Cross, "Newly Found Inscriptions," 6-7.

17. See Milik, "An Unpublished Arrow-Head with Phoenician Inscription of the 11th-10th Century B.C.," *BASOR* 143 (1956) 3, 5-6, and Cross, "The Origin," 19* and 19* n. 72. The Biqaᶜ Arrowhead has the name Bin-ᶜAnat (*bnᶜn[t]*). One also recalls the mention of *Šamgar ben-ᶜănāt* in Judg 3:31 and 5:6.

18. Cf. Cross ("The Origin," 13* and 13* n. 33; "Newly Found Inscriptions," 7) and Milik (in the article by Milik and Cross [5 n. 1], 6-7; "Unpublished Arrow-Head," 3-6). *ᶜbdlbiʾt* occurs in a Ugaritic census list of archers (*UT* 321.3.38).

19. Milik and Cross, 8-9. Milik comments: "As for the lioness-goddess there is an embarrassing choice between the three chief Canaanite goddesses: *ʾAṯirat*, *ᶜAṯtart* and *ᶜAnat*. The first seems preferable, as she, under the epithet *Qudšu*, is represented standing on a lion in the numerous Egyptian stelae dedicated to her, together with Min and Rašpu, by the workers of the Deir el-Medîneh Necropolis . . . But Asherah is rather mother and fertility-goddess, and in names of bowmen one might perhaps expect a war divinity. Usually ᶜAṯtart and ᶜAnat are characterized as goddesses of war in the Canaanite and Egyptian texts and representations" (Milik and Cross, 8).

20. *CMHE*, 33. Earlier, Cross had equated the Lion Lady with ᶜAnat ("The Origin," 13* and 13* n. 33).

21. Cf. Cross, "Newly Found Inscriptions," 7.

22. See Milik in Milik and Cross, 8.

23. Milik and Cross, 8-9.

24. See Albright's discussion of the name of a princess which appears in the Amarna Letters and which may be "taken from an appellation of the goddess Qudshu (Asherah . . .)" ("Two Little Understood Amarna Letters from the Middle Jordan Valley," *BASOR* 89 [1943] 15-7 and 15 n. 49).

25. Cross, *CMHE*, 33.

26. Previously, ʾAšerah was thought to be mentioned in an Akkadian cuneiform letter (TT 1, from the fifteenth century B.C.) discovered at Tell Taᶜannek, but this reading (*ᵈA-ši-rat*, line 21) must now be discarded. See Anson F. Rainey, "Verbal Usages in the Taanach Texts," *Israel Oriental Studies* 7 (1977) 59.

27. Paul W. Lapp, "The 1968 Excavations at Tell Taᶜannek," *BASOR* 195 (1969) 42.

28. For the reconstructed stand, see Lapp, 43 fig. 29 (black and white photo of front of stand); Albert E. Glock,

"Taanach," *Encyclopedia of Archaeological Excavations in the Holy Land* 4 (ed. Michael Avi-Yonah and Ephraim Stern; Englewood Cliffs, N.J.: Prentice-Hall, 1978) 1142 (color photo showing front and a side of the stand; see also his discussion of the piece, 1147); and A. Reichert, "Kultgeräte," *Biblisches Reallexikon* (2nd ed.; ed. Kurt Galling; Tübingen: J. C. B. Mohr [Paul Siebeck], 1977) 191 fig. 45 (drawing of stand as it was shown in the preceding photo; discussion, 191). A third photo (black and white) appears in Glock's "*Taanach," *IDB* Supplementary Volume (1976) 856.

29. Glock, "Taanach," 1147; Lapp, 42.

30. Lapp, 42. Each side of the topmost square bears the complete relief of a winged beast, which Lapp calls a "griffin" (42, 44).

31. Lapp, 44. Lapp writes that the "crudely formed fingers of the female grasp at the ears of the lions." After examining the photos and picture I prefer to describe the fingers as touching (not grasping) the animals' ears. The next highest square displays a pair of winged sphinxes of female appearance (their hair style resembles the Hathor wig). In the front panel of the third square from the bottom "the traditional scene of two goats [or ibexes?] eating from a stylized tree of life is flanked by a pair of lions, virtually identical with those in the lowest register" (Lapp, 44). The front panel of the topmost square shows in the center a young standing "bovine" facing to the viewer's left, "surmounted by a winged sun disc. The bovine is flanked by what is apparently intended to represent a pair of voluted columns. The columns are flanked by objects which might perhaps represent cultic stands" (Lapp, 44). Lapp thinks that this piece from Taanach might have been used for libation (there is "absolutely no trace of smoke or burning to be associated with its use"), but chooses to refer to the object by "the noncommital designation 'cultic stand'" (44).

32. See Zeʾev Meshel, "Kuntillet ʾAjrud [*sic*]: An Israelite Religious Center in Northern Sinai," *Expedition* 20 (1978) 50-4; *Kuntillet ʿAjrud: A Religious Centre from the Time of the Judaean Monarchy on the Border of Sinai* (Jerusalem: Israel Museum, Cat. 175, 1978); "Did Yahweh Have a Consort?," *BAR* 5 (1979) 24-35; also William G. Dever, "Material Remains and the Cult in Ancient Israel: An Essay in Archeological Systematics," in *The Word of the Lord Shall Go Forth* (ed. Carol L. Meyers and M. O'Connor; Winona Lake, In.: Eisenbrauns, 1983) 571-87; and Dever, "Asherah, Consort of Yahweh? New Evidence from Kuntillet ʿAjrûd," *BASOR* 255 (1984) 21-37.

33. Meshel, "Consort?," 28.

34. With regard to the inscriptions (and pictures), pertinent references in addition to those mentioned above (n. 32) include Debra A. Chase, "A Note on an Inscription from Kuntillet ᶜAjrūd," *BASOR* 246 (1982) 63-7; Dever, "Recent Archaeological Confirmation of the Cult of Asherah in Ancient Israel," *Hebrew Studies* 23 (1982) 37-43; J. A. Emerton, "New Light on Israelite Religion: The Implications of the Inscriptions from Kuntillet ᶜAjrud," *ZAW* 94 (1982) 2-20; Lemaire, "Who or What?," 44-51; Joseph Naveh, "Graffiti and Dedications," *BASOR* 235 (1979) 28-30; and Ziony Zevit, "The Khirbet el-Qôm Inscription Mentioning a Goddess," *BASOR* 255 (1984) 44-7. For further references, see Lemaire, "Who or What?," 51 nn. 4 and 5.

35. I use the word "apparently" because, as Prof. Cross has explained to me, "ʾEl" and "Baᶜl" seem to be in parallel in these inscriptions; thus "ʾEl" may = "Baᶜl." It is unknown if "ʾEl" and "Baᶜl" are distinct from "Yahweh," or if they are alternate designations of Yahweh at Kuntillet ᶜAjrud.

36. For this decipherment cf. Meshel, *A Religious Centre* (unnumbered); "Consort?," 30; and Naveh, 28.

37. Naveh, 28.

38. An earlier proposal had been that *šmrn* perhaps should be rendered "our guardian" (Naveh, 28 and 29 n. 9; cf. Meshel, *A Religious Centre*, and "Consort?," 31), but today the scholarly consensus is that "Samaria" is correct. Aside from the orthographical problem of translating "our guardian" (defective spelling), another ᶜAjrud inscription reads in part *yhwh htmn wʾšrth*, "Yahweh of the South Land and his *ʾašrh*" (private conversation with Prof. Cross, but the translation is my own; cf. Dever, "Recent Confirmation," 37 and 41 n. 3; also Emerton, 2-13). Parallel constructions from cognate languages include, for example, "ʾAṯirat of Tyre" and "ʾElat of Sidon" in the Ugaritic Kirta Epic (*CTA* 14.4.197-206; see Chap. 1, text no. 17), and "Ištar of Nineveh" who was worshipped in Egypt (Chap. 3, n. 100). Moreover, influences from Israel (/Northern Kingdom), as well as from Phoenicia, are clear at Kuntillet ᶜAjrud, being partly seen in the frequent *-yw* (*yaw*) names, the Phoenicianizing inscriptions, certain ceramic vessels, and the Syro-Phoenician background of the artistic motifs (Dever, "Asherah, Consort?," 26, and "Recent Confirmation," 39; Lemaire, "Who or What?," 44-5; and Meshel, "Consort?," 32, 34).

A portion of an inscription on the second large ᶜAjrud pithos with a number of drawings reads: ". . . brktk.lyhwh [ ] wlʾšrth.ybrk.wyšmrk wyhy ᶜm. ʾdny . . .," ". . . I bless you by Yahweh [ ] and by his *ʾašrh*. May He bless and keep you and be with my lord . . ." (for the Hebrew reading and translation cf. Meshel, *A Religious Centre*; "Consort?," 31-2; and Naveh, 28). In the lacuna after *lyhwh* Meshel has restored *tymn*, "Teman" (Dever, "Asherah, Consort?," 32 n. 5; see also Lemaire, "Who or What?," 44).

Zevit, in connection with his study of Inscription No. 3 from Tomb 2 at Khirbet el-Kom (treated in the next section of this chapter), proposes that *ʾšrth* of the Kuntillet ʿAjrud inscriptions is *ʾašērátā*, "ʾAšerata" (the double feminization of the name *ʾšrt*). See the next section.

39. Lemaire ("Les inscriptions de Khirbet el-Qôm et l'ashérah de Yhwh," *RB* 84 [1977] 597-608, esp. 603-8) discusses the first three of the following four proposals with regard to his reading of *ʾšrh* in Khirbet el-Kom Inscription No. 3. He discusses the last three of the following four proposals in his article dealing with both the Khirbet el-Kom inscription and the Kuntillet ʿAjrud inscriptions ("Who or What?," 44-51). Lemaire himself understands *ʾšrh* of Kuntillet ʿAjrud, Khirbet el-Kom, and biblical *ʾăšērāh* to be a cultic object; more precisely, a sacred tree or grove.

40. E.g., Meshel, "Consort?," 31. Meshel holds that *ʾšrh* in this and other ʿAjrud inscriptions could have the generic meaning of a female deity who was Yahweh's consort.

41. E.g., Meshel, *A Religious Centre*; "Consort?," 31. For discussions of the ʾašerah, see, e.g., Emerton, 15-8; William L. Reed, *The Asherah in the Old Testament* (Fort Worth: Texas Christian University, 1949); and Reed, "Asherah," *IDB* 1 (1962) 250-2.

42. E.g., Meshel, *A Religious Centre*; and "Consort?," 31. Dever, "Material Remains," 576, puts forward "Asherah-shrine" as a possibility. Cf. Edward Lipiński, "The Goddess A̱tirat in Ancient Arabia, in Babylon, and in Ugarit," OLP 3 (1972) 101-19, who writes: "The Hebrew words *ʾašērā*, *ʾašērīm*, *ʾašērōt* must be understood in the same sense as the corresponding Akkadian, Phoenician and Aramaic terms which designate the shrine, chapel or sanctuary. It seems that no biblical passage mentions the goddess A̱tirat or her emblem" (116).

43. E.g., Dever, "Recent Confirmation," 37-9; "Material Remains," 576; "Asherah, Consort?," 22-31; Meshel, "Consort?," 31.

44. Mention should again be made of *ʾaṯrty* in *UT* 1002.2.39 (App. B, text no. 4), which could be analyzed as the 1st s. c. suffix on *ʾaṯrt*. However, because the text was so badly preserved, *ʾaṯrty* remained untranslatable.

45. See Emerton, 15-8.

46. See Lipiński, "Aṯirat," 114-6. For Phoenician attestation, note *KAI* no. 19, line 4, and see Richard S. Tomback, *Comparative Semitic Lexicon of the Phoenician and Punic Languages* (SBLDS 32; Missoula, Mont.: Scholars Press, 1978) 36; also Lemaire, "Who or What?," 50 and 51 n. 16. In addition, Prof. Cross has shown me a photograph of an unpublished sherd from ᶜAkko written in Phoenician on both sides. On the side having four lines of writing ᵓšrt, with the meaning "(holy) place," appears in the second line. The sherd dates approximately to the fifth century B.C., and likely should be placed toward the end of that century (see the forthcoming article of Moshe Dothan). For Aramaic attestation, note *KAI* no. 222 B, line 11; also *KAI* no. 260 B, line 3 (ᵓ*trh*); and see Lemaire, "Who or What?," 50 and 51 n. 15.

47. For a fuller treatment of the proposed translations of ᵓ*šrth*, including a discussion of relevant material from Elephantine, see Emerton, 13-8.

48. Meshel, "Consort?," 30, 31; Dever, "Asherah, Consort?," 24; see Pirhiya Beck, "The Drawings from Ḥorvat Teiman (Kuntillet ᶜAjrud)," *Tel Aviv* 9 (1982) 35-6.

49. "Recent Confirmation," 37-9, "Asherah, Consort?," 22-31. Dever thinks that the object on which the woman sits is "the common ancient Near Eastern 'sphinx-throne' of kings and deities" ("Recent Confirmation," 38; see also "Asherah, Consort?," 24-5). This may be correct, but it is conceivable that the piece of furniture depicted was merely a chair. One may ask whether lion- or sphinx-like features were limited only to thrones in the ancient Near East, or if they could appear with other pieces of furniture.

50. Cf. 1 Kgs 12:28-30.

51. E.g., cf. Meshel, "Consort?," 31.

52. The central image -- between the standing figure to the (viewer's) left and the seated woman on the right -- could be female, because of the two circles which possibly indicate feminine breasts (note the same markings on the seated woman). However, cf. Beck, 30-1. The object hanging between the legs of the central image in Beck's reproduction (9 fig. 5.T) resembles more a tail than a phallus. Further, it is questionable whether this object is actually visible on the pithos itself (Beck, pl. 5.2; Lemaire, "Who or What?," photo at top of p. 45). See also Emerton, 10.

53. Cf. Meshel, "Consort?," 31; also Mordechai Gilula, "To Yahweh Shomron and His Asherah," *Shnaton* 3 (1978-9) 129-37 (Hebrew; English summary, pp. xv-xvi). For other drawings on this and the second pithos see the figures,

plates, and discussion of Beck; also Meshel, "Consort?" Both agree that the majority of the artistic motifs at ᶜAjrud were derived from the Syro-Phoenician world.

54. See Beck, 60.

55. Beck, 46. Beck thinks that the inscription was added after both standing figures were already drawn (46).

56. Beck, 47.

57. Beck, 29.

58. Beck, 29.

59. Beck, 36.

60. Beck, 36.

61. Cf. RS 24.245, rev. lines 5-8 (*Ug 5*, 558).

62. See n. 64. Dever has argued forcefully (esp. in "Asherah, Consort?," 21-34; but note his remarks at the bottom of the first column and top of the second column of p. 30) for identifying the seated lyre player as ᵓAšerah, and thus for translating the inscription "Yahweh and his ᵓAšerah [the goddess]," but I still feel that the lyre player does not necessarily represent a goddess (and if it does, that she need not be ᵓAšerah). Should the figure's garments and coiffure, which Dever adduces as evidence for regarding her as a female deity ("Asherah, Consort?," 22-4), be associated only with a goddess? Dever himself points out that the coiffure recalls "the Phoenician style hairdo of . . . the 'Lady-at-the-Window' (a sacred prostitute) depicted on the 8th century B.C. ivories of Samaria, Arslan-Tash, and Nimrud" ("Asherah, Consort?," 23). Also, see above, n. 49. Further, Dever refers to "other clear cultic scenes" ("Asherah, Consort?," 25) on the two pithoi mentioning "Yahweh and his ᵓ*šrh*" ("Asherah, Consort?," 25-9). Yet in my opinion it is uncertain whether all the scenes discussed by Dever (e.g., the lion, the cow suckling her calf) and other scenes on the pithoi (e.g., horses [Beck, 7 fig. 4.A; 9 fig. 5.V; 19; 20-2], a boar [Beck, fig. 4.B; 20] and an archer [Beck, fig. 6.K; 40-1]) have to be viewed, or exclusively have to be viewed, as cultic, and thus question whether this is the only possible interpretation of the lyre player. Nevertheless, granting that the seated female figure is a cultic image, and taking into consideration the general cultic context of the ᶜAjrud finds, which is undisputable, this still would not be conclusive for determining that the lyre player represents a goddess, and more importantly, that the inscription should be connected specifically with this figure. In such a cultic environment the person responsible for the inscription may have been

moved to write "I bless you by Yahweh of Samaria and his ᵓšrh," with no special view, however, simply to the figure of the seated lyre player (if it was already drawn; cf. n. 55 above).

63. Cf. Beck, 35-6.

64. Beck, 27-31. Beck notes that similar to "the cow-and-calf motif [also on this pithos], the lyre player and Bes figures were very popular and widely distributed throughout Western Asia" (36).

65. Beck, 30.

66. Cf. Beck, 30.

67. Although there is no clear external evidence for interpreting ᵓšrth at ᶜAjrud as "his consort," it must be remembered that for most of the ancient Semitic languages the corpus of texts from which vocabulary has been derived is relatively small.

68. The passages will only be cited and briefly examined (without detailed critical treatment). An interesting consideration, as Prof. Coogan has reminded me, is whether ᵓšrth should be translated "its ᵓašerah."

69. Cf. 1 Kgs 14:23, which accuses the people of the Southern Kingdom of making ᵓašerahs during the reign of Rehoboam.

70. Cf. 2 Kgs 21:3, according to which Manasseh made an *ᵓăšērāh* [MT] *kaᵓăšer ᶜāśāh ᵓaḥᵓāb melek yiśrāᵓēl.* The account goes on to say that Manasseh put this ᵓašerah in the Jerusalem temple (v. 7), and, further on (23:6), that Josiah brought this cult symbol out of the temple and burned it. 2 Kgs 18:4 of the MT reports Hezekiah's cutting down *ᵓet-hāᵓăšērāh*, but for text critical reasons I think that the plural ("the ᵓašerahs") is the better reading.

71. The biblical material does not tell of a succeeding Israelite king cutting down this ᵓašerah in the capital. In the climactic condemnation of Israel (2 Kgs 17:7-23), the list of the people's sins includes their making "an ᵓašerah" (v. 16).

72. Theoretically, there might have been other "major" ᵓašerahs in various cities and religious centers throughout Israelite and Judaean territory (cf. 2 Kgs 23:15). The ᶜAjrud blessing which uses the phrase "Yahweh of the South Land and his ᵓašerah" (n. 38) could be understood as invoking the protection of the God who comes from that region (cf. Hab 3:3) on a traveller in the south, and as having issued from a man who worshipped Yahweh in some place other than the South Land (Emerton, 9-10, 12-3, 19). Emerton explains that "the phrase

'Yahweh of Teman' did not denote a deity different from 'Yahweh of Samaria', or perhaps 'Yahweh of Jerusalem' or whatever it was, but the needs of the situation led him to recall the one Yahweh's traditional connexion with Teman when he invoked a blessing on a friend" (13). According to this explanation, the ʾašerah mentioned in the phrase *yhwh htmn wʾšrth* could refer to a specific cult object in Israel (not necessarily in Samaria) or Judah. Or, it could refer to any such cult object, indicating that for the man who wrote this phrase an ʾašerah was always associated with Yahweh and his worship.

While suggesting that the precise meaning of *ʾšrh* in the ʿAjrud inscriptions is "cult object," I wonder how the people as a whole or in part actually viewed the object. It is conceivable, for example, that they may have regarded the ʾašerah (at least in some localities) as the manifestation of ʾAšerah or a related goddess, whom they believed to be the consort of Yahweh. Thus, in the people's minds there could have been, theoretically, an overlapping or blending of "ʾašerah [object]" with "consort."

73. Cross prefers a date ca. 700 B.C. or perhaps slightly later for the inscription; Dever (with whom Albright was in agreement) favors a date in the mid-eighth century. See Dever, "Iron Age Epigraphic Material from the Area of Khirbet el-Kôm," *HUCA* 40-1 (1969-70) 165 and 165 n. 53.

74. The site is located 8.5 miles west of Hebron, 6.5 miles southeast of Lachish, and 6 miles northeast of Tell Beit Mirṣim (Dever, "Khirbet el-Kôm," 140; see 141 fig. 1).

75. ʾUriyahu is mentioned in the inscription's first line.

76. Zevit reads, for the first word, *brkt*, "I blessed," and translates line 2 "I blessed Uryahu to YHWH" (43-4).

77. "Khirbet el-Kôm," 159-62. For photos of Inscription No. 3 see, e.g., "Khirbet el-Kôm," pls. 6B and 7 (pp. 200-1); Dever, "כתובות ממערות-קבורה ישראליות בהר חברון," *Qadmoniot* 4 (1971) 91; Lemaire, "Les inscriptions," pl. facing p. 600; and Zevit, 45 fig. 6.

78. Lemaire, "Les inscriptions," 599-602; "Who or What?," 42-4.

79. Naveh, 28.

80. Siegfried Mittmann, "Die Grabinschrift des Sängers Uriahu," *ZDPV* 97 (1981) 142-4.

81. Zevit, 41-6.

82. Dever ("Khirbet el-Kôm," 159, 161), too, reads these letters, however as *lʾšr th-*. Mittmann incorporates an additional *l* into his rendering: *lʾl šrth* (144). Lemaire ("Les inscriptions," 598-9; "Who or What?," 44) and Zevit (43; 44 fig. 5) read *lʾšrth* at the bottom of this same stone piece from Khirbet el-Kom.

83. I hesitantly offer my understanding of the line, since it is very tentative, but hope that the reader will be stimulated to attempt his/her own reading of the text. After the *waw* at the beginning the line becomes messy. I see next a *mem*, which in its upper portion is somewhat unclear (perhaps the *mem* appearing below and to the right was written by the original or a later scribe for the purpose of clarification). Above and slightly to the left of the *mem* of line 3 an *ʾaleph* seems to have been inscribed, which is followed, in my opinion, by a *ṣade* (on the same level as the *waw* and *mem* and the rest of the line). Reasons for the *ʾaleph* being in the elevated position could be that it was originally omitted (by mistake), or that the letter was written on the same level as the others but then was inadvertently overlapped by the *ṣade*, which took the two horizontals of the *ʾaleph* (a possible vertical stroke for this *ʾaleph* may have been part of a longer scratch on the stone). Whatever, the scribe then wrote the *ʾaleph* in the closest "clear" spot which provided enough room for the letter. The rest of the line I read as *r*, *y*, *h*, *l*, *ʾ*, *š*, *r*, *t*, *h*, *h*, *w*, *š*, *ʿ*, *l*, *h*, grouping the letters *wmʾṣryh lʾšrth hwšʿ lh*, and translating, "and <u>his</u> treasures/stored goods [*pual* or *hophal* ptc. of $\sqrt{ʾṣr}$, which occurs in Biblical Hebrew, though, only in the *qal*, *niphal*, and *hiphel*] belonging to his place. May he save him." Thus, I understand lines 2 and 3 to be saying essentially, "May Yahweh bless ʾUriyahu and the stored goods/treasures of his place. May Yahweh save him."

84. Zevit, 45. Note his accompanying discussion (45-6, and 46 n. 2).

85. Zevit, 46.

86. In his discussion Zevit cites no personal names with this "double feminization" (45-6).

87. This site, roughly fifty miles southeast of Carchemish, was the location in the seventh century B.C. of the Assyrian town Ḫadattu ("New-town" in Aramaic). A 1928 French archaeological expedition, under the direction of F. Thureau-Dangin, excavated at Arslan Tash, clearing the remains of an Assyrian palace built originally by Tiglath-pileser III about 730 B.C. (Albright, "An Aramaean Magical Text in Hebrew from the Seventh Century B.C.," *BASOR* 76 [1939] 5).

88. Albright, "Aramaean Magical Text," 5 and 5 n. 1; Cross and Richard J. Saley, "Phoenician Incantations on a Plaque of the Seventh Century B.C. from Arslan Tash in Upper Syria," *BASOR* 197 (1970) 42 and 42 n. 1; and Gaster, "A Canaanite Magical Text," *Or* n.s. 11 (1942) 42.

89. See the bibliographical references provided by Cross and Saley, 42 n. 2 and 43 n. 3. Javier Teixidor and Pierre Amiet think that this and another plaque from Arslan Tash are a forgery of the 1930s, but I find their arguments unconvincing. See Teixidor, "Les tablettes d'Arslan Tash au Musée d'Alep," *Aula orientalis* 1 (1983) 105-8, and Teixidor's comments in his review of Gibson's *Textbook of Syrian Semitic Inscriptions.* Vol. 3: *Phoenician Inscriptions Including Inscriptions in the Mixed Dialect of Arslan Tash* (*JBL* 103 [1984] 454); also Amiet, "Observations sur les 'Tablettes magiques' d'Arslan Tash," *Aula orientalis* 1 (1983) 109.

90. Cross and Saley, 42; see also Albright, "Aramaean Magical Text," 6-7.

91. Cross and Saley, 42; Albright, "Aramaean Magical Text," 7, 11. Cross and Saley, while pointing out that the orthography of these inscriptions is normally Phoenician (that is, without the use of final vowel letters), list a few Aramaisms appearing in them (48).

92. The Phoenician article, Cross and Saley explain, is not used in the four poetic inscriptions, "even where it might be expected in Phoenician prose of the period. This is as it should be. The Canaanite article developed only in the era after the loss of case endings, i.e., between the thirteenth and tenth centuries B.C., after the classical period of Canaanite prosody. Its use in archaic and archaizing Hebrew poetry is also exceedingly rare" (48). Moreover, lines 5-18 (the incantation proper) of the main inscription fit "precisely into the strict canons of Canaanite poetry" (Cross and Saley, 47; see also 45 and 45-6 n. 22, and Albright, "Aramaean Magical Text," 7 and 7 n. 5). In addition, Canaanite *b* with the meaning "from" occurs in two of the short inscriptions (Cross and Saley, 46 and 46 nn. 23, 26; cf. Albright, "Aramaean Magical Text," 9 and Gaster, "Canaanite Magical Text," 44).

93. Cross and Saley, 44-8. The plaque's size (8.2 cm. x 6.7 cm. x 2.2 cm.), inscriptions, shape, and hole drilled through the top indicate that it was hung up by a thong to protect a house, very likely in the doorway where it would be seen by the demons attempting an entrance (Cross and Saley, 48). Most of the treatments of the plaque prior to that of Cross and Saley (who were aided by two new sets of photographs provided by the Direction

des Antiquités et des Musées of Syria -- Cross and Saley, 44 and 44 n. 4) had regarded the text as being connected with child-birth -- e.g., Albright, "Aramaean Magical Text," 5, 9-11, and Gaster, "Canaanite Magical Text," 42, 44.

94. The transliteration is that of Cross and Saley (44), who note with regard to *k{r}rt* in lines 8-9 that the plaque's scribe had a tendency to commit dittographies when shifting from the end of a line to a new line (see 44 n. 7 for other examples). Albright has the same transliteration, except for a minor difference at the end of line 8 -- *k (k?)* -- and for line 12, which he renders *wrb . -(?) w(?)kl . qdš(t?)* ("Aramaean Magical Text," 8). Gaster's reading for this portion of the text matches that of Cross and Saley, except for slight differences at the end of lines 8 -- *k k* -- and 12 -- *qdš[m]* ("Canaanite Magical Text," 44). Cross and Saley state that the *nun* (*qdšn*) "could not be clearer on the new photographs" (44 n. 10).

95. "Aramaean Magical Text," 8. Concerning *ʾšr* (line 10), Albright says: "We must probably supply a *t*, inadvertently omitted because of the proximity of other sequences of the letters *r-t*" (8 n. 16).

96. "Aramaean Magical Text," 44. Regarding his translating *ʾšr* as "Ašur," Gaster writes: "The invocation of the name of Ašur, chief deity of the Assyrian pantheon is perfectly natural when we remember that at the time when our tablet was written Arslan Tash (Ḫadatu) was an Assyrian colony" (58).

97. Cross and Saley, 45. About their translating *ʾšr* as "Asherah" Cross and Saley comment: "The spelling *ʾšr* for *ʾaširo* is interesting. Usually the form in Phoenician is *ʾAširt*. The dialect of the plaque at this point has an isogloss with Hebrew. There is no reason to restore a 〈*t*〉 (Albright)" (45 n. 17). See n. 91 above regarding the Phoenician orthography of the inscriptions. In reconstructing forms in the text which do not have final vowel letters -- e.g., *ln/lanū*, *ʾšr/ʾaširo*, *bn/banê*, *rb/rabbê*, *ly/liyū* (Cross and Saley, 48) -- Cross and Saley presume the Phoenician shifts á > o (as well as ā > ō > ū), etc., which had taken place by the seventh century B.C. (48 n. 46).

H. Torczyner, understanding the language of the inscription to be Biblical Hebrew, transliterates lines 8-11 as do Cross and Saley, but translates, "thou hast concluded for us a covenant of eternity, which [*ʾšr*] thou hast concluded with us, and (so) every divine being . . ." ("A Hebrew Incantation Against Night-Demons from Biblical Times," *JNES* 6 [1947] 19, 22, 28). The language, however, is Phoenician; yet, as Propp has pointed out, one could theoretically argue for a "which" translation of *ʾšr* in the incantation by citing an isogloss with Hebrew (10). Decisively against this interpretation, however, is the parallelism yielded by the reading of Cross and Saley: *ʿlm* // *ʾšr* (Propp, 10; see main body).

98. See Cross and Saley, 45-6. They suggest that *kl* of line 12 is probably secondary in the text, partly because the "cliche is *dr ʾlm*, or *dr qdšm*" (45 n. 19).

99. On the sherd from ʿAkko (n. 46) is an example of a similar isogloss -- *bʿt lbn ḥdš*, "in the time of the new moon" (cf. Hebrew *lbnh ḥdšh*) -- unless *lbn* is a "new" masculine. It is theoretically possible, given the location and historical background of Arslan Tash (n. 87), that *ʾšr* on the plaque is "Aššur." An argument could be made that such a rendering would not necessarily disrupt the prosody of lines 8-12. However, because of the other Canaanite features in this text, I feel that "Aššur" is highly unlikely.

100. Cross discusses this title of ʾEl in *CMHE*, 16-20, 25.

101. See the translation and discussion of Cross and Saley, 45, 47-8.

102. The following was initiated by the discussion of Cross, *CMHE*, 31 and 31-2 n. 112.

103. See H. Hamburger, "A Hoard of Syrian Tetradrachms and Tyrian Bronze Coins from Gush Ḥalav," *IEJ* 4 (1954) 207-8, no. 137; 224, no. 137; pl. 20.137. Cf. a very similar Tyrian coin (without the Phoenician inscription), dated to 218-22 A.D., in Hill, *Catalogue of the Greek Coins of Phoenicia* (Catalogue of Greek Coins in the British Museum 25; London: British Museum, 1910) pl. 44.9; discussion, pp. cxli and 277 no. 410.

104. E.g., Hamburger writes: "A Phoenician [instead of Greek] legend would be used [on this and certain other contemporary coins] . . . because the reverses [which the legends explain] were chosen from the oldest past of Tyre and depicted ancient Phoenician heroes. Dido is here shown metaphorically as 'Goddess of Tyre'" (208). Cf. Hill, *Coins of Phoenicia*, cxli.

105. In a recent article Betlyon makes reference to an excavation of a temple complex (identified by some as that of ʾEšmun) by Maurice Dunand at Bostan esh-Sheikh, near Sidon ("The Cult of ʾAšerah/ʾĒlat at Sidon," *JNES* 44 [1985] 53-4, 56). One room (dating perhaps to the sixth century B.C.) contains a massive throne of simple design; around the throne was a pool of water which apparently served no ritualistic function. Betlyon convincingly argues that this room was probably dedicated to ʾAšerah/ʾElat ("Cult," 54-6).

106. The reverse of a contemporary Tyrian coin (Hamburger's no. 138, pp. 207-8, 225; pl. 21.138), reading ΔΙ Δω

and (in Phoenician) ʾ*lt* [*ṣwr*], shows a female figure, with rule and scepter, building Carthage; in the field is a murex shell. For like coins having the building scene, with the name "Dido" in Greek (but without a Phoenician inscription), see Hill, *Coins of Phoenicia*, cxli; 277 no. 409; 284 no. 440; pls. 33.6, 34.5, 44.8.

On the first coin described above (Hamburger's no. 138) Dido perhaps is being identified with "ʾElat," or with "the goddess [of Tyre]," that is, ʾAšerah (Albright, *YGC*, 122-3 n. 30 points to the same understanding). Dido was identified at Carthage with Tannit/Caelestis. According to Timaeus (ca. 356-260 B.C.) her name at Tyre was Elissa; when she came to the future site of Carthage, she was given the name "Dido" because of all her "wanderings." However, a number of scholars interpret "Dido" as "Beloved" ("Dido," *The Encyclopaedia Britannica* 7 [13th ed., 1926] 206; O. Rossbach, "Dido," PW 5 [1905] cols. 426, 431).

The situation of this historical (?) and mythical figure being regarded as both woman and goddess and having two names is puzzling. Was "Dido" originally an epithet of ʾAšerah which was secondarily given to the woman who founded Carthage? This could have been a result of, or helped to result in, her later deification. Without clarifying evidence the problem of the relationships between Dido, Elissa, and ʾAšerah/Tannit remains unresolved.

107. As noted earlier, the worship of Atargatis (comprehending ʾAšerah, ʿAštart, and ʿAnat) continued at least into the third century of the Christian Era (Chap. 2); Tannit was still venerated in that century (Chap. 3); and Ascalonite coins portraying Derketo and Phanebalos (to which cf. the Tyrian coins just discussed) date as late as 217/8 A.D. and 230/1 A.D. respectively (Chap. 3).

108. Cf. the cornucopiae held by Tannit/Qudšu on the stelai from the Ghorfa (Chap. 3), and the cornucopia raised by a Triton on the second series of Derketo coins from Ascalon discussed in Chap. 3.

CONCLUSIONS

The corpus of mythological accounts in which ʾAšerah plays a direct or indirect role consists of the *Phoenician History*, Ugaritic texts, and the myth (in Hittite) of El-kuniřša, Ašertu, and the Storm God.[1] These separate bodies of literature actually are complementary, each supplying key points of information not contained in the other two sources. Several titles of the goddess are provided by the Ugaritic literature: "Lady ʾAṯirat of the Sea," "ʾElat," "Creatress of the Gods" (cf. ʾEl's epithet "Father of the Gods"),[2] possibly "Mother (of the Gods)," "ʾAṯirat of Tyre," "ʾElat of Sidon," "Raḥmay," and "Qudšu." Further, in Ugaritic mythology especially, but also in the Canaanite myth preserved in Hittite, one is able to learn more specifically about ʾAšerah's personality (as presented by the myths). She is depicted as an active goddess, willing to use her position as chief wife/consort of the head of the pantheon (ʾEl) for the benefit of those she chooses to help and for the ruin of those she decides to punish. The general conclusions concerning ʾAšerah to be derived from an examination of all three sources are that she was: 1) the chief wife/consort of the supreme god; 2) a mother/fertility goddess -- as shown by her numerous children; 3) a goddess of eroticism -- which is linked with the preceding, but also suggested by her relationship with ʾEl in the Ugaritic texts and strongly indicated in the Hittite myth; 4) a goddess with marine connections -- "Lady ʾAṯirat of the Sea," and "Fisherman," her servant (cf. also Diodorus's account); and 5) a goddess with a violent, combative, warlike, and/or angry side to her nature -- evidenced in the Kirta Epic, clear enough in the Hittite myth, and perhaps implied in the *Phoenician History*, since she was sent (together with ᶜAštart) to kill Kronos/ᵓEl by stealth.

One or more of these characteristics, together with epithets of ᵓAšerah known from Ugarit, help identify and/or clarify worship of the goddess in other regions and periods, under various representational forms and "new" titles. Specifically, the Qudšu representations, *d̲t bt̲n*, *bᶜlt gbl*, Tannit, Derketo, Phanebalos, and *lbᵓt* should be identified with ᵓAšerah, and she is one of the deities comprehended in Atargatis. Certain members of this group, in turn, shed light on other members of the group. For example, that the Qudšu figure holds serpents leads to the association of *d̲t bt̲n* with Qudšu (= ᵓAšerah). The Qudšu figure itself is to be seen behind the sign of Tannit (who was the "Serpent Lady"), and the serpents of the former in the caduceus of the latter. Tannit was called "face of Baᶜl," and "Phanebalos" is the name of the goddess pictured on an Ascalonite coin beside a Tannit sign. Derketo, too, is to be identified with Tannit (/ᵓAšerah), and therefore also with Phanebalos; Atargatis, moreover, is to be partially identified with Derketo. The Hierapolis σημήιον was in essence the same object as the Punic caduceus, a symbol of Tannit.

There still remains the question concerning the meaning of "ᵓAšerah." No evidence as yet has been uncovered which provides a decisive answer for this question; thus the following is only theory.[3] Very briefly, *aširatum* (Akkadian), *aširtu* (Akkadian), *aširta* (Amarna), and *ᵓăšērāh* (Hebrew Bible) point to an original form *ᵓat̲irat( )* for the goddess's name. **ᵓat̲irat( )*, in turn, may be viewed as a noun or verb involving the same root: *ᵓt̲r*, "to step, tread, advance, go on, proceed." Taken as a noun (*ᵓat̲iratu*), the name would mean "(holy) place," "shrine";[4] as a verb (formally stative, perfect, 3rd f. s.), "she stepped/s, trod/treads, advanced/s."

The verbal explanation perhaps is preferable, since *ᵓat̲rt ym* (of Ugaritic literature) could have been a primitive cultic sentence/phrase and the origin of the goddess's name: *ᵓat̲irat yamma*, "She Treads the Sea" or "She Trod(/Treads) the Sea(-dragon)."[5] As the female counterpart of the chief male deity (ʾEl), the goddess possibly was first called "ʾElat." In her were centered the functions of greatest importance to her worshippers: providing for their needs, bestowing life and fertility, ensuring victory over enemies, granting protection and healing, and watching over the dead. It is conceivable that one description of ʾElat was ʾ*aṯrt ym*. Hypothetically, at a relatively early stage the use of "ʾElat" began to decrease, while ʾ*aṯrt ym* became more common as a designation for the goddess; this sentence/phrase could be and was frequently abbreviated to its first element. "ʾAṯirat/ʾAšerah" (*yamma*) predominated in Syria-Palestine, but, as already stated, the same goddess was referred to under different epithets elsewhere.

ʾ*aṯrt ym* may indicate that there was a mythic tradition about ʾElat having fought and defeated the Sea(-dragon)/Chaos. Such an interpretation of the phrase is not disproven by the Ugaritic texts, in which Yam is a son of ʾAṯirat, Baʿl defeats Yam, and ʿAnat claims to have done likewise. When dealing with the myths, a tendency to over-rationalize must be avoided. An alternate explanation of ʾ*aṯrt ym* is that merchants, sailors, and fishermen in coastal cities and territories believed that ʾElat trod the sea, accompanying their ships as guide, guardian, and grantor of success to their endeavors. However ʾ*aṯrt ym* is understood, the goddess seems to have been associated with the sea either originally or at a very early time. Her marine connections were later preserved in her worship as Tannit, Derketo, and Atargatis.

In the end, one is impressed by two aspects of ʾAšerah's worship seen throughout this study. The first is its diffusion (from Hierapolis and the Near East to Spain) and endurance (from the second millennium B.C. to the Christian Era); the second, its basic consistency over the centuries.

NOTES TO CONCLUSIONS

1. Diodorus's account of Derketo is not included in this corpus, since it is so heavily embellished with features which are not relevant to a study of ʾAšerah.

2. E.g., *CTA* 32.1.25, 33. See Cross, *CMHE*, 15-6.

3. My thanks to Prof. Cross for his advice concerning the following discussion.

4. Of interest is the fact that *qdš*, "holiness," possibly also could be translated "holy (place)," "sanctuary."

5. What "Sanctuary of the Sea" would signify is unclear. In Chap. 1, because *ʾaṯrt* was rendered simply as "ʾAṯirat," *ʾaṯrt ym* was vocalized and translated *ʾaṯiratu yammi*, "(Lady) ʾAṯirat of the Sea."

Appendix A

MESOPOTAMIAN AND ARABIC EVIDENCE

This appendix briefly reviews textual data concerning ᵓAšerah from Mesopotamia and Arabia.

Mesopotamia

Certain Babylonian texts mention an Ašratum (Ašratu, Aširtu, Aširatum). The writer concurs with the scholarly opinion holding that the goddess was an Amorite deity who had been brought to Babylonia from the West, and thus should be identified with ᵓAšerah.[1] She appears in old god lists,[2] as, for example, one from Nippur,[3] which probably dates to the first part of the second millennium B.C., to a period corresponding to the beginning of the First Dynasty of Babylon.[4] A text naming a number of Babylonian temples indicates that Ašratum possessed such a structure.[5] The second line of a hematite cylinder with Old Babylonian script reads ^{d}*aš-ra-tum*; the first line gives the name of the goddess's consort, ^{d}*ra-ma-a-nu-um*.[6] From the time of Hammurabi comes the personal name ^{d}*aš-ra-tum-um-mi*, "Ašratum is my mother."[7]

As various Babylonian texts make clear, Ašratum was considered to be consort of Amurru,[8] who was regarded as the son of Anum, the god of the heavens. A Sumerian votive inscription[9] set up on behalf of the life of Hammurabi and dedicated to the goddess calls her (line 2) the great (or chief) daughter-in-law (*é-gi-a-g*[*al*], *kallatum rabītum*) of Anum (*an-na*).[10] The text (line 4) connects the goddess with "abundance" and "jubilation" (*ḫi-li-ma-az-bi*, *kuzbi u ulṣi*), which may in part be an allusion to eroticism and fertility, and refers to her (line 7) as the "merciful Lady" (*nin-šà-lá-sù, bēltum rēmēnītum*). In addition, the text indicates (lines 5-6) that Ašratum was lovingly honored "on the mountain" (*ḫur-sag-gá, ina šadêm*). This phrase recalls the usual epithet of Amurru, *bēl šadê*, "Lord of the mountain."[11] Edzard has observed that the terms *kur* and *ḫur-sag* -- and consequently their Akkadian equivalent *šadûm* -- did not have to necessarily designate mountain chains in the proper sense, but only the desert plateau (*Hohe der Steppe*).[12] Ašratum was often referred to later under the title "(Ašratum,) Lady of the Steppe," (*ᵈgú-bar-ra*) *gašan-gú-edin-na*, (*Ašratum*) *bēlet ṣēri*.[13] The epithet suited perfectly the consort of Amurru; it perhaps also both characterized Ašratum as the goddess of Amorite nomads and pointed back to the Syrian steppe.[14]

Arabia

The literary evidence from Arabia cited in discussions of ʾAšerah is meager and not entirely clear. South Arabian attestation[15] of the goddess possibly includes portions of two Qatabanian inscriptions: *wbny wsḥdṯ byt wdm wʾṯrt wmḫ̮tn mlkn*,[16] which has been translated "and he built and restored the temple of Wadd and ʾAṯirat and the *mḫ̮tn* of the king,"[17] and *wkl mhlk wḥdṯn byt wdm wʾṯrt wmḫ̮tn mlkn*,[18] rendered "and all the execution and restoration of the temple of Wadd and ʾAṯirat and the *mḫ̮tn* of the king."[19] These texts could be regarded as indicating that the consort of Wadd, the lunar deity of the Minaean and Awsanian kingdoms, was ʾAṯirat (= ʾAšerah).[20] However, an alternate interpretation of the inscriptions is to view them as speaking of the temple of Wadd and the king's *ʾṯrt* and *mḫ̮tn*. Thus, *ʾṯrt* in both inscriptions conceivably designates a structure possessed by the king.[21]

There are additional examples of similarly ambiguous portions of texts. Part of a Qatabanian text -- *rdʾ lʾṯrt tsʿn bḥtn* -- has been interpreted "have dedicated/vowed to ʾAṯirat nine young she-camels,"[22] but "have vowed to the *ʾṯrt*" is another possibility. The phrase *sqny ʾṯrt*, translated "he dedicated to ʾAṯirat,"[23] could be interpreted "he dedicated an ʾ*ṯrt*."[24] The expression *ḏ-ʾṯrt*, appearing as the name of a month in a Minaean inscription,[25] has been rendered "the one of ʾAṯirat,"[26] yet this is indefinite.[27] Likewise, though a territory in the kingdom of Qataban was also called *ḏ-ʾṯrt*,[28] the phrase does not necessarily mean "that of ʾAṯirat."[29]

Certain Qatabanian texts, in the writer's opinion, indicate somewhat more clearly that a goddess named *ʾṯrt* was worshipped in southern Arabia. Specifically, they seem to suggest that ʾAṯirat was the consort of the principle Qatabanian god ʿAmm, a lunar deity.[30] The recurring phrase is *wdm wbntm wšptm lʿm wʾṯrt*,[31] "voluntary offering and gift and promise to ʿAmm and ʾAṯirat."[32]

North Arabian attestation of ʾAṯirat/ʾAšerah may perhaps be seen in Thamudic personal names, *bi-ʾaṯirat*, *ṯūr-ʾaṯirat*, and *mʿdʾṯr*, if *ʾṯr* is a shortened form of *ʾṯrt*.[33] An Aramaic inscription from Tema, dating to about the fifth century B.C.,[34] has been understood to contain the goddess's name (as *ʾšyrʾ*, though the letter between the *yod* and *ʾaleph* is very unclear).[35] However, Cross has shown on the basis of another (unpublished) inscription from Tema that the correct reading is *ʾšymʾ*.[36]

NOTES TO APPENDIX A

1. For a reference to scholars who have held this viewpoint see William L. Reed, *The Asherah in the Old Testament* (Fort Worth: Texas Christian University, 1949) 73 n. 15. Helpful discussions of the Amorites include Giorgio Buccellati's *The Amorites of the Ur III Period* (Ricerche 1; Naples: Istituto Orientale di Napoli, 1966); I. J. Gelb's "The Early History of the West Semitic Peoples," *JCS* 15 (1961) 27-47, esp. 44-7; Alfred Haldar's *Who Were the Amorites*? (Monographs on the Ancient Near East 1; Leiden: E. J. Brill, 1971); and M. Liverani's "The Amorites," in *Peoples of Old Testament Times* (ed. D. J. Wiseman; Oxford: Clarendon, 1973).

2. For these lists consult the references provided by Edward Lipiński, "The Goddess Aṯirat in Ancient Arabia, in Babylon, and in Ugarit," OLP 3 (1972) 104 n. 20, and Reed, *The Asherah*, 74 n. 23. Ašratum continued to be mentioned in the god lists down to Assyrian times.

3. Edward Chiera, *Sumerian Lexical Texts from the Temple School of Nippur* (OIP 11; Chicago: University of Chicago, 1929) no. 122, rev., col. v, 17 (pl. 63) = no. 124, rev., col. vii, 21 (pl. 68).

4. Chiera, *Lexical Texts*, 1, 3, and *Lists of Personal Names from the Temple School of Nippur* (University of Pennsylvania Museum Publications, Babylonian Section 11; 3 pts.; Philadelphia: University Museum, 1916-19) 17-8.

5. K. 3089, line 12, in Theophilus G. Pinches's "The Temples of Ancient Babylonia, I.," *Proceedings of the Society of Biblical Archaeology* 22 (1900) 359. Ašratum was also connected with the Temple Eḫilikalamma, and the Ezida (*aš-rat ša é-zida*) and Esagil (*aš-rat ša é-sagil*); see Erich Ebeling, "Ašratu," *Reallexikon der Assyriologie* 1 (ed. Erich Ebeling and Bruno Meissner; Berlin and Leipzig: Walter de Gruyter, 1932) 169, and Knut Tallqvist, *Akkadische Götterepitheta* (StudOr 7; Helsingforsiae: Societas Orientalis Fennica, 1938) 265.

6. A. H. Sayce, "Babylonian Cylinders in the Hermitage at St. Petersburg," *ZA* 6 (1891) 161-2. Sayce originally read "Ratanum" with uncertainty. Since that time the scholarly consensus (with which I am in agreement) has

been that "Ramanum" is the correct reading: see, e.g., Fritz Hommel, *Aufsätze und Abhandlungen* (3 pts.; München: G. Franz, 1892-1901) 210; Ebeling, "Ašratu," 169; and Reed, *The Asherah*, 73 and 73 n. 18. The epithet *ram(m)ān(um)*, perhaps "the Thunderer," was, as Frank Moore Cross points out (*Canaanite Myth and Hebrew Epic* [Cambridge: Harvard University, 1973; hereafter *CMHE*] 58), given to both Amurru (see Tallqvist, 251, 438) and Hadad (cf. "Hadad-rimmon," Zech 12:11, and see, e.g., John Gray, "Rimmon, 2," *IDB* 4 [1962] 99). Since other Babylonian evidence links Ašratum with Amurru (next par. of main body), I think that "Ramanum" on this cylinder is better identified with Amurru than Hadad (= Baᶜl).

7. Fr. Thureau-Dangin, *Lettres et contrats de l'epoque de la première dynastie babylonienne* (Musée du Louvre, Département des Antiquités Orientales, Textes Cunéiformes 1; Paris: Paul Guethner, 1910) nos. 89, 7; 98, 8; 99, 8; (pp. 4, 16, 59; pls. 53, 56, 57). Jean-Robert Kupper (*L'iconographie du dieu Amurru dans la glyptique de la Iʳᵉ dynastie babylonienne* [Académie Royale de Belgique, Classe des Lettres, Mémoires, 2nd series, 55/1; Bruxelles: Palais des Académies, 1961] 63 n. 2) explains that the texts cited in the preceding reference are not Cappadocian tablets, as some have affirmed, but Babylonian documents.

8. Kupper, *Amurru*, 59, 61-2, 62 n. 2.

9. The inscription may be found in L. W. King's *The Letters and Inscriptions of Ḫammurabi* (3 vols.; New York: AMS, 1976; a reprint of the 1898-1900 work) 1: no. 66, pls. 126-127. A photograph of the text is provided by Charles J. Ball, *Light from the East* (London: Eyre and Spottiswoode, 1899) 65. I wish to express my thanks to Prof. William Moran for his help in translating portions of this text. Cf. also the translations of King, 3: 196 (transliteration, 195), and Edmond Sollberger and Jean-Robert Kupper, *Inscriptions royales sumeriennes et akkadiennes* (Littératures anciennes du Proche-Orient; Paris: Editions du Cerf, 1971) 219, no. IVC6o.

10. See the comment of Julius Lewy, "Amurritica," *HUCA* 32 (1961) 31 n. 3.

11. Kupper, *Amurru*, 62.

12. Dietz Otto Edzard, *Die "Zweite Zwischenzeit" Babyloniens* (Wiesbaden: Otto Harrassowitz, 1957) 31-2 n. 131; Kupper, *Amurru*, 62; see also Jean Ouellette, "More on ʾÊl Šadday and Bêl Šadê," *JBL* 88 (1969) 471. Thorkild Jacobsen has a similar understanding of *ḫur-sag*, explaining that the term "can denote the foothills and near mountain ranges of the Iranian highlands in the East, but also the stony Arabian desert bordering the alluvium of Southern Mesopotamia in the west. Basically, therefore, it would seem to denote 'stony ground', 'rock'" ("Notes

on Nintur," *Or* n.s. 42 [1973] 281). Such an interpretation, Jacobsen comments, "is suggested by the fact that Abiak on the Áb-gal (*apkallatu*) canal in the extreme west of the Mesopotamian alluvial bordered on the hur-sag̃ according to the text giving borders fixed by Ur-Nammu . . . In the region where we must locate Abiak no mountains, only the stony Arabian plateau, can come into consideration" ("Nintur," 281-2 n. 25).

13. Kupper, *Amurru*, 62 and 62 nn. 2, 6; cf. Lipiński, "Aṯirat," 104. For *gú-bar-ra* = *Ašratum*, see Ebeling, "Ašratu," 169 (citing texts from the Neo-Babylonian and Greek periods) and Kupper, *Amurru*, 62-3 n. 6. Kupper adds that under her Sumerian name "Gubarra" Ašratum was invoked in several psalms of penitence (*Amurru*, 62 n. 6, with references). The goddess *šá-ra-a-ḫi-i-tú*, mentioned in contracts of the Seleucid period, may have been Ašratum: = *aš-rat a-ḫi-i-tum* (?) = "foreign Ašratum" (?); see Ebeling, "Ašratu," 169.

14. Cf. Kupper, *Amurru*, 62-3; Lipiński, "Aṯirat," 104. For Amurru as "Lord of the Steppe," see Kupper, *Amurru*, 67-8, 76. Cross has discussed the possibility of identifying Amurru with Amorite ᵓEl (*CMHE*, 57-9); cf. Kupper, *Amurru*, 87-8, and Jimmy J. M. Roberts, *The Earliest Semitic Pantheon* (Baltimore: Johns Hopkins University, 1972) 16.

15. Inscriptional South Arabic (Old South Arabic: Sabaean, Minaean, Qatabanian) is dated from the eighth century B.C. to the fourth century of the Christian Era, with the bulk of the material coming from and after the third century B.C. While attempting to show the relative uncertainty of seeing the goddess's name in the texts dealt with in the first and second paragraphs of the "Arabia" section of App. A, I do, nevertheless, think that this is the likeliest interpretation.

16. Hommel, 206; *Répertoire d'épigraphie sémitique* (Académie des Inscriptions et Belles-lettres; 8 vols.; Paris: 1900-68; hereafter *RES*) 3550, 4-5.

17. Hommel, 207; James B. Pritchard, *Palestinian Figurines in Relation to Certain Goddesses Known Through Literature* (AOS 24; New Haven: American Oriental Society, 1943; hereafter *PF*) 63.

18. Hommel, 206; *RES* 3534 B.

19. Pritchard, *PF*, 64; cf. Hommel, 207.

20. Lipiński, "Aṯirat," 102; Pritchard, *PF*, 63-4; Reed, *The Asherah*, 75. Lipiński proposes that although the two inscriptions are actually Qatabanian, the temple, whose restoration is commemorated, may have been originally Awsanian (102 n. 8). Since the name "Wadd" derives from

a root meaning "to love," Pritchard suggests that the possible association of the cults of ʾAṯirat and Wadd may point to the goddess's having some fertility characteristic (*PF*, 64).

21. Reed, *The Asherah*, 76; also, note (with caution) C. C. Torrey's comment in Albert T. Clay's *The Antiquity of Amorite Civilization* (New Haven, Conn.: privately printed, 1924) 24 n. 6.

22. *RES* 856, 3-4.

23. See *RES* 3534 bis and 4274, 1 (Qatabanian texts); also Hommel, 207 (Qatabanian). Cf. *RES* 3902, pl. 13, fig. 5, 1 (Qatabanian).

24. See Torrey's remark in Clay's *Amorite Civilization*, 24 n. 6.

25. *RES* 3306 A, 7-8.

26. Lipiński, "Aṯirat," 102; Hommel also regards the second element in the month name as "ʾAṯirat" (157 n. 2), as does, apparently, Pritchard (*PF*, 64).

27. Torrey, in Clay's *Amorite Civilization*, 24 n. 6. Torrey explains that "the list of South-Arabian month-names known to us gives us no reason for expecting the name of a deity here."

28. *RES* 4330, 2.

29. The translation "that of ʾAṯirat" is Lipiński's ("Aṯirat," 102). A. Jamme, too, translates *ʾaṯrt* of *RES* 4330, 2 as "ʾAṯirat": ". . . on the top of the fortified hill (2) D̲û-Mawẓadum, for his ground D̲û-Daraᶜat and D̲û-ʾAṯirat; and he entrusted it to the care of . . ." ("South-Arabian Inscriptions," in *Ancient Near Eastern Texts Relating to the Old Testament* [3rd ed. with Supplement; ed. James B. Pritchard; Princeton: Princeton University, 1969] 668 no. 15). Other texts which may mention ʾAṯirat are *RES* 4203 (Qatabanian) and 2886, 3 (Minaean; see *RES* 7 [1935] 143).

30. Lipiński, "Aṯirat," 102 and 102 n. 6; Pritchard, *PF*, 64 and 64 nn. 28-30.

31. *RES* 3689, 5; 3691, 4-5; 3692, 3.

32. Jamme, 668-9 no. 16.

33. See Lipiński, "Aṯirat," 101 and 101 n. 3, 103 and 103 n. 16. Lipiński ("Aṯirat," 102 n. 5, 103) interprets *ṯūr-ʾaṯirat* as "uplifted by ʾAṯirat."

34. Herbert Donner and Wolfgang Röllig, *Kanaanäische und aramäische Inschriften* (3 vols.; Wiesbaden: Otto Harrassowitz, 1966-69; hereafter *KAI*) no. 228 A.

35. E.g., *KAI* 2: 278-9; Lipiński, "Aṯirat," 103; Pritchard, *PF*, 64; and Reed, *The Asherah*, 79. See *Corpus Inscriptionum Semiticarum* (Ab Academia inscriptionum et litterarum humaniorum; Paris: e Republicae typographeo, 1881-) Pars Secunda, no. 113, line 16; cf. line 3.

36. Lecture delivered in the Harvard Semitic Museum, Sept. 29, 1983.

Appendix B

ADDITIONAL UGARITIC TEXTUAL MATERIAL

Appendix B contains excerpts from the Ugaritic mythological texts which probably or possibly mention ʾAṯirat/ʾElat and are not included in Chapter 1 (nos. 1-4 below), and a Ugaritic god list with its Akkadian equivalent (no. 5 below).

1. *CTA* 1.4.13-15

ʾEl is in the process of giving another name to one of his sons. Due to the poor condition of *CTA* 1 in general, and of column 4 specifically, the following are only a very tentative vocalization and translation. "ʾElat" perhaps occurs in line 14.

(13) wayaʿnī luṭ<pā>nu ʾilu dū pa[ʾidu]
(14) šimu biniya yawu[a] ʾilatu[ ]
(15) wapaʿarū šimu yammi[ ]

(13) And Luṭpan ʾEl the Compassionate answered . . .
(14) "The name of my son is Yaw,[a] (O) ʾElat . . .
(15) And they proclaimed the name of Yam . . .

Note

a) This word has received more than a little scholarly attention. See, e.g., Gibson (4 n. 2), Gordon (*UT*, 410 no. 1084) and esp. *TOML* (309 and 309 n. n).

2. *CTA* 3.1.13-15

In column 1 of Tablet 3 Baᶜl is being served food and drink. Lines 10-15 deal with an impressive cup.

(13) kāsa qaduša (14) la-tipāhunnahu[a] ᵓaṯṯatu
karpāna (15) la-taᶜīnu[b] ᵓaṯiratu[c]

(13) a holy cup (14) which a woman should not view,[a]
a goblet (15) which ᵓAṯirat[c] should not see.[b]

Notes

a) Possibly "did/does/has not view(ed)," or "cannot/could not view." Jirku translates "a holy cup, which indeed the woman/wife sees" (26).
b) Cf. note a.
c) There is no compelling reason for understanding ᵓ*aṯrt* other than as "ᵓAṯirat" (contra Driver [83]; Gibson [46 n. 4]; Ginsberg [136 n. 1]; and Obermann [10 n. 14]).

3. *CTA* 8.1-6

Any translation of these lines is uncertain. Further, the question remains as to where *CTA* 8 fits into the Baᶜl cycle (between *CTA* 3.5 and 3.6?), if at all.

(1) [ᵓê]ka[a] magganu rabbati ᵓaṯirati (2) [yammi]
maǵẓu qāniyati ᵓilīma
(3) [la-]tattinu[b] bêta la-baᶜli kī-mā (4) [ᵓi]līma
wa-ḥaẓira kī banī (5) [ᵓa]ṯirati[c]
gā-ma la-ǵalmêhu (6) baᶜlu yaṣīḥu

(1) "Why is there[a] a present for Lady ᵓAṯirat (2) of the Sea,
a gift for the Creatress of the Gods?
(3) Indeed she will give [?][b] a house to Baᶜl as she did (4-5) to the (other) gods,
and a court as she did to ᵓAṯirat's sons."[c]
Aloud to his two lads (6) Baᶜl shouts,

Notes

a) Or, "should there be."

b) Reading [*l*]*ttn* instead of Herdner's *wtn* (which would be an imperative of *ytn*, and somewhat awkward in this context).[1] In light of *CTA* 4.2 - 4.5.81, "she will give" of line 3 perhaps means that ʾAṯirat as newly won ally will bring about, through her speaking to ʾEl, the wish of Baʿl.

c) See Chapter 1, text no. 10, n. j.

4. *UT* 1002 (*PRU 2* 2)

Gordon describes this text as a mythological poem (*UT*, 267), but the bad state of preservation prevents the translation of a single complete line. Pertinent to this study are lines 39, 43, and 60, which are given below, together with their preceding and following lines.

(38)] . hw[ ]y . h[ ]r . wrgm . ank
(39)](i/h)ddt[ ]l . aṯrty[a]
(40)]ptm . ṣḥ(t/q)[ ]

(42)]k . yritn . mǵy . hy . wkn
(43)] . ḥln . db . dmt . um . il[m?][b]
(44)]d̲yn . bʿd[ ]d̲yn . wl .

(59)]ṣlm . pny[ ]tlkn
(60)]rḥbn . hm . laṯr[t][c]
(61)]šy . wydn [.] bʿ[ ]n .

Notes

a) The *-y* on *aṯrt* is intriguing. Is this the 1st s. c. suffix? If so, should ʾ*aṯrty* be translated "my ʾAṯirat" or "my ʾaṯirat," the latter referring to a cult object or idol? Or does ʾ*aṯrt* in line 39 have a different meaning (e.g., "place"; cf. Akkadian *aširtu*)? Cf. ʾ*šrth* at Kuntillet ʿAjrud (see Chapter 4).

b) Perhaps, with Gordon (*UT*, 386 no. 679), "window [cf. Hebrew *ḥallôn*, "window"] which is in the *dmt* [cf. Akkadian *dimtu* I, "tower"] of the mother of the gods"? Cf. text no. 6 n. d in Chapter 1, and ʾAṯirat's epithet *qnyt ʾilm*, "Creatress of the Gods."

c) Should a *-y* be restored here (*laṯr*[*ty*]) on the basis of line 39?

5.

RS 24.264 + 280[2]	RS 20.24[3]
ʾilʾib	DINGIR a-bi
ʾil	ilum^{lum}
dgn	^{d}da-gan
bʿl ṣpn	^{d}adad be-el ḫuršân ḫa-zi
bʿlm	^{d}adad II
bʿlm	^{d}adad III
bʿlm	^{d}adad IV
bʿlm	^{d}adad V
bʿlm	^{d}adad VI
bʿlm	^{d}adad VII
ʾarṣ wšmm	^{d}IDIM ù IDIM
kṯ[r]t	^{d}sa-sú-ra-tum
yr[ḫ]	^{d}sîn
[ṣ]pn	^{d}ḫuršân ḫa-zi
kṯr	^{d}é-a
pdry	^{d}ḫé-bat
ʿṯtr	^{d}aš-ta-bi
ǵrm w[	^{d}ḫuršânu^{M} u a-mu-tu[m]
[ʾaṯ]rt	^{d}aš-ra-tum
ʿnt	^{d}a-na-tum
špš	^{d}šamaš
ʾ(!)arṣy[a]	^{d}al-la-tum
ʾušḫry	^{d}iš-ḫa-ra
ʿṯtrt	^{d}ištar$^{iš\text{-}tar}$
ʾil [t]ʿḏr bʿl	ilânu^{M} til-la-at ^{d}adad
r[š]p	^{d}2nergal

	ddmš	^{d}dá-ad-mi-iš
	pḫr ʾilm	^{d}pu-ḫur ilâni^{M}
	ym	^{d}tâmtum
(30)	ʾuṯḫ[t]	$^{d\,DUG}$BUR.ZI.NÍG.NA
	knr	$^{d\;is}$ki-na-rum
	mlkm	^{d}MA.LIK.MEŠ
	šlm	^{d}sa-li-mu

Note

a) Erroneously printed ʿ*arṣy*; cf. the drawing of Herdner (NTA, 2).

NOTES TO APPENDIX B

1. An examination of the photograph (see *CTA*, Figures and Plates volume, pl. 1; also fig. 30) indicates that Herdner, taking into consideration the amount of tablet which has been worn away, judges the first mark of line 3 to be the final horizontal stroke of a *w*. However, I think it is equally plausible, after estimating the original space, that the preserved first mark is actually a *t*, and that it could have been preceded by a *l*, or less likely a *k*.

2. NTA, 1-3.

3. *Ug 5*, 44-5.

Appendix C

HATHOR

Egyptian religion is characterized by, to borrow Gardiner's phrase, a "chaotic polytheism."[1] A tendency to create new forms of a god/goddess by instituting his/her worship in new local centers persisted throughout the whole course of Egyptian history.[2] One god/goddess could easily be identified with another on the basis of a common feature or embodied power.[3] In discussing Hathor, the purpose of this appendix is not to give a detailed, complete review of the worship of the goddess throughout Egyptian history, but rather to present some of the main aspects of this worship, focusing specifically on those which may relate to the subject matter of Chapter 3.

Hathor was one of the oldest, most esteemed divinities of ancient Egypt and was worshipped throughout the whole country. Her name perhaps means "House of Horus," but other interpretations have been proposed.[4] Most scholars agree that the goddess's *Urform*[5] was that of a cow.[6] Acknowledgment of this original form was tenaciously maintained when Hathor was later represented as a woman.[7] She was shown with a headpiece of (two) cow horns, and/or sometimes with a pair of cow ears; infrequently she was given a cow's head.[8] Due to the significance which Hathor soon gained, other cow goddesses, who were worshipped in several Egyptian nomes, were early identified with her.[9]

Already in the Old Kingdom Dendera was considered to be Hathor's main cult place, where she had connections with Horus of Edfu.[10] At Dendera her cult symbol appears to have been a round pillar, which had at the top two heads of the goddess looking in opposite directions.[11] Another cult symbol of Hathor was the sistrum.

Hathor drew to herself not only cow cults; she was also identified with a number of other goddesses, as, for example, a serpent goddess of Upper Egypt.[12] She furthermore absorbed into herself tree goddesses. In particular Hathor took possession of an old Memphite tree cult (a sycamore near that city on the desert fringe of the cultivated land was thought to be occupied by a benevolent goddess) under the name "Lady of the (Southern) Sycamore."[13] Moreover, the tree goddess who offered food and drink to the dead was often identified as Hathor (at other times she was identified as Nut). Pictures of the tree involved reproduce the sycamore tree of Memphis.[14] These pictures are not encountered before the Eighteenth Dynasty, but already in the Coffin Texts the tree goddess Hathor was believed to be a helper of the dead.[15]

Hathor was worshipped as goddess of the dead in the necropolis of Thebes, where she was not viewed as a tree divinity. Rather, she had the form of a cow and is depicted as looking forth from the steep mountainside which borders the Theban necropolis.[16] Tuthmosis III (ca. 1490-1436) and Amenophis II (ca. 1436-1413) constructed for her a sanctuary which was situated in the cliffs of Deir el-Bahri.[17] As a very highly esteemed deity of the necropolis Hathor was called the "Cow of Gold," "Lady of the Necropolis," the one who "lived on the steep mountainside of the west,"[18] or simply "Lady of the West."[19]

In addition, Hathor blended together with the celestial cow Methyer, which probably in part established her significance for the dead. Formerly, the dead man had been promised help from Methyer for his entrance into the heavenly land of light; now, after the assimilation of the two goddesses, he set his hope upon Hathor, who received the sun setting in the west and promised him thereby light and warmth also in the dark of the night.[20] His desire, therefore, was "to be in the retinue of Hathor."[21]

The understanding of Hathor as goddess of the heavens was related to the long-standing and various connections of Hathor with the sun. It is not unlikely that she was originally viewed as the mother of Re; however, already in sun sanctuaries of the Old Kingdom she was worshipped as the feminine complement of Re;[22] but finally, and most prominently, Hathor became the eye of the sun (therefore, the sun itself), which meant that she was the daughter of Re. This last development is tied together with the sun disk which was so commonly pictured between the horns of Hathor.[23] First Hathor was regarded as the carrier of the eye of the sun, and then she became that herself.[24]

An Egyptian myth relates how the gods suggested to Re, who had grown old, that he send his eye (that is, the sun) as the goddess Hathor to smite rebellious mankind which was conspiring against him. The goddess, having been sent, slew many men. Thereby she was identified with Sakhmet (the "Powerful One").[25] Re had compassion on humanity, yet Hathor wanted to continue her slaughter. Through trickery Re succeeded in getting Hathor drunk, with the result that she did not see and/or recognize her victims and mankind was saved from her wrath.[26]

Hathor overlapped Nut, with whom she coincided not only as guardian of the dead, but also as goddess of the heavens. Inevitably one goddess was comprehended as a form of the other and both were fused under the names Hathor-Nut or Nut-Hathor. Occasionally Hathor was addressed as the daughter of Nut.[27] Also, Hathor was identified with the lion goddess Tefnut, who cunningly led her father Re from Nubia back home to Egypt. Finally, it is not surprising that Hathor came to be understood as the eye of the moon.[28]

Concerning her worship outside the Land of the Nile, the Egyptians recognized Hathor in the goddess of Byblos. Eventually for the natives themselves their goddess entered into the form of the Egyptian deity.[29] The "Lady of Byblos" became a popular form of Hathor in Egypt.[30] A sanctuary was built for Hathor at Serabiṭ el-Ḫadem on the Sinai peninsula, where she was worshipped as "Lady of the Turquoise" (this temple fell into disuse by the end of the New Kingdom). Another title of the goddess in the Sinai region was "Lady of the Turquoise Land," and later the cult of "Hathor, Lady of the Turquoise Land" continued in Egypt to the time of the Ptolemies, being practiced particularly in the eastern Delta, but also in Alexandria.[31] In the lands to the south of Egypt Hathor was worshipped as the "Ruler" of Nubia and the "Lady of Punt."[32]

As the traditions attached to the goddess were varied, so also the character of Hathor was diverse, but for the sake of simplification it can be discussed under two basic aspects. The first was connected to her being identified with the burning, fire-emitting eye of the sun. She became a "Lady of Terror," joyful in battle and full of fury, who annihilated the enemies of the sun god.[33]

The other side of her character, and probably the better known, was the maternal, feminine aspect. She was a mother herself,[34] and the bestower of children's blessings.[35] Childbirth was aided and protected by Hathor.[36] In royal propaganda dealing with their divine birth, different Pharaohs claimed her as mother and/or wet nurse. For example, Pepi I (ca. 2327-2278?) proclaimed himself the son of Hathor, Lady of Iuny.[37] Amenemhet III (ca. 1842-1797), Tuthmosis III, Horemheb (ca. 1333-1303), and Psammetichus I (ca. 664-610) are depicted as being suckled by the great cow goddess, Hathor.[38] Further, she was (especially at Dendera) the goddess of love, joy, festivity, and dance.[39] At her festivals, which were many, drink flowed freely, resulting in much intoxication.[40] These maternal, feminine characteristics undoubtedly lay in the original essence of the goddess.[41]

In conclusion, even this brief sketch of Hathor makes apparent her complexity. Murray summarizes the matter nicely:

> The main difficulty in the study of Hathor is that she absorbs into herself the identity of many of the other goddesses. She is the Sky-goddess, she is Sekhmet the lioness, and finally she and Isis are so intermingled that it is often impossible to distinguish one from the other. The Greeks, however, regarded these two great goddesses as entirely different; to them Isis was

> Demeter, and Hathor Aphrodite, but no indication is given as to why they were differentiated.[42]

Therefore, that the Egyptians identified Qudšu with Hathor, and that the Qudšu representations were influenced by this identification, is not surprising, for two reasons: a) Qudšu (ʾAšerah) and Hathor shared more than a few similar functions and characteristics, and b) Hathor had an amazing capacity to assimilate other goddesses and to assume different roles.

NOTES TO APPENDIX C

1. Alan H. Gardiner, "Egypt: Ancient Religion," *Encyclopaedia Britannica* 9 (11th ed., 1910-11) 48.

2. Gardiner, "Egypt: Ancient Religion," 50. The opposite tendency, operating simultaneously, explains Gardiner, made national out of local gods.

3. Gardiner, "Egypt: Ancient Religion," 52; Eberhard Otto, "Egyptian Religion," *The New Encyclopaedia Britannica* Macropaedia 6 (1980) 503.

4. See Hans Bonnet, *Reallexikon der ägyptischen Religionsgeschichte* (Berlin: Walter de Gruyter, 1952) 277.

5. Bonnet, 277.

6. Jaroslav Černý comments that cows impressed the peasant folk by their motherly care (*Ancient Egyptian Religion* [Hutchinson's University Library, World Religions; London: Hutchinson House, 1952] 24-5).

7. Often her face, when frontally viewed, is broad, kindly, and surrounded by the thick "Hathor wig." According to Margaret A. Murray, Hathor is the only goddess who is (at times) represented full-face in the Egyptian bas-reliefs (*The Splendour that was Egypt* [London: Sidgwick and Jackson, 1963] 116-7).

8. Bonnet, 277. In many temples the head of Hathor (wearing various headpieces) was used as the capital of pillars. The finest example of such capitals is the Ptolemaic temple dedicated to her at Dendera (Murray, 116-7, 156).

9. Bonnet, 278; Černý, 24-5.

10. At different times and locations in Egypt Hathor was considered to be either the mother of Horus (early on Isis took over this role) or his wife (as at Dendera). See Bonnet, 277-8, 280, and "Hathor," *The New Encyclopaedia Britannica* Micropaedia 4 (1980) 946.

11. Bonnet, 278 and 278 fig. 71. Hathor is in certain other examples also represented only by her face/head.

12. Bonnet, 279.

13. Bonnet, 279; Černý, 25. The Memphite sycamore cult stood in high repute especially during the Old Kingdom. Bonnet explains that through this cult Hathor came into connection with Ptah. From the time of the New Kingdom come reports of a procession in which Ptah was led to the sycamore goddess, who thereby was considered as his daughter (279).

14. Bonnet, 279; Černý, 25; Pierre Montet, *Eternal Egypt* (trans. Doreen Weightman; New York: Praeger, 1964) 141; Murray, 116-7.

15. Bonnet, 279.

16. For a picture of Hathor, the cow goddess, looking out from the mountainside of western Thebes see Bonnet, 279 fig. 72 and E. A. Wallis Budge, *The Gods of the Egyptians* (2 vols.; New York: Dover, 1969; a reprint of the 1904 work) 1: (plate facing) 427. In this picture her (cow's) head appears among papyrus stalks; Montet comments that Hathor's favorite abode was among these plants (89).

17. Bonnet, 279, 799. See also Murray, 116-7. The Ptolemaic temple of Deir el-Medina was dedicated to Hathor (Bonnet, 799-800).

18. Bonnet, 279-80, 799.

19. "Hathor," *The New Encyclopaedia Britannica*, 946; cf. Bonnet, 800.

20. Bonnet, 280; Alfred Wiedemann, *Religion of the Ancient Egyptians* (New York: G. P. Putnam's Sons, 1897) 29-30.

21. Bonnet, 280.

22. Similarly, Hathor was at one time identified with the "Lady of Hetepet," the companion of Atum. She was thus regarded as the helpmate of the great creator god of Heliopolis, who was placed at the top of the Ennead by old local tradition and named "Bull" (Bonnet, 71, 280). Atum's cult later merged with that of Re (see Otto, 505 table 1). Černý points out that in Egyptian religion women seem to have taken no part in the liturgy proper, their role being limited to singing, dancing, and playing music in the temple and at the appearance of the god in public during processions. These women musicians, according to Černý, impersonated the god's harem and their leader was regarded as the wife of the god. In every case this wife was supposed to be the goddess Hathor, evidently under the influence of the sun cult of Heliopolis in which Hathor was the sun god's (Atum's) wife (118-9).

23. One way of representing Hathor was to show her as a cow wearing the solar disk and two plumes between her horns (Alan W. Shorter, *The Egyptian Gods* [London: Kegan Paul, Trench, Trubner, 1937] 130-1). A picture of this may be seen in Budge, 1: (page facing) 427.

24. Bonnet, 280-1; 733-5, esp. 735.

25. Sakhmet was a fierce, warlike lion goddess, represented as a lioness or woman with a lion's head, on which she wore the solar disk and uraeus. Her main cult place was Memphis, where she was worshipped under the title "Beloved of Ptah" as the wife of the great creator god (of Memphite theology) and mother of Nefertum (Bonnet, 643; Otto, 505 table 1). This triad came into existence only shortly before the New Kingdom; further, the union of Sakhmet with Ptah is not much older. Originally the Memphite Hathor stood much closer to Ptah. For this reason some have questioned whether Memphis was really the home of Sakhmet. Perhaps her home is to be located in the second nome of Lower Egypt, where Sakhmet had a sanctuary in its capital city Letopolis. However, for the history of the goddess the cult in Memphis is of fundamental significance. Through it she entered into the circle of the great *Residenzgötter* and had contact with the kingship. She was considered to be mother of the king, whom she also nursed (Bonnet, 643-4).

    Sakhmet became the eye of Horus and also the eye of Re. Occasionally she was named "Disk of the Sun" (Bonnet, 645). As the "Powerful One" she smote the enemies of Re and of Osiris; she felled Apophis, and slew the companions of Seth (Bonnet, 644).

    The goddess was regarded as having the power both to create epidemics and bring them to an end, and was called upon in magical spells. The priests of Sakhmet were generally considered to have a special magical knowledge. Moreover, doctors needed such knowledge, in view of the close connection of magic and the medical arts; thus at times doctors were priests of Sakhmet (Bonnet, 645; also Rainer Stadelmann, *Syrisch-Palästinensische Gottheiten in Ägypten* [Probleme der Ägyptologie 5; Leiden: E. J. Brill, 1967] 142).

    In spite of this patronage of the medical arts, the belief predominated that Sakhmet through her "messengers" sent sickness. Annual epidemics especially were attributed to her. Therefore, the deity's worshippers lived in fear of the rage of the goddess (in which the unpredictability of her animal, the lion, was reflected), and sought to appease her (Bonnet, 645-6).

26. Černý, 48; Shorter, 9. See also Bonnet, 282.

27. Bonnet, 281.

28. Bonnet, 281.

29. Stadelmann's comment puts the proper perspective on this matter, namely, that despite how the Egyptians may have viewed her, the *bʿlt gbl* was not actually a local form of Hathor, but was always in her real essence a Near Eastern (i.e., not an Egyptian) goddess, even when she was outwardly assimilated to the Hathor type. The decisive portion of Egyptian influence on the religion of Syria-Palestine was not in the altering of the essence of the divinities, but in the development and establishment of certain external types (145-6).

30. Bonnet, 281.

31. Bonnet, 281. See also Stadelmann, 1-4.

32. Bonnet, 281. As a counterpart to this Hathor of the foreign lands a "Hathor, Lady of Egypt" was worshipped (Bonnet, 281-2).

33. Bonnet, 282.

34. Budge's discussion of Hathor (perhaps somewhat overly exuberant) emphasizes this point (1: 431-2).

35. Bonnet, 282.

36. Bonnet, 282; J. R. Harris, "Medicine," in *The Legacy of Egypt* (2nd ed.; ed. J. R. Harris; Oxford: Clarendon, 1971) 120.

37. Montet, 157.

38. Montet, 33-4; Wiedemann, 184-5 n. 1.

39. Bonnet, 282; "Hathor," *The New Encyclopaedia Britannica*, 946; Wiedemann, 142.

40. Wiedemann, 61-2 n. 1, 142. Bonnet, as an example of a Hathor festival, refers to the "'Fest der Trunkenheit der Herrin von Dendera,'" in which "der König tanzend den Weinkrug zur Göttin trägt" (282). Interestingly, Bonnet understands the music and dance of the festivals as being two-sided: not only expressing joy, but also appeasing (the eye of the sun).

41. Bonnet, 282. The so-called "seven Hathors" were actually minor goddesses or "fairies" (Gardiner, "Egypt: Ancient Religion," 53) who appeared at birth and announced what the future of the child would be. They obtained the name "Hathor" secondarily, which as a result increased their prestige. In Greco-Roman times each of the seven was designated as the Hathor of a known Hathor cult place (Bonnet, 282).

42. Murray, 116-7. Of note here is the observation of Montet that the most popular deities of Egypt (including Hathor)

were called upon to take action in so many matters that it would be difficult to assign to them any one particular activity. On the whole, he explains, the Egyptians did not think in terms of a deity having one specialized function, and the Greeks were mistaken in assuming that the forms and names of their own deities had earlier parallels in the Nile Valley (151).

Appendix D

CORRESPONDING TEXT NUMBERS

Appendix D lists on the left the texts cited (in Chapters 1-4) from *CTA* and other sources, and on the right the corresponding numbers in M. Dietrich, O. Loretz, and J. Sanmartín's *Die keilalphabetischen Texte aus Ugarit.*

CTA	1	1.1
	2	1.2
	3	1.3
	4	1.4
	5	1.5
	6	1.6
	8	1.8
	12	1.12
	14	1.14
	15	1.15
	16	1.16
	17	1.17
	18	1.18
	19	1.19
	23	1.23
	29	1.47
	30	1.65
	32	1.40
	34	1.39
	35	1.41
	36	1.46
	37	1.49
	38	1.50
	App. II	1.87
PRU 2	2 (*UT* 1002)	2.31
	4	1.81
	24	4.141
	91	4.216

PRU 5	1	1.92
RS	8	7.56-59
	20.24	
	24.244	1.100
	24.245	1.101
	24.247	1.103
	24.256	1.112
	24.258	1.114
	24.263	1.117
	24.264 + 280	1.118
	24.271	1.123
	24.302	1.140
	24.643	1.148
	26.142	
UT	321	
	1002 (*PRU 2* 2)	2.31

Drawings

Drawing 1. Craigie, "The Tablets from Ugarit," 65
Drawing 2. *ANEP*, 163 fig. 471
Drawing 3. Bisi, *Le Stele Puniche*, pl. 30.2
Drawing 4. Bisi, *Le Stele Puniche*, pl. 31
Drawing 5. Bisi, *Le Stele Puniche*, pl. 30.1
Drawing 6. Berthier and Charlier, *Le sanctuaire punique*, pl. 22.A
Drawing 7. Hours-Miedan, "Les représentations," pl. 12.f (*CIS*, Pars Prima, no. 4569)
Drawing 8. Bisi, *Le Stele Puniche*, pl. 27.3
Drawing 9a. Berthier and Charlier, *Le sanctuaire punique*, pl. 24.B
Drawing 9b. Bisi, *Le Stele Puniche*, pl. 20.1
Drawing 10a. Berthier and Charlier, *Le sanctuaire punique*, pl. 5.C
Drawing 10b. Bisi, *Le Stele Puniche*, pl. 26.3
Drawing 11a. Berthier and Charlier, *Le sanctuaire punique*, pl. 17.C
Drawing 11b. *CIS*, Pars Prima, no. 689
Drawing 12. Berthier and Charlier, *Le sanctuaire punique*, pl. 27.C
Drawing 13. *CIS*, Pars Prima, no. 2235
Drawing 14. Bisi, *Le Stele Puniche*, pl. 25.1

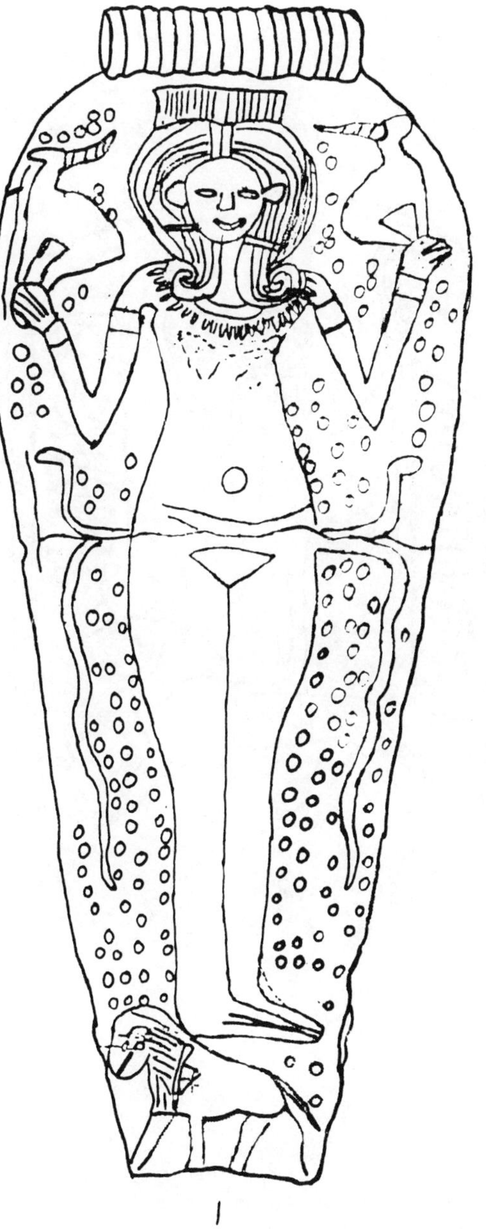

1

2

3

4

5

6

7

8

9a

9b

10a

10b

11a

11b

13

12

14

BIBLIOGRAPHY

Abou-Assaf, Ali; Bordreuil, Pierre; and Millard, Alan R. *La statue de Tell Fekherye et son inscription bilingue assyro-araméenne*. Etudes Assyriologiques, Cahier 7. Paris: Editions Recherche sur les civilisations, 1982.

Acquaro, Enrico. *I Rasoi Punici*. Studi Semitici 41. Roma: Consiglio Nazionale delle Ricerche, 1971.

Aharoni, Yohanan. *The Archaeology of the Land of Israel*. Ed. Miriam Aharoni, trans. Anson F. Rainey. Philadelphia: Westminster, 1982.

Albright, William Foxwell. "An Aramaean Magical Text in Hebrew from the Seventh Century B.C.," *BASOR* 76 (1939) 5-11.

________. *Archaeology and the Religion of Israel*. Baltimore: Johns Hopkins, 1942.

________. "Astarte Plaques and Figurines from Tell Beit Mirsim." In *Mélanges syriens*: offerts à monsieur René Dussaud, secrétaire perpétuel de l'Académie des Inscriptions et Belles-lettres, par ses amis et ses élèves, vol. 1, 107-20. Paris: Paul Geuthner, 1939.

________. "A Catalogue of Early Hebrew Lyric Poems (Psalm LXVIII)," *HUCA* 23 (1950-51) 1-39.

________. "The Early Alphabetic Inscriptions from Sinai and their Decipherment," *BASOR* 110 (1948) 6-22.

________. "The Evolution of the West-Semitic Divinity ᶜAn-ᶜAnat-ᶜAttâ," *AJSL* 41 (1925) 73-101. "Further Observations on the Name *ᶜAnat-ᶜAttah*," *AJSL* 41 (1925) 283-5. "Note on the Goddess ᶜAnat," *AJSL* 43 (1927) 233-6.

________. *From the Stone Age to Christianity*. 2nd ed. Garden City, N.Y.: Doubleday, 1957.

________. "Neglected Factors in the Greek Intellectual Revolution," *Proceedings of the American Philosophical Society* 116 (1972) 225-42.

_______. "The North Canaanite Epic of ʾAlʾêyân Baʿal and Môt," *JPOS* 12 (1932) 185-208.

_______. "A Prince of Taanach in the Fifteenth Century B.C.," *BASOR* 94 (1944) 12-27.

_______. *The Proto-Sinaitic Inscriptions and Their Decipherment.* HTS 22. Cambridge: Harvard University, 1966.

_______. "Some Observations on the New Material for the History of the Alphabet," *BASOR* 134 (1954) 26.

_______. "Two Little Understood Amarna Letters from the Middle Jordan Valley," *BASOR* 89 (1943) 7-17.

_______. "A Vow to Asherah in the Keret Epic," *BASOR* 94 (1944) 30-1.

_______. *Yahweh and the Gods of Canaan.* Garden City, N.Y.: Doubleday, 1968.

Amiet, Pierre. "Observations sur les 'Tablettes magiques' d'Arslan Tash," *Aula orientalis* 1 (1983) 109.

Ap-Thomas, D. R. "The Phoenicians." In *Peoples of Old Testament Times*, ed. D. J. Wiseman, 259-86. Oxford: Clarendon, 1973.

Archi, Alfonso. "Les dieux d'Ebla au IIIe millenaire avant J. C. et les dieux d'Ugarit," *Les Annales Archéologiques Arabes Syriennes* 29-30 (1979-80) 167-71.

_______. "The Epigraphic Evidence from Ebla and the Old Testament," *Bib* 60 (1979) 556-66.

_______. "Further Concerning Ebla and the Bible," *BA* 44 (1981) 145-54.

Astour, Michael C. "Ugarit and the Great Powers." In *Ugarit in Retrospect*, ed. Gordon D. Young, 3-29. Winona Lake, In.: Eisenbrauns, 1981.

Attridge, Harold W. and Oden, Robert A., Jr. *Philo of Byblos: The Phoenician History.* CBQMS 9. Washington, D.C.: Catholic Biblical Association of America, 1981.

_______. *The Syrian Goddess (De Dea Syria). Attributed to Lucian.* SBLTT 9. Missoula, Mont.: Scholars Press, 1976.

Aubet, Maria E. See Ferron, Jean.

Bailey, Lloyd R. "Israelite *ʾĒl Šadday* and Amorite *Bêl Šadê*," *JBL* 87 (1968) 434-8.

Ball, Charles J. *Light from the East.* London: Eyre and Spottiswoode, 1899.

Barr, James. "Philo of Byblos and his 'Phoenician History,'" *BJRL* 57 (1974) 17-68.

Barrelet, Marie-Thérèse. "Deux déesses syro-phéniciennes sur un bronze du Louvre," *Syria* 35 (1958) 27-44.

Beck, Pirhiya. "The Drawings from Ḥorvat Teiman (Kuntillet ᶜAjrud)," *Tel Aviv* 9 (1982) 3-68.

Beit-Arieh, Itzhaq. "Fifteen Years in Sinai," *BAR* 10 (1984) 26-54.

Benz, Frank L. *Personal Names in the Phoenician and Punic Inscriptions.* Studia Pohl 8. Rome: Biblical Institute Press, 1972.

Berthier, André and Charlier, René. *Le sanctuaire punique d'El-Hofra à Constantine.* Plates and Text. Paris: Arts et Métiers Graphiques, 1952, 1955.

"Bes," *The New Encyclopaedia Britannica,* Micropaedia 1 (1980) 1023.

Best, Jan. "*yaššaram!*," *UF* 13 (1981) 291-3.

Betlyon, John Wilson. *The Coinage and Mints of Phoenicia.* HSM 26. Chico, Ca.: Scholars Press, 1980.

________. "The Cult of ᵓAšerah/ᵓĒlat at Sidon," *JNES* 44 (1985) 53-6.

Beyers Brink, Marthinus. "A Philological Study of Texts in Connection with Aṯtrt and Aṯirat in the Ugaritic Language." Doctor in Literature diss., University of Stellenbosch, 1977.

Bisi, Anna Maria. *Le Stele Puniche.* Studi Semitici 27. Roma: Istituto di Studi del Vicino Oriente, Università di Roma, 1967.

Bonnet, Hans. *Reallexikon der ägyptischen Religionsgeschichte.* Berlin: Walter de Gruyter, 1952.

Bordreuil, Pierre. See Abou-Assaf, Ali.

Boreux, Charles. "La Stèle C.86 du Musée du Louvre et les stèles similaires." In *Mélanges syriens*: offerts à monsieur René Dussaud, secrétaire perpétuel de l'Académie des Inscriptions et Belles-lettres, par ses amis et ses élèves, vol. 2, 673-87. Paris: Paul Geuthner, 1939.

Brancoli, Isabella; Ciasca, Antonia; Garbini, Giovanni; et al. *Mozia-III*. Studi Semitici 24. Roma: Istituto di Studi del Vicino Oriente, Università di Roma, 1967.

Breasted, James Henry. *A History of Egypt*. New York: Charles Scribner's Sons, 1912.

Bright, John. *A History of Israel*. 3rd ed. Philadelphia: Westminster, 1981.

Brockelmann, Carl. *Grundriss der vergleichenden Grammatik der semitischen Sprachen*. 2 vols. Hildesheim: Georg Olms, 1961; a reprint of the 1908, 1913 work.

Buccellati, Giorgio. *The Amorites of the Ur III Period*. Ricerche 1. Naples: Istituto Orientale di Napoli, 1966.

Budge, E. A. Wallis. *Egyptian Religion*. London: Routledge and Kegan Paul, 1972; a reprint of the 1899 work.

________. *The Gods of the Egyptians*. 2 vols. New York: Dover, 1969; a reprint of the 1904 work.

Caquot, André and Sznycer, Maurice. *Ugaritic Religion*. Iconography of Religions 15/8. Leiden: E. J. Brill, 1980.

Caquot, André; Sznycer, Maurice; and Herdner, Andrée. *Textes ougaritiques. I. Myths et légendes*. Littératures anciennes du Proche-Orient 7. Paris: Editions du Cerf, 1974.

Černý, Jaroslav. *Ancient Egyptian Religion*. Hutchinson's University Library, World Religions. London: Hutchinson House, 1952.

Charlier, René. See Berthier, André.

Chase, Debra A. "A Note on an Inscription from Kuntillet ʿAjrūd," *BASOR* 246 (1982) 63-7.

Chiera, Edward. *Lists of Personal Names from the Temple School of Nippur*. 3 pts. University of Pennsylvania Museum Publications, Babylonian Section 11. Philadelphia: University Museum, 1916-19.

________. *Sumerian Lexical Texts from the Temple School of Nippur*. OIP 11. Chicago: University of Chicago, 1929.

Ciasca, Antonia. See Brancoli, Isabella.

Clapham, Lynn Roy. "Sanchuniathon: The First Two Cycles." Ph.D. diss., Harvard University, 1969.

Clay, Albert T. *The Antiquity of Amorite Civilization.* New Haven, Conn.: privately printed, 1924.

Clemen, Carl. *Lukians Schrift über die syrische Göttin.* Der Alte Orient 37/3,4. Leipzig: J. C. Hinrichs, 1938.

________. *Die phönikische Religion nach Philo von Byblos.* Mitteilungen der vorderasiatisch-ägyptischen Gesellschaft 42/3. Leipzig: J. C. Hinrichs, 1939.

Clifford, Richard J. *The Cosmic Mountain in Canaan and the Old Testament.* HSM 4. Cambridge: Harvard University, 1972.

________. "Recent Scholarly Discussion of *CTCA* 23 (*UT* 52)." In *SBL 1975 Seminar Papers*, ed. George MacRae, vol. 1, 99-106. Missoula, Mont.: Scholars Press, 1975.

Cogan, Morton. *Imperialism and Religion: Assyria, Judah and Israel in the Eighth and Seventh Centuries B.C.E.* SBLMS 19. Missoula, Mont.: Scholars Press, 1974.

Coogan, Michael David, ed. and trans. *Stories from Ancient Canaan.* Philadelphia: Westminster, 1978.

Coote, R. B. "The Serpent and Sacred Marriage in Northwest Semitic Tradition." Ph.D. diss., Harvard University, 1972.

Corpus Inscriptionum Semiticarum. Ab Academia inscriptionum et litterarum humaniorum. Paris: e Republicae typographeo, 1881-.

Craigie, Peter C. "The Tablets from Ugarit and their Importance for Biblical Studies," *BAR* 9 (1983) 62-73.

Cross, Frank Moore, Jr. *Canaanite Myth and Hebrew Epic.* Cambridge: Harvard University, 1973.

________. "The Cave Inscriptions from Khirbet Beit Lei." In *Near Eastern Archaeology in the Twentieth Century*, ed. James A. Sanders, 299-306. Garden City, N.Y.: Doubleday, 1970.

________. "The Evolution of the Proto-Canaanite Alphabet," *BASOR* 134 (1954) 15-24.

________. "Newly Found Inscriptions in Old Canaanite and Early Phoenician Scripts," *BASOR* 238 (1980) 1-20.

________. "The Origin and Early Evolution of the Alphabet," *Eretz-Israel* 8 (1967) 8*-24*.

________. "Prose and Poetry in the Mythic and Epic Texts from Ugarit," *HTR* 67 (1974) 1-15.

________. Lectures on Phoenicians in the West and an unpublished Aramaic inscription from Tema, delivered in the Harvard Semitic Museum, Sept. 29, 1983.

________. See also Milik, J. T.

Cross, Frank Moore, Jr. and Saley, Richard J. "Phoenician Incantations and a Plaque of the Seventh Century B.C. from Arslan Tash in Upper Syria," *BASOR* 197 (1970) 42-9.

de Moor, Johannes C. "The Semitic Pantheon of Ugarit," *UF* 2 (1970) 187-228.

de Tarragon, Jean-Michel. *Le Culte à Ugarit*. Cahiers de la Revue Biblique 19. Paris: J. Gabalda, 1980.

Dever, William G. "Asherah, Consort of Yahweh? New Evidence from Kuntillet ʿAjrûd," *BASOR* 255 (1984) 21-37.

________. "Iron Age Epigraphic Material from the Area of Khirbet el-Kôm," *HUCA* 40-41 (1969-70) 139-204.

________. "כתובות ממערות-קבורה ישראליות בהר חברון," *Qadmoniot* 4 (1971) 90-2.

________. "Material Remains and the Cult in Ancient Israel: An Essay in Archaeological Systematics." In *The Word of the Lord Shall Go Forth*, ed. Carol L. Meyers and M. O'Connor, 571-87. Winona Lake, In.: Eisenbrauns, 1983.

________. "Recent Archaeological Confirmation of the Cult of Asherah in Ancient Israel," *Hebrew Studies* 23 (1982) 37-43.

"Dido," *The Encyclopaedia Britannica* 7 (13th ed., 1926) 206.

Dietrich, M.; Loretz, O.; and Sanmartín, J. *Die keilalphabetischen Texte aus Ugarit*. AOAT 24. Neukirchen-Vluyn: Butzon and Bercker Kevelaer, 1976.

"Dione," *Encyclopaedia Britannica* 8 (11th ed., 1910-11) 283.

Donner, Herbert, and Röllig, Wolfgang. *Kanaanäische und aramäische Inschriften*. 3 vols. Wiesbaden: Otto Harrassowitz, 1966-69.

Dothan, M. "A Sign of Tanit from Tel ʿAkko," *IEJ* 24 (1974) 44-9.

Dowling, Herndon G. "Snake," *The Encyclopedia Americana* 25 (1973) 85-101.

Dowson, V. H. W. *Dates and Date Cultivation of the ᵓIraq.* 3 parts. Agricultural Directorate, Ministry of Interior, Mesopotamia, Memoir 3. Cambridge, England: Heffer, for The Agricultural Directorate of Mesopotamia, 1921-3.

Driver, Godfrey Rolles. *Canaanite Myths and Legends.* Edinburgh: T. and T. Clark, 1956.

Duthie, Alexander. *The Greek Mythology.* Edinburgh: Oliver and Boyd, 1949.

Dyer, Louis. *Studies of the Gods in Greece at Certain Sanctuaries Recently Excavated.* London: MacMillan, 1891.

Ebeling, Erich. "Ašratu," *Reallexikon der Assyriologie* 1, ed. Erich Ebeling and Bruno Meissner, 169. Berlin and Leipzig: Walter de Gruyter, 1932.

________. See also Knudtzon, Jørgen Alexander.

Edwards, I. E. S. "A Relief of Qudshu-Astarte-Anath in the Winchester College Collection," *JNES* 14 (1955) 49-51.

Edzard, Dietz Otto. *Die "Zweite Zwischenzeit" Babyloniens.* Wiesbaden: Otto Harrassowitz, 1957.

Eissfeldt, Otto. "Phönikische und griechische Kosmogonie," *Kleine Schriften* 3 (1966) 501-512.

Emerton, J. A. "New Light on Israelite Religion: The Implications of the Inscriptions from Kuntillet ᶜAjrud," *ZAW* 94 (1982) 2-20.

Erman, Adolf. *A Handbook of Egyptian Religion.* Trans. A. S. Griffith. London: Archibald Constable, 1907.

Escher-Bürkli, J. "Dione," PW 5 (1905) cols. 878-880.

Fensham, F. C. "The Numeral Seventy in the Old Testament and the Family of Jerubbaal, Ahab, Panammuwa and Athirat," *PEQ* 109 (1977) 113-5.

Ferron, Jean. *Mort-Dieu de Carthage.* Collection Cahiers de Byrsa Série Monographies 2. Text and Plates. Paris: Librairie Orientaliste Paul Geuthner, 1975.

Ferron, Jean and Aubet, Maria E. *Orants de Carthage.* Collection Cahiers de Byrsa Série Monographies 1. Text and Plates. Paris: Librairie Orientaliste Paul Geuthner, 1974.

Garbini, Giovanni. Review of *The Phoenicians*, by Donald Harden. *OrAnt* 1 (1962) 296-8.

________. See Brancoli, Isabella.

Gardiner, Alan Henderson. "Egypt: Ancient Religion," *The Encyclopaedia Britannica* 9 (11th ed., 1910-11) 48-57.

________. *Egypt of the Pharaohs.* Oxford: Oxford University, 1961.

Garstang, John and Strong, Herbert A. *The Syrian Goddess.* London: Constable, 1913.

Gaster, Theodor H. "A Canaanite Magical Text," *Or* n.s. 11 (1942) 41-79.

________. "The Magical Inscription from Arslan Tash," *JNES* 6 (1947) 186-8.

________. *Thespis: Ritual, Myth, and Drama in the Ancient Near East.* Garden City, N.Y.: Doubleday, 1961.

Gates, Marie-Henriette. "Dura-Europos: A Fortress of Syro-Mesopotamian Art," *BA* 47 (1984) 166-81.

Gauckler, P. See La Blanchère, F. Du Coudray.

Gelb, I. J. "The Early History of the West Semitic Peoples," *JCS* 15 (1961) 27-47.

Gibson, J. C. L. *Canaanite Myths and Legends.* Edinburgh: T. and T. Clark, 1977.

Gilula, Mordechai. "To Yahweh Shomron and His Asherah," *Shnaton* 3 (1978-9) 129-37 (Hebrew; English summary, pp. xv-xvi).

Ginsberg, H. L., trans. "Ugaritic Myths, Epics, and Legends." In *Ancient Near Eastern Texts Relating to the Old Testament*, 3rd ed. with Supplement, ed. James B. Pritchard, 129-55. Princeton: Princeton University, 1969.

Giveon, Raphael. "Some Egyptological Considerations Concerning Ugarit." In *Ugarit in Retrospect*, ed. Gordon D. Young, 55-8. Winona Lake, In.: Eisenbrauns, 1981.

Glock, Albert E. "A New Taᶜannek Tablet," *BASOR* 204 (1971) 17-30.

________. "Taanach," *Encyclopedia of Archaeological Excavations in the Holy Land* 4, ed. Michael Avi-Yonah and Ephraim Stern, 1138-47. Englewood Cliffs, N.J.: Prentice-Hall, 1978.

________. "*Taanach," *IDB* Supplementary Volume (1976) 855-6.

Goetze, Albrecht, trans. "Hittite Myths, Epics, and Legends." In *Ancient Near Eastern Texts Relating to the Old Testament*, 3rd ed. with Supplement, ed. James B.

Pritchard, 120-8, 519. Princeton: Princeton University, 1969.

Gollob, Hedwig. *Die Götter am Nil*. Vienna: Gerold, 1959.

Gordon, Cyrus H. *Ugaritic Literature*. Rome: Pontifical Biblical Institute, 1949.

________. *Ugaritic Textbook: Grammar, Texts in Transliteration, Cuneiform Selections, Glossary, Indices*. AnOr 38. 3 pts. Rome: Pontifical Biblical Institute, 1965.

Graf, Alfred Byrd. *Tropica: Color Cyclopedia of Exotic Plants and Trees from the Tropics and Subtropics*. 1st ed. East Rutherford, N.J.: Roehrs, 1978.

Graves, Robert. *The Greek Myths*. 2 vols. Baltimore: Penguin Books, 1955.

Gray, John. *I and II Kings*. 2nd ed. Old Testament Library. London: SCM, 1970.

________. *The KRT Text in the Literature of Ras Shamra*. 2nd ed. Leiden: E. J. Brill, 1964.

________. "Resheph," *IDB* 4 (1962) 36-7.

________. "Rimmon, 2.," *IDB* 4 (1962) 99.

Greenfield, Jonas C. Review of *Ugaritic-Hebrew Philology*, by Mitchell Dahood. *JAOS* 89 (1969) 174-8.

Gröndahl, Frauke. *Die Personennamen der Texte aus Ugarit*. Studia Pohl Dissertationes Scientificae de Rebus Orientis Antiqui 1. Rome: Pontifical Biblical Institute, 1967.

Gsell, Stéphane. *Histoire ancienne de l'Afrique du nord*. Vol. 4, *La civilisation carthaginoise*. Paris: Hachette, 1920.

Guthrie, W. K. C. *The Greeks and their Gods*. Boston: Beacon Press, 1951.

Haldar, Alfred. *Who Were the Amorites*? Monographs on the Ancient Near East 1. Leiden: E. J. Brill, 1971.

Hallo, William W. and Simpson, William K. *The Ancient Near East*. New York: Harcourt Brace Jovanovich, 1971.

Hamburger, H. "A Hoard of Syrian Tetradrachms and Tyrian Bronze Coins from Gush Ḥalav," *IEJ* 4 (1954) 201-26.

Hamilton, R. W. "Beth-shan," *IDB* 1 (1962) 397-401.

Hanson, Paul D. *The Dawn of Apocalyptic.* Philadelphia: Fortress Press, 1975.

Harden, Donald. *The Phoenicians.* Harmondsworth, Middlesex, England: Pelican Books, 1971.

Harding, Lankester. See Tufnell, Olga.

"Harness and Saddlery," *The New Encyclopaedia Britannica* Macropaedia 8 (1980) 657-9.

Harris, James R. "Medicine." In *The Legacy of Egypt*, 2nd ed., ed. James R. Harris, 112-37. Oxford: Clarendon, 1971.

"Hathor," *The New Encyclopaedia Britannica* Micropaedia 4 (1980) 946.

Heckenbach, J. "ʽΡέα," PW 1 (Zweite Reihe; 1914) cols. 339-341.

Helck, Wolfgang. *Die Beziehungen Ägyptens zu Vorderasien im 3. und 2. Jahrtausend v. Chr.* Ägyptologische Abhandlungen 5. Wiesbaden: Otto Harrassowitz, 1962.

Herdner, Andrée. *Corpus des tablettes en cunéiformes alphabétiques découvertes à Ras Shamra-Ugarit de 1929 à 1939.* Mission de Ras Shamra 10. Text, and Figures and Plates. Paris: Imprimerie Nationale, 1963.

________. "Nouveaux textes alphabétiques de Ras Shamra - XXIVe campagne, 1961." In *Ugaritica VII*, 1-74. Mission de Ras Shamra 18. Paris: Mission Archéologique de Ras Shamra, 1978.

________. See also Caquot, André.

Hill, George Francis. *Catalogue of the Greek Coins of Palestine.* Catalogue of the Greek Coins in the British Museum 27. London: British Museum, 1914.

________. *Catalogue of the Greek Coins of Phoenicia.* Catalogue of the Greek Coins in the British Museum 25. London: British Museum, 1910.

Hillers, D. R. "An Alphabetic Cuneiform Tablet from Taanach," *BASOR* 173 (1964) 45-50.

Hommel, Fritz. *Aufsätze und Abhandlungen.* 3 pts. München: G. Franz, 1892-1901.

Hours-Miedan, Magdeleine. "Les représentations figurées sur les stèles de Carthage," *Cahiers de Byrsa* 1 (1951) 15-160.

Hrozný, Friedrich. "Keilschrifttexte aus Taᶜannek," *Denkschriften der Kaiserlichen Akademie der Wissenschaften in Wien*, Philosophisch-Historische Klasse 50 (1904) 113-22.

Hvidberg-Hansen, F. O. *La Déesse TNT*. Trans. Françoise Arndt. 2 vols. Copenhague: G. E. C. Gad's Forlag, 1979.

Inge, Charles H. See Tufnell, Olga.

Jacobs, Paul F. "Tell Halif/Lahav 1983 Season," *ASOR Newsletter* 36 (1985) 4-5.

Jacobsen, Thorkild. "Notes on Nintur," *Or* n.s. 42 (1973) 274-98.

________. *The Treasures of Darkness*. New Haven: Yale University, 1976.

Jacoby, Felix. *Die Fragmente der griechischen Historiker*. Dritter Teil, C. Leiden: E. J. Brill, 1958.

Jamme, A., trans. "South-Arabian Inscriptions." In *Ancient Near Eastern Texts Relating to the Old Testament*, 3rd ed. with Supplement, ed. James B. Pritchard, 663-70. Princeton: Princeton University, 1969.

Jenkins, G. K. and Lewis, R. B. *Carthaginian Gold and Electrum Coins*. London: Royal Numismatic Society, 1963.

Jirku, A. *Kanaanäische Mythen und Epen aus Ras Schamra - Ugarit*. Gütersloh: Gütersloher Verlagshaus Gerd Mohn, 1962.

Kautzsch, E., ed., and Cowley, A. E., trans. *Gesenius' Hebrew Grammar*. 2nd English ed. Oxford: Clarendon, 1946.

Kees, Hermann. *Der Götterglaube im alten Ägypten*. 2nd ed. Berlin: Akademie, 1956.

Kerényi, C. *The Gods of the Greeks*. Trans. Norman Cameron. London: Thames and Hudson, 1951.

King, L. W. *The Letters and Inscriptions of Ḫammurabi*. 3 vols. New York: AMS, 1976; a reprint of the 1898-1900 work.

Knudtzon, Jørgen Alexander; Weber, Otto; and Ebeling, Erich. *Die El-Amarna-Tafeln*. 2 vols. Leipzig: J. C. Hinrichs, 1915.

Kupper, Jean-Robert. *L'iconographie du dieu Amurru dans la glyptique de la Iʳᵉ dynastie babylonienne*. Académie Royale de Belgique, Classe des Lettres, Mémoires, 2nd series, 55/1. Bruxelles: Palais des Académies, 1961.

________. See also Sollberger, Edmond.

La Blanchère, F. Du Coudray and Gauckler, P. *Musée Alaoui.* Catalogue des Musées et Collections Archéologiques de l'Algérie et de la Tunisie 7. Paris: 1897.

Landsberger, Benno. "Assyrische Königsliste und 'Dunkles Zeitalter' [Continued]," *JCS* 8 (1954) 47-73.

________. *The Date Palm and its By-products according to the Cuneiform Sources.* *AfO* 17. Graz: Ernst Weidner, 1967.

Langlois, Arthur C. *Supplement to Palms of the World.* Gainesville, Fla.: University of Florida, 1976.

Lapp, Paul W. "The 1968 Excavations at Tell Taᶜannek," *BASOR* 195 (1969) 2-49.

Laroche, Emmanuel. "Textes mythologiques hittites en transcription, 2e partie: Mythologie d'origine étrangère," *Revue Hittite et Asianique* 26 (1968) 5-92.

________. See also Nougayrol, Jean.

L'Heureux, Conrad E. *Rank Among the Canaanite Gods.* HSM 21. Missoula, Mont.: Scholars Press, 1979.

Lemaire, André. "Les inscriptions de Khirbet el-Qôm et l'ashérah de Yhwh," *RB* 84 (1977) 595-608.

________. "Who or What Was Yahweh's Asherah?," *BAR* 10 (1984) 42-51.

Levine, Baruch A. "The Descriptive Ritual Texts from Ugarit: Some Formal and Functional Features of the *Genre*." In *The Word of the Lord Shall Go Forth*, ed. Carol L. Meyers and M. O'Connor, 467-75. Winona Lake, In.: Eisenbrauns, 1983.

Lewis, R. B. See Jenkins, G. K.

Lewy, Julius. "Amurritica," *HUCA* 32 (1961) 31-74.

Lidzbarski, Mark. *Handbuch der nordsemitischen Epigraphik.* 2 vols. Weimar: Emil Felber, 1898.

Linder, Elisha. "A Cargo of Phoenicio-Punic Figurines," *Archaeology* 26 (1973) 182-7.

Lipiński, Edward. "Aḫat-milki, reine d'Ugarit, et la guerre du Mukiš," OLP 12 (1981) 79-115.

________. "The Goddess Aṯirat in Ancient Arabia, in Babylon, and in Ugarit," OLP 3 (1972) 101-19.

Liverani, M. "The Amorites." In *Peoples of Old Testament Times*, ed. D. J. Wiseman, 100-33. Oxford: Clarendon, 1973.

Løkkegaard, F. "Some Reflexions on Reading F. O. Hvidberg-Hansen's Book La Déesse Tnt, Une étude sur la religion canaanéo-punique," *UF* 14 (1982) 129-140.

Loretz, O. See Dietrich, M.

Macalister, Robert A. S. *The Excavation of Gezer, 1902-1905 and 1907-1909*. 3 vols. London: John Murray, 1912.

McCurrach, James C. *Palms of the World*. New York: Harper and Brothers, 1960.

Maier, Walter A., III. "A Study of ʾAšerah: The Extrabiblical Evidence." Ph.D. diss., Harvard University, 1984.

Merlin, Alfred. *Le sanctuaire de Baal et de Tanit près de Siagu*. Notes et Documents 4. Paris: Direction des Antiquités et Arts, 1910.

Meshel, Zeʾev. "Did Yahweh Have a Consort?," *BAR* 5 (1979) 24-35.

________. *Kuntillet ʿAjrud: A Religious Centre from the Time of the Judaean Monarchy on the Border of Sinai*. Jerusalem: Israel Museum, Cat. 175, 1978.

________. "Kuntillet ʾAjrud [*sic*]: An Israelite Religious Center in Northern Sinai," *Expedition* 20 (1978) 50-4.

Meyers, Carol L. *The Tabernacle Menorah: A Synthetic Study of a Symbol from the Biblical Cult*. ASOR Dissertation Series 2. Missoula, Mont.: Scholars Press, 1976.

Milik, J. T. "An Unpublished Arrow-head with Phoenician Inscription of the 11th-10th Century B.C.," *BASOR* 143 (1956) 3-6.

Milik, J. T. and Cross, Frank M., Jr. "Inscribed Javelin-heads from the Period of the Judges: A Recent Discovery in Palestine," *BASOR* 134 (1954) 5-15.

Millard, Alan R. See Abou-Assaf, Ali.

Miller, Patrick D. "Animal Names as Designations in Ugaritic and Hebrew," *UF* 2 (1970) 177-86.

"Min," *The New Encyclopaedia Britannica* Micropaedia 6 (1980) 905.

Mittmann, Siegfried. "Die Grabinschrift des Sängers Uriahu," *ZDPV* 97 (1981) 139-52.

Montet, Pierre. *Eternal Egypt*. Trans. Doreen Weightman. New York: Praeger, 1964.

More, Brookes, trans. "Atalanta." In *Great Classical Myths*, ed. F. R. B. Godolphin, 327-33. Modern Library. New York: Random House, 1964.

Mosca, Paul G. "Child Sacrifice in Canaanite and Israelite Religion." Ph.D. diss., Harvard University, 1975.

________. "The Offerants and Their Professions." Paper presented at the Carthage Symposium held at the national conference of the Society for Biblical Literature/ American Schools of Oriental Research, San Francisco, 1981.

Moscati, Sabatino. "L'origine del 'segno di Tanit,'" *Atti della Accademia Nazionale dei Lincei*, Rendiconti della Classe di scienze morali, storiche e filologiche, series 8, vol. 27 (1972) 371-4.

________. *The World of the Phoenicians*. Trans. Alastair Hamilton. London: Weidenfeld and Nicolson, 1968.

Mras, Karl. *Eusebius Werke*. Achter Band, *Die Praeparatio Evangelica*. GCS 43. Berlin: Akademie, 1954.

Mullen, E. Theodore, Jr. *The Divine Council in Canaanite and Early Hebrew Literature*. HSM 24. Chico, Ca.: Scholars Press, 1980.

Müller, Hans-Peter. "Religionsgeschichtliche Beobachtungen zu den Texten von Ebla," *ZDPV* 96 (1980) 1-19.

Müller, L. *Numismatique de l'ancienne Afrique*. 3 vols. Copenhague: Bianco Luno, 1860-62.

________. *Numismatique de l'ancienne Afrique. Supplément*. Copenhague: Bianco Luno, 1874.

Murray, Margaret A. *The Splendour that was Egypt*. London: Sidgwick and Jackson, 1963.

Naveh, Joseph. "Graffiti and Dedications," *BASOR* 235 (1979) 27-30.

Negbi, Ora. *Canaanite Gods in Metal*. Tel Aviv University Institute of Archaeology 5. Tel Aviv: Peli, 1976.

Nougayrol, Jean. *Le Palais Royal d'Ugarit III*. Mission de Ras Shamra 6. Text and Plates. Paris: Imprimerie Nationale, 1955.

Nougayrol, Jean; Laroche, Emmanuel; Virolleaud, Charles; and Schaeffer, Claude F. A. *Ugaritica V*. Mission de Ras Shamra 16. Paris: Imprimerie Nationale, 1968.

Obermann, J. *Ugaritic Mythology.* New Haven: Yale University, 1948.

Oden, Robert A., Jr. "Philo of Byblos and Hellenistic Historiography," *PEQ* 110 (1978) 115-26.

________. *Studies in Lucian's De Syria Dea.* HSM 15. Missoula, Mont.: Scholars Press, 1977.

________. See also Attridge, Harold.

Oldfather, C. H., trans. *Diodorus of Sicily I.* LCL. London: William Heinemann, 1933.

Otten, Heinrich. "Ein kanaanäischer Mythus aus Boğazköy," *Mitteilungen des Instituts für Orientforschung,* Deutsche Akademie der Wissenschaften zu Berlin 1 (1953) 125-50.

Otto, Eberhard. "Egyptian Religion," *The New Encyclopaedia Britannica* Macropaedia 6 (1980) 503-9.

Ouellette, Jean. "More on ʾÊl Šadday and Bêl Šadê," *JBL* 88 (1969) 470-1.

Patai, Raphael. *The Hebrew Goddess.* New York: Avon, 1978.

Paton, Lewis B. "Atargatis," *Encyclopaedia of Religion and Ethics* 2, ed. James Hastings, 164-7. New York: Charles Scribner's Sons, 1910.

Perlman, Alice Lenore. "Asherah and Astarte in the Old Testament and Ugaritic Literature." Ph.D. diss., Graduate Theological Union, Berkeley, Ca. Ann Arbor, Mich.: University Microfilms, 1978.

Peters, James A. "Serpentes," *The New Encyclopaedia Britannica* Macropaedia 16 (1980) 559-67.

Pettinato, Giovanni. "Culto ufficiale ad Ebla durante il regno di Ibbi-Sipiš," *OrAnt* 18 (1979) 85-215.

Picard, Colette. *Carthage.* Paris: Société d'Edition "*Les Belles Lettres,*" 1951.

________. "Genèse et évolution des signes de la bouteille et de Tanit à Carthage," *Studi Magrebini* 2 (1968) 77-87.

________. See also Picard, Gilbert.

Picard, Gilbert. *Carthage.* Trans. Miriam and Lionel Kochan. New York: Frederick Ungar, 1964.

________. *Le Monde de Carthage.* Paris: Buchet/Chastel, 1956.

Picard, Gilbert and Picard, Colette. *The Life and Death of Carthage*. Trans. Dominique Collon. London: Sidgwick and Jackson, 1968.

Pinches, Theophilus G. "The Temples of Ancient Babylonia, I," *Proceedings of the Society of Biblical Archaeology* 22 (1900) 358-71.

Pomponio, F. "I nomi divini nei testi di Ebla," *UF* 15 (1983) 141-56.

Pope, Marvin H. *El in the Ugaritic Texts*. Leiden: E. J. Brill, 1955.

________. Review of *Rank Among the Canaanite Gods, El, Baᶜal, and the Rephaim*, by Conrad E. L'Heureux. *BASOR* 251 (1983) 67-9.

Popenoe, Paul B. *Date Growing in the Old World and the New*. Altadena, Ca.: West India Gardens, 1913.

________. *The Date Palm*. Ed. Henry Field. Miami, Fla.: Field Research Projects, 1973.

Pritchard, James B., ed. *The Ancient Near East in Pictures Relating to the Old Testament*. Princeton: Princeton University, 1954.

________. "Les fouilles de Sarepta," *Bible et terre sainte* 157 (1974) 4-14.

________. *Palestinian Figurines in Relation to Certain Goddesses Known Through Literature*. AOS 24. New Haven: American Oriental Society, 1943.

________. *Recovering Sarepta, A Phoenician City*. Princeton: Princeton University, 1978.

Propp, William H. "The Goddess ʾ*Aṯiratu* and the Israelite Asherah." Senior Honors thesis, Harvard University, 1979.

Rainey, Anson F. "Notes on Some Proto-Sinaitic Inscriptions," *IEJ* 25 (1975) 106-16.

________. "Some Minor Points in Two Proto-Sinaitic Inscriptions," *IEJ* 31 (1981) 92-4.

________. "Verbal Usages in the Taanach Texts," *Israel Oriental Studies* 7 (1977) 33-64.

Redford, Donald B. "New Light on the Asiatic Campaigning of Ḥoremheb," *BASOR* 211 (1973) 36-49.

Reed, William L. "Asherah," *IDB* 1 (1962) 250-2.

________. *The Asherah in the Old Testament.* Fort Worth: Texas Christian University, 1949.

Reichert, A. "Kultgeräte," *Biblisches Reallexikon*, 2nd ed., ed. Kurt Galling, 189-94. Tübingen: J. C. B. Mohr (Paul Siebeck), 1977.

Répertoire d'épigraphie sémitique. Académie des Inscriptions et Belles-lettres. 8 vols. Paris: 1900-68.

Roberts, Jimmy J. M. *The Earliest Semitic Pantheon.* Baltimore: Johns Hopkins University, 1972.

Robinson, James M. "Claude Frederic-Armand Schaeffer-Forrer (1898-1982)," *BAR* 9 (1983) 56-61.

Roeder, Günther. *Ägypter und Hethiter.* Alte Orient 20. Leipzig: J. C. Hinrichs, 1919.

Röllig, Wolfgang. See Donner, Herbert.

Rose, Herbert Jennings. "Juno," *The Oxford Classical Dictionary* (1949) 471-2.

Rossbach, O. "Dido," PW 5 (1905) cols. 426-433.

Rostovtzeff, M. "Hadad and Atargatis at Palmyra," *AJA* 37 (1933) 58-63.

Saley, Richard J. See Cross, Frank Moore, Jr.

Sanmartín, J. See Dietrich, M.

Sayce, A. H. "Babylonian Cylinders in the Hermitage at St. Petersburg," *ZA* 6 (1891) 161-3.

Schaeffer, F.-A. "Les fouilles de Minet-el-Beida et de Ras Shamra," *Syria* 10 (1929) 285-97.

________. See also Nougayrol, Jean.

Seger, Joe D. Review of *Canaanite Gods in Metal: An Archaeological Study of Ancient Syro-Palestinian Figurines*, by Ora Negbi. *BASOR* 249 (1983) 95-6.

Seibert, Ilse. *Women in the Ancient Near East.* Trans. Marianne Herzfeld, rev. George A. Shepperson. New York: Abner Schram, 1974.

"Sekhmet," *The New Encyclopaedia Britannica* Micropaedia 9 (1980) 37.

Shorter, Alan W. *The Egyptian Gods.* London: Kegan Paul, Trench, Trubner, 1937.

Simon, Hilda. *The Date Palm.* New York: Dodd and Mead, 1978.

Simpson, William K. See Hallo, William W.

Smith, William Robertson. *The Religion of the Semites.* 3rd ed., Stanley A. Cook. London: Black, 1927.

Sollberger, Edmond and Kupper, Jean-Robert. *Inscriptions royales sumeriennes et akkadiennes.* Littératures anciennes du Proche-Orient. Paris: Editions du Cerf, 1971.

Stadelmann, Rainer. *Syrisch-Palästinensische Gottheiten in Ägypten.* Probleme der Ägyptologie 5. Leiden: E. J. Brill, 1967.

Stager, Lawrence E. "I. The Rite of Child Sacrifice at Carthage." In *New Light on Ancient Carthage*, ed. John Griffiths Pedley, 1-11. Ann Arbor: University of Michigan, 1980.

Stager, Lawrence E. and Wolff, Samuel R. "Child Sacrifice at Carthage -- Religious Rite or Population Control?," *BAR* 10 (1984) 30-51.

Steindorff, Georg. *The Religion of the Ancient Egyptians.* New York: G. P. Putnam's Sons, 1905.

Stocks, H. "Studien zur Lukians 'De Syria Dea,'" *Berytus* 4 (1937) 1-40.

Strong, Herbert A. See Garstang, John.

Sznycer, Maurice. See Caquot, André.

Tallqvist, Knut. *Akkadische Götterepitheta.* StudOr 7. Helsingforsiae: Societas Orientalis Fennica, 1938.

Teixidor, Javier. "Les tablettes d'Arslan Tash au Musée d'Alep," *Aula orientalis* 1 (1983) 105-8.

________. Review of *Textbook of Syrian Semitic Inscriptions. Vol. 3: Phoenician Inscriptions Including Inscriptions in the Mixed Dialect of Arslan Tash*, by J. C. L. Gibson. *JBL* 103 (1984) 453-5.

Thureau-Dangin, Fr. *Lettres et contrats de l'époque de la première dynastie babylonienne.* Musée du Louvre, Département des Antiquités Orientales, Textes Cunéiformes, 1. Paris: Paul Geuthner, 1910.

Tomback, Richard S. *A Comparative Semitic Lexicon of the Phoenician and Punic Languages.* SBLDS 32. Missoula, Mont.: Scholars Press, 1978.

Toombs, Lawrence E. "Baal, Lord of the Earth: The Ugaritic Baal Epic." In *The Word of the Lord Shall Go Forth*, ed. Carol L. Meyers and M. O'Connor, 613-23. Winona Lake, In.: Eisenbrauns, 1983.

Torczyner, H. "A Hebrew Incantation Against Night-demons from Biblical Times," *JNES* 6 (1947) 18-29.

Tufnell, Olga; Inge, Charles H.; and Harding, Lankester. *Lachish II: The Fosse Temple*. The Wellcome-Marston Archaeological Research Expedition to the Near East Publications 2. London: Oxford University, 1940.

Ullendorff, Edward. "Ugaritic Marginalia," *Or* n.s. 20 (1951) 270-4.

Unger, Merrill F. *Archaeology and the Old Testament*. Grand Rapids, Mich.: Zondervan, 1954.

Ussishkin, David. *Excavations at Tel Lachish 1978-1983: Second Preliminary Report*. Tel Aviv University Institute of Archaeology Reprint Series 6. Tel Aviv: "Achdut" Press, 1983.

Vanel, A. "Six *ostraca* phéniciens trouvés au temple d'Echmoun, près de Saïda," *Bulletin du Musée de Beyrouth* 20 (1967) 45-95.

Viganò, Lorenzo. "The Ebla Tablets," rev. and ed. Dennis Pardee, *BA* 47 (1984) 6-16.

Virolleaud, Charles. *Le Palais Royal d'Ugarit II*. Mission de Ras Shamra 7. Paris: Imprimerie Nationale, 1957.

________. *Le Palais Royal d'Ugarit V*. Mission de Ras Shamra 11. Paris: Imprimerie Nationale, 1965.

________. See also Nougayrol, Jean.

Wallace, Howard Neil. "The Eden Narrative." Th.D. diss., Harvard University, 1982.

Walton, F. R. "Atargatis," *RAC* 1 (1950) cols. 854-860.

Weber, Otto. See Knudtzon, Jørgen Alexander.

Whitaker, Richard E. *A Concordance of the Ugaritic Literature*. Cambridge: Harvard University, 1972.

Wiedemann, Alfred. *Religion of the Ancient Egyptians*. New York: G. P. Putnam's Sons, 1897.

Wolff, Samuel R. See Stager, Lawrence E.

Woolley, Charles Leonard. *Alalakh*. Reports of the Research Committee of the Society of Antiquaries of London 18. Oxford: University Press, 1955.

Xella, Paola. *I testi rituali di Ugarit-I*. Studi Semitici 54. Roma: Consiglio Nazionale delle Ricerche, 1981.

Yadin, Yigael. "Symbols of Deities at Zinjirli, Carthage and Hazor." In *Near Eastern Archaeology in the Twentieth Century*, ed. James A. Sanders, 199-231. Garden City, N.Y.: Doubleday, 1970.

Zevit, Ziony. "The Khirbet el-Qôm Inscription Mentioning a Goddess," *BASOR* 255 (1984) 39-47.

BL 1605 .A7 M35 1986

Maier, Walter A., 1952-

Aserah, extrabiblical evidence 470110